Praise for
It Takes More Than Good Looks

"*Wayne Freedman knows how to make a television news story memorable. He tells you how to do it by using as examples stories he told on the air. More than being a solid writer, he's also a crackerjack producer, interviewer, on-camera talent, photographer and author.*"

Mervin Block—Television Newswriting Workshop
Author, *Writing Broadcast News Shorter, Sharper, Stronger:*
A Professional Handbook

"*I wish more reporters captured the essence and emotion of a story like Wayne does. I have recommended his book to countless journalism students and young reporters I have met, mentored or hired. Hopefully they've learned the best stories are not a list of facts, but a well-crafted tale.*"

Tracey Watkowski Silva—News Director
KFSN-TV/ABC30, Fresno, California

"*This just might be the first "how to" book for television storytelling. It's all about attitude. Watch TV in a few years and you'll quickly see who hasn't read this book.*"

David Busse—News Photographer, KABC-TV

"*As the industry changes and more journalists make the jump from print to television, this should be required reading. It was for me.*
What better teacher is there?"

Cecilia Vega—ABC News Correspondent
Former Reporter, *San Francisco Chronicle*

"*For TV reporters who want to find and tell better stories, Wayne Freedman provides a terrific road map. He's one of those rare journalists who both produces excellent work and can explain how he does it. In other words, he's a gifted teacher. Learn from him!*"

Deborah Potter—President and Executive Director, Newslab
Former CBS News Correspondent

"*Easy to read. Educational. And fun. Yes, fun. This should be given to all journalism students—it'll show them how good TV is done. Veterans will learn a lot too, like how to shoot a thorough, creative story in 30 minutes.*

Wayne makes it seem possible with his explanations and real-life examples.

This book made me realize how obsolete and lame my journalism textbooks were. If I had read this, then maybe I could've skipped that stint at a small TV station located in a cornfield.

Even though Wayne has been in the business awhile, he's not one of those jaded journalists. He'll teach you how to do more with less, and how to make each day manageable. This world-class television writer might even teach some old photographers new tricks."

Anne Herbst—Multimedia Journalist, Denver Post

"*Wayne Freedman is one of the finest storytellers in the field, masterfully weaving video, sound and just the right words to tell stories that no one else seems to find. More important, he has found a way to tell OTHERS how to do this. As a professor of broadcast journalism, I can tell you, that is no small accomplishment. If you are a serious student of television journalism (and no, that is NOT an oxymoron), you need to have this book. You also need to read it.*"

Judy Muller—Associate Professor
USC Annenberg School of Communication
Former Correspondent, ABC News
National Public Radio Commentator

"*MTGL feels like you've bellied up to the bar for some brews and war stories that will educate, illuminate and inspire the storyteller in us all.*

My students love MTGL and often say they can't put it down to do their other assigned readings.

This smart, savvy, streetwise guide is seasoned with decades of experience and told with the brutal truth, flair and humor we've come to expect from a Wayne Freedman story. It's an avalanche of nuggets of wisdom, gems of advice and tips of pure gold."

Greeley Kyle—Assistant Professor
School of Journalism, University of Missouri

"*I'll bet when Wayne Freedman is hypnotized, we discover he was Moliere or Shakespeare in an early life. He gets every little detail. No one living is better at telling stories. He sees things mere mortals do not, and is truly gifted at conveying those insights. This latest edition is as much a fun, intelligent read as it is instructive. If my students internalize all of this, then I do not need to teach. Wayne knows everything about broadcast news and it's all in here. Read this, learn the skills, and you'll be a better electronic journalist. Period.*"

David Hazinski—Head, Digital and Broadcast News
Meigs Distinguished Teaching Professor
Jim Kennedy Professor
Grady School of Journalism, University of Georgia

"Landing a TV reporting job is not tough. Make a tape, be persistent and someone somewhere will put you on the air.

Leaning the craft of television news reporting is a different ball game. Wayne Freedman shows what it takes to become one of the very best.

This book offers practical, easy to use tips to anyone in the business. The challenges and frustrations Wayne describes will happen to you, count on it. Just as important, he explains ways to overcome those obstacles. Regardless of your experience level, this book is crammed full of useful tips that can improve your work.

But this is not only a collection of "how to" tips.

It Takes More than Good Looks to Succeed at TV News Reporting, inspired me. Those of us lucky enough to make a career of TV news have the best, most interesting jobs around. Thanks to Wayne we now have a playbook to make ourselves, and our work, even better!"

Robert Wilson

"Just finished the book this morning on the train ride in to work. I have to say that I enjoyed it from beginning to end! It was jam packed FULL of useful tips and great anecdotes that would help ANYONE to become a great news reporter or multimedia journalist PERIOD.

My favorite part? I could no sooner pick a favorite star in the sky. This book was sooo informative, interesting, and absolutely HILARIOUS. It's all you would ever want or need in a non-fiction book. It's like going on a ride through his MOST INTERESTING LIFE!!

While reading this book, I often paused and said to myself, "Wow, it's like he read my mind and answered my most pressing questions without me having to ask."

What did I learn . . . ?

. . . That I'm in the right field! I read the bulk of the book on the train with people looking at me weird every couple of minutes as I laughed aloud, mumbled "NICE!" at his scripts, and sighed "awww" at his experiences. This book is an absolute Godsend—a true journalist's handbook. I cannot thank Mr. Freedman enough for sharing!"

Tilesha Brown—Journalism Student

"If you want to write television news stories that simply sing, this is a must-have book. I'm a reporter at a station in Allentown, PA, and I bought this book a while ago and have re-read it several times . . . each time I get something new out of it. More important, it's absolutely packed with "tricks of the trade" that are useful and creative.

If you're serious about good reporting and telling people's stories that will linger in the minds of your viewers long after the newscast has ended, I suggest you give this book a try."

D. Parker

SECOND EDITION

IT TAKES MORE THAN GOOD LOOKS

To Succeed at Television News Reporting

WAYNE FREEDMAN

A Wealth of Wisdom llc
Keauhou Hawaii

First Edition: Bonus Books, 2003, 978-1-5662518-8-4 (hardcover)
Second Edition: A Wealth of Wisdom, 2011
  ISBN: 978-0-9843125-3-5   (softcover)
  ISBN: 978-0-9843125-4-2   (eBook)
  ISBN: 978-0-9843125-5-9   (ePub)

Library of Congress Control Number: 2011935871

Book Design: Renée Robinson
Cover Design: Lauren P Freedman

Published by A Wealth of Wisdom LLC, Hawaii USA
www.AWealthOfWisdom.com
Printed in the United States of America

Preface

It didn't seem right.

Not when original copies of *It Takes More than Good Looks* sold on the internet at obscene multiples of the original cover price.

Not when young reporters continued to contact me, asking for rogue copies.

Not when college professors asked if they could use pdf files because the book was out of print.

That's when I knew it was high time for seat time, and a second edition. I secured the rights, found a good, new publisher, and went to work.

So, here it is, same as it always was—updated with more recent and relevant examples reflecting the changes in our business. Don't worry. Most of the first edition remains. That first book drew from two decades of reporting experiences. This new edition draws from three.

In culling it together, I am reassured that even as our business models change, the fundamentals of solid visual storytelling remain the same. What worked in the 60s, 70s, 80s, and 90s still applies in the new millennium.

Since the first edition, I have changed too, becoming older, wiser, more efficient, more newsy, and more jaded. I remain just as committed to telling stories well, and seeing them told well.

"Your writing this book is better than my listening to you shout at the television," said my wife.

She's right. This book is a brain dump. Everything I know about how to produce a quality television news story is in these pages.

The business has been good to me. I have been relatively successful. Maybe, after reading this, it will help you have a successful career, too.

To Susan and Lauren.

For my parents, Mike and Alicia.

And to the old schoolers, wherever you are. Pass it on.

Table of Contents

Part Three: Pragmatics

Part One

MINDSET

CHAPTER 1

Pursuit

When news people look at clocks, they invariably wish the hands would move slower, not faster. If you report, you may have days, hours, minutes, or seconds to finish a story. It doesn't matter. You will always be aware of time's relentless forward march. You cannot help feeling hurried, and sometimes worried.

For television news crews, every day brings a new challenge. Some of those days are more trying than others, and none more so than a Wednesday in June, 2000. KGO-TV photographer Doug Laughlin and I had gone to Pebble Beach, California for general news coverage of the U.S. Open Golf tournament. Our troubles began early, when a security man stopped us near the first tee.

"That is only a press pass," he said with authority. "Your press pass is not a photo pass. You need a photo pass to take that camera on the course."

"Where do we get a photo pass?"

"It's too late if you don't already have one," he said indifferently.

"But we need a photo pass."

"Everybody needs a photo pass."

Clearly, this man had perfected something in life—his imitation of a brick wall. We had planned to do a story about watching golf from the gallery at that scenic venue, but he cared only about rules and technicalities. "Your press pass grants access to the press tent, but nowhere else," he droned with the charm of a customs agent. "See here. Your press pass does not say 'photo.' It says 'press.'"

What a predicament. I had begged for this assignment and promised to deliver one quality piece every day. With a deadline approaching, we could not get to our story.

"Now what?" I asked of no one in particular. If you work in this business, you have probably asked that question, too. Angst comes with the job, and at that moment I felt buried beneath a mountain of it. "What do we do now?"

As if to answer my question, a golf cart pulled up and stopped a few feet away. Two tournament officials climbed out. One of them carried a small, ornate piece of silver. It looked familiar—very familiar. Doug caught my nod, grabbed his camera, and began shooting as we approached.

"Excuse me," I asked, "But isn't that…?"

"It is, indeed," the driver boasted. "This is the lid to the U.S. Open Trophy."

Only the lid, mind you, disembodied from its much larger cup. "Where's the rest?"

"Back in its carrying case," said the man, who identified himself as Rand Jerris, a librarian for the United States Golf Association. "We're taking the lid in for repairs."

"You mean the trophy is broken?"

"Of course it's not broken. We certainly have all the parts for it. We're just going for a quick fix." Rand Jerris appeared to be enjoying his moment in front of the lens. He even let me hold the lid, which features a famous winged, female victory figure. One of those wings was missing. Then he dangled a clear plastic sandwich bag. Inside—the severed appendage. Jerris had done everything but pack it in ice.

Clearly we'd struck, if not gold, then silver. The U.S. Open trophy, the holy icon of American golf, had been maimed, cracked, ravaged, savaged, or abused. Better yet for our purposes, the USGA would be taking it to a place beyond the hoopla and the press passes. Someone in the neighborhood would be fixing it, and that could make a good story. "So who's doing the work for you?" I asked innocently.

"We're not sure, yet. There have to be some silversmiths in town," Jerris speculated. "We'll try one of them."

"Mind if we go along?"

Rand Jerris, the mild-mannered, bookish USGA librarian, looked at us as if we were insane. "Why would you care about that? I'll check. Wait here."

Jerris walked into the press tent and spoke with his superior. Doug and I held back. Five minutes passed. Then ten. We became anxious. No sign. No word.

We watched as Jerris showed the lid to his boss, who looked over at us. I smiled benignly. He scowled back.

All the while, countless golf writers sauntered past. They kept their eyes glued to pairing sheets, or glanced at the scoreboard, or spoke into mobile telephones. Amazingly, none seemed to notice or care about the broken lid of the U.S. Open Trophy. How could no one else be curious?

Finally, I couldn't take it anymore. Doug and I approached Jerris and his boss, who gave me a disdainful once-over. "We at the USGA don't believe this would be conducive to a positive image of the Open," his superior said dismissively. "We won't help."

"But how did the trophy break?"

"It just did," he replied.

"Who broke it? And when?"

"Now, really," he tut-tutted. "This is an internal matter."

"Come on," I persisted. "It's the US Open Trophy. How many people pay dues to the USGA? It's a good human interest angle."

"Not to us," he said icily.

The official seemed determined to act like a jerk, so I followed his lead. "Okay, but, you should know, we already have nice tight shots of the wrecked lid and that wing in the plastic bag," I said. "We already have enough for a story. But here's a deal. Give us a photo pass with full access to the course for the next four days, and we'll be happy to hold this."

"Nice try," huffed the boss. He marched off without even saying goodbye. Maybe he thought we were bluffing—and we certainly would have kept our part of the offer—but I was partly relieved. The man had been so snootily rude that he'd turned this into a contest between us and them. Besides, the broken trophy made a richer story, and I had an idea.

Find Small Stories in the Big Ones, and Big Stories in the Small Ones

At heart, I'm just like anybody else who enjoys spinning a good yarn. As a guy who does it for a living, I must deal with the added element of competition. Every reporter feels the same pressure. To excel and win, we search constantly for novel angles, and develop our own methods of finding them. One of my techniques is to keep an eye on other reporters and, when possible, to work in an opposite direction. Note what they're getting, and also what they're missing.

It's my philosophy that in most every story, large or small, we tell the news of the day. Taken at face value, that news is often fairly forgettable. By looking deeper into those everyday stories, however, you may find something simple, approachable, or telling about the world. That's my joy in this business—finding stories within stories. *There are big stories in the small ones, and small stories in the big ones. They reveal the meaningful truths about life.*

I'll take a story like that, anytime. Viewers tend to remember and appreciate them.

Back in the press tent, Doug and I knew we had such a segment within reach, but first we would have to find the person fixing that trophy. If the United States Golf Association didn't want to cooperate, so be it. "Let's get the story without them," I told Doug.

We returned to town, killed some time with a couple of coffees, and then opened the Yellow Pages. They listed only one silversmith for all of Pacific Grove. I gave Jerris about a one-hour head start and then called the number for Colonial Silver. "Hello?" answered a pleasant man with an Italian accent.

I identified myself, and realized the next line would be crucial. Uncertainty might have given us away. "Are you the man who is single-handedly saving the U.S. Open?" I asked in a congratulatory manner.

Silence.

I dropped a name. "Has Rand Jerris stopped by with the trophy yet?"

"His trophy is right here." The man on the phone identified himself as Carmelo Tringali, and said that he owned the place.

It felt like progress, but I still had to be careful. I rambled casually by using the few facts we knew. Remember, we had held the lid and seen the broken wing. Jerris told us he was taking it for repairs. Having established some semblance of credibility, I made my pitch. "Mr. Tringali, we want to do a report about the man repairing the trophy."

"What about the golf people?" he asked.

"The USGA knows we want to do this story." It was an absolutely truthful statement—enough for Mr. Tringali, thankfully. He invited us over.

In person, we found Carmelo Tringali to be a gentle, soft-spoken man with black glasses, a gray beard, and a tarnish-stained apron. Doug put a microphone on him and quickly set some lights. Mr. Tringali led us to the back of his shop, where, on a table piled with family heirlooms, he unceremoniously lifted a soiled piece of denim, revealing the damaged trophy lid.

"What did the USGA tell you?" I asked.

"They said, 'See if you can fix this thing.'"

A thing?

Clearly, Mr. Tringali did not play golf, and knew nothing of the trophy's hallowed tradition. "To me, this is just a piece of silver," he said with a chuckle. "It's just another broken lid." He saw no difference between the U.S. Open Trophy, grandma's tea service, Billy's first trumpet, or any of the other golf trophies around the room. "I fixed those, too."

What a change in fortune. Two hours earlier, we had been despondent, but the fun of working in journalism is that, on any given day, you never know what you're going to find, where you're going to go, or whom you're going to meet. Every new assignment is a learning experience. While this one wasn't typical, our pursuit of that trophy exemplifies several of the themes and survival skills in this book:

1. Never give up.
2. Recognize opportunities.
3. Be willing to change plans at a moment's notice.
4. If you identify a main character, you can always tell a story.
5. Layer your story. Speak to viewers at several factual and emotional levels.
6. A news report does not need to change the world to be memorable. A small story can make just as big an impression.

Our trophy segment fit all of those criteria. Carmelo Tringali gave us a wonderful contrast to the USGA's pretentious pomp. That humble, unassuming craftsman would leave his mark on a crown jewel of golf and, in a world-wide competitive journalistic environment, nobody else even knew about the story.

Back at his shop, Mr. Tringali clamped the broken wing before torching it into place. Our piece needed an ending. He still wore a microphone as I asked off-handedly, "Mr. Tringali, did you ever consider how the entire golfing world will see your work, but never know you did it, and never hear your name?"

"That's okay. I'll try to do a good job," he said intently. "When do they need this thing, again? Sunday?"

Yes. Of course. Sunday. And on that day, with millions watching, a young and seemingly innocent Tiger Woods hoisted the very same U.S. Open trophy. He would follow that victory with others at the British Open, the PGA Championship, and then the Masters—four consecutive majors.

No one knew it at the time, but that U.S. Open trophy became the first of what some writers called the Grand Slam, and others, the Tiger Slam. By any measure, it made golf history.

Imagine—four major championship trophies on Tiger Woods's mantle, and if anyone looked closely, he would have seen that one of them had a broken wing.

Tiger's Trophy
June 2000

See players practicing

AMONG THE POSSIBLE HEROES AT THIS YEAR'S U.S. OPEN, HERE'S A NAME YOU HAVEN'T HEARD— CARMELO TRINGALI.

(SOT)
Tringali: "I'm just a lucky person, I guess."

WE WOULD NEVER HAVE MET HIM, IF NOT FOR TWO USGA OFFICIALS WHO TOOK A RIDE IN A GOLF CART WITH A PIECE OF SILVER IN THEIR HANDS. BUT WAIT…

(SOT)
File tape, crowd cheers as past champions hold the trophy, shots of trophy and lid

DOESN'T THAT PIECE LOOK A LOT LIKE THIS?

COULD IT BE?

(SOT)
Rand Jerris: "Yes, that is the lid to the U.S. Open trophy."

JUST THE LID, MIND YOU, DISEMBODIED FROM THE CUP.
AND IF YOU LOOK CLOSELY, NOTE THE WING BROKEN OFF FROM
THE VICTORY FIGURE. THE USGA WRAPPED IT IN A PLASTIC BAG,
LIKE A SEVERED LIMB.

(SOT)
Wayne: "WAIT A MINUTE. YOU'RE TELLING ME THE U.S. OPEN
TROPHY IS BROKEN?"

Jerris: "Of course it's not broken. We certainly have all the parts
for it. We're just going to go for a quick fix on it."

(WAYNE STAND-UP)
AND THAT IS ALL THEY WOULD TELL US. THE MORE WE
QUESTIONED USGA OFFICIALS, THE LESS THEY SAID . . .
NOT HOW THE CUP BROKE, OR BY WHOM, OR WHEN.
"NO BIG DEAL," THEY KEPT INSISTING. "ACCIDENTS HAPPEN."

Exterior, the Colonial Silver

AND ACCIDENTS GET FIXED. BUT, IN NEARBY PACIFIC GROVE,
THE YELLOW PAGES LIST ONLY ONE SILVERSMITH.

(SOT)
Wayne to Tringali: "WHAT DID THEY TELL YOU WHEN THEY
CAME IN?"

Tringali: "They said, 'See if you can fix this broken thing.'"

Wayne: "THING?"

Tringali: "Yeah. Thing."

We see historical footage of famous golfers receiving the trophy

THIS THING, ALSO KNOWN AS THE HOLY GRAIL OF

AMERICAN GOLF. THIS THING, WHICH HAS PASSED FROM
HAND TO HAND OF GOLFING LEGENDS, LIVING AND DEAD,
FOR ONE-HUNDRED AND FIVE YEARS.
PAYNE STEWART . . .JACK NICKLAUS . . .

(SOT)
Wayne to Tringali: "BEN HOGAN HAD THIS TROPHY."

Tringali: "Ben Hogan? Never heard of him."

CARMELO TRINGALI NEVER HEARD OF MOST OF THEM.
UNTIL TODAY, HE NEVER EVEN KNEW THIS TROPHY EXISTED.
FIXING IT SHOULDN'T BE A PROBLEM, HE SAYS.

(SOT)
Tringali: "To me it's just another piece of silver.
It's just another lid."

. . . NO DIFFERENT FROM GRANDMA'S TEA SERVICE,
OR ANY OTHER GOLF TROPHY . . .

File of more victorious golfers

EXCEPT THAT THIS ONE MEANS JUST A LITTLE MORE.
AND NOW CARMELO TRINGALI CAN CLAIM A PIECE OF
THE CUP'S ILLUSTRIOUS HISTORY. MAYBE IT'S BEST THAT
HE DOESN'T KNOW.

(SOT)
Wayne to Tringali: "MR. TRINGALI, DID YOU EVER CONSIDER
HOW THE ENTIRE GOLFING WORLD WILL SEE YOUR WORK,
BUT NEVER KNOW YOUR NAME?"

Tringali: "I'll try to do a good job."

HE SAYS HE'LL HAVE IT READY BY SUNDAY.

Part Two

FUNDAMENTALS

CHAPTER 2

Find a Person, Tell a Story

Try to remember the last time you passed a fender bender on the road. Do you recall the exact location, or any details about the cars? Probably not. Like most people, you glanced over, assessed the damage, drove on, and forgot about it within a couple of minutes. You didn't know the people involved, so why dwell on it?

You would be less indifferent, however, if you recognized a car in the wreck as one belonging to a friend or neighbor. In that case, you would probably stop to help, and you would certainly remember the accident for longer than two minutes.

That fender bender helps describe how people watch television news. Stories are not accidents, of course, but viewers always care more about the news when they feel they have a stake in it. Unfortunately, many reporters neglect that simple formula. They fail to make the facts relevant to viewers.

In a perfect world, every news story would affect everyone directly. In reality, this rarely happens, but good reporters will always find ways to make the material compelling. They recognize that television news in its purest form can and should give viewers an experience—anger, fear, wonder, enlightenment, laughter, sadness. They know intuitively that, in our business, *the road to a viewer's head passes through the gut. Television is a visceral medium. People remember what they feel. If you reach a person on that level, you will get all of him.*

Use Characters to Tell Stories

Sometimes I wonder why we call our work television news "stories" when so many of us overlook the "story" part. We get distracted by details and deadlines, and forget a basic fundamental: stories have characters.

It's so simple. Events have impacts on people. When you put the people element into your stories, viewers pay attention, especially when they see a little of themselves, or someone they know. *Characters help reporters ground stories in the real world.*

Joey

A few years ago, photographer Randy Davis and I covered a highway closure in a snowstorm. The producer asked for a live shot wrapped around a short segment. Randy and I pulled into a checkpoint where drivers either installed tire chains, or else paid people to do the job for them. There, we spotted Joey Cattrell crouching in the snow next to a small sedan. He gave the story a different twist. Joey had been riding with five friends, any of whom would have happily split the cost of a chain installer. But that didn't sit right with Joey, who asked, "Why waste money?"

Joey Cattrell is the kind of person you might call a "doer." We all know someone like him. As Randy and I watched, he removed his parka, rolled around on his back in the dirty, frozen muck, and attached those chains by himself. By interviewing Joey, showing his friends standing around, and then developing all of them as characters, we made the story of that traffic jam a little more approachable by finding a universal and simple truth:

> AT A TIME LIKE THIS, IT'S ALWAYS NICE TO HAVE A GUY
> LIKE JOEY CATTRELL AROUND.

The Formula

Joey exemplifies a simple and reliable journalistic formula. *Find a person. Tell a story. Weave the facts of the news inside of it.* See news events as daily dramas, and the people within them as role-players. When you look beyond a newsmaker's function and examine the individual instead, you can make almost anyone interesting, from an embattled politician to an overworked detective, to a man on the street, to a civil engineer with a clipboard.

The Math Wiz

In 2002 the Port of Oakland, California, purchased four monstrous cargo cranes from a company in Japan, which then sent them across the Pacific Ocean aboard an ungainly looking, top-heavy ship. Those cranes towered above the water, and could not have been built any taller. Having traveled several thousand miles, they would pass beneath the San Francisco/Oakland Bay Bridge with only twenty-six inches of clearance.

The port felt confident about that number because it employed an engineer who had worked the calculations. The day before those cranes arrived, we tracked him down for a story. During the interview he showed us the math, which prompted me to ask if he had done well in his SAT college entrance exam.

"Perfect score," boasted the engineer. That small fact made the story, and turned a public servant into a regular guy. Any viewer who ever struggled with a math problem could relate to him. It also gave the piece an opening line:

(SOT)
Pencil scratches paper as the engineer calculates aloud

IF YOU EVER WONDERED WHAT KIND OF PERSON GETS A PERFECT MATH SCORE ON HIS SAT, HERE IS YOUR ANSWER. TOMORROW, YOU WILL BE GLAD HE DID.

Interviews as Salesmanship

The Unemployment Line

In July 1991, CBS News made cost cuts, and I was one of them. Such misfortune happens to almost everyone in this business. Don't take it personally. Four months later, I went to work for KGO-TV in San Francisco, beginning as a freelance reporter.

Fittingly, in my very first week the producers asked me to do a story about California's unemployment rate reaching double digits. Our desk had already set up an interview with a state official who would tell us what the numbers meant. No, it wasn't the most compelling human angle, but a reporter should never argue with his employer when, technically, he's still an unemployment statistic himself. Photographer Pam Partee and I went to the bureaucrat's office and tried to keep our eyes open during the interview.

Surely, though, there had to be a better way to approach the assignment. I called the desk. "What if we go to an unemployment office and talk with the people waiting there?" Just two weeks earlier I had stood in such a line, and I remembered how we had commiserated with one another. If Pam and I could capture that for the news, it would give the piece some of that missing humanity. The desk cleared us to go ahead and try.

In theory, it was a good idea. In reality, the people waiting to make unemployment claims wanted nothing to do with a television crew. "You have to be kidding," said one man.

Clearly, we would have to do a sales job before conducting any interviews. This isn't unusual. If you report from the field, you already know that for every person who asks to be on the news, ten others won't want anything to do with you.

This is where persuasion comes into play. You need to find the right people and convince them to talk. We ask for their time. We ask for their honesty. Adding to our difficulties, we're television news reporters, and many civilians distrust us.

Reporters As Chameleons

When asking someone for an on-camera interview, follow a proven method of salesmanship. Let the buyer buy. In the same way a skilled salesman allows a client to describe his needs before pitching a product, let your subject convince himself that it's in his best interest to talk with you. This may require you to become an emotional chameleon, of sorts, as you find a tone that resonates with him. Honesty works in these situations, as does being an active, sympathetic listener. Try to truly understand your subject's position and motivations.

I remember a story in which San Francisco's district attorney made a show of filing charges against an unscrupulous landlord. We tried repeatedly to get that landlord's reaction, but he would not return our calls. Clearly, he didn't want to talk, so we gave him a reason. I called his machine one last time and left the following question: "Do you think the district attorney would make such a big deal about you if he weren't running for re-election? What's your side of the story?"

That landlord took the bait and agreed to go on camera. Ultimately, his interview enraged the district attorney even more.

Interviews As Real Estate

By now, perhaps you're beginning to understand that reporters should avoid taking no for an answer. Do not give up easily. Often, I revert to a real estate analogy. "We will be giving this story almost two minutes, tonight," I might say. "The other side has already agreed to speak with us. It's kind of like playing *Monopoly*. If time is real estate, they have already claimed some of it. We are trying to get this story straight, and to be fair about granting equal time. The other side is talking about you. If you go on camera, you get to speak for yourself."

It works.

Avoid Settling For Statements

In our increasingly media-savvy world, individuals and companies have taken to issuing carefully worded statements. Those releases are typically a form of damage control, designed and crafted to limit dialogue or embarrassing questions. Reporters settle for statements much too often.

If a newsmaker tells me that he is not available, I often ask if he might appear via Skype, or if I can record a telephone interview. That person will usually decline, and defer back to the statement with no further comment.

Good taste does not allow my barnyard analogy describing the use of such tactics. Unless you're faced with an immediate deadline, don't make it easy for them. As a means of gaining leverage, I often advise statement makers that my report will note the questions they would not answer. It's only fair. Occasionally, my statement in reaction to their statement gets the interview, after all.

Handling Gatekeepers

We can't blame newsmakers for protecting their self-interests. We do need to learn to deal with them. Often, an obstacle manifests itself in the form of an administrative assistant who may take a message, or say that the person is not in the office. Again, do not acquiesce easily.

"Can you get in touch with her?" I recently asked a lawyer's assistant.

"I can connect you with her voicemail."

"But you just said she is not in. Will she be picking up that voicemail?"

"I can't speak for her," the assistant said.

"Do you know where she is?" I pressed.

"She is not in."

The assistant might have thought, by then, that we had reached a stalemate. Not yet. After reporters do this job for a few years, they acquire extra tools. I pulled out an old standard. "Let's say your building was burning down. You could reach her then, right?"

"Of course I could reach her," the assistant said with authority.

"Well, I don't mean to be difficult, but this is kind of like that," I continued. "ABC7 News needs to speak with her, and she will want to talk with us. Could you pretend we're a fire? It's really important."

David Hazinski, a former NBC News correspondent who is now a journalism professor at The University of Georgia, espouses a different method.

"My tactic is to ask their name. They always ask why. I say, because I want to say on the air whom I spoke with. You're saying they're not available and have no comment. I just want to make sure I get your name right. I usually hear, 'just a moment.' Then the official comes on."

Hazinski was based in Atlanta, and remains old-school savvy. "Those gatekeepers are fine with keeping you out if it doesn't involve any risk for them personally. When I make it about them, the game sometimes changes. I don't blame them," says Hazinski, "but I have little patience with playing it their way. This is our game, as well."

Suffice it to say, if you don't hear from a person after such persuasive efforts, there is a good chance he or she really is avoiding you.

When I described these methods to my wife, she said, "No wonder people hate the press."

I took a deep breath. "Dear, it is better to be a righteous nuisance than a wimpy dittohead."

No Interview Is Worth More Than Your Reputation

Just accept that, no matter how hard you try, you will not make every sale. Don't take it personally. Remain courteous. Retain your dignity. Don't bully, threaten, or follow up with nasty emails. Thank the person for listening to your pitch, cut your losses, and move on. Don't hide microphones or surreptitiously roll tape in the hope of stealing a sound bite. Reporters are not in the exploitation business. Respect your subjects as viewers, and your viewers as consumers. Try to keep them on our side. No story should be more important than your reputation.

Sometimes, You Push

That day in the unemployment office, however, instinct told me to push with the man who said he didn't want to talk. Although he'd effectively told us to get lost, he pursued the conversation and didn't hold back his feelings. Since he wasn't bashful, I suspected he was mostly worried about what he might say and then be unable to take back. If only we could capture his passion on tape.

"It's my job to convince you to go on camera," I said candidly. "You can help us, and we can help you. California just reached ten percent unemployment. We can hear about it from a bureaucrat, or from someone who's living it. Name one person who understands the numbers better than you."

"Why should I trust you?" the man asked.

"Because two weeks ago I was unemployed, and stood in this very same line."

The man paused. Then he opened up. "It sucks," he finally said. "I'm not a cost-cutting measure. I'm a person. I busted my butt for that company. I gave it four years, and now I'm on the street. They scratched me out like a line item on a balance sheet."

"You need to say that on camera," I told him. "You know what you're going through, and so do I. But the rest of the world—they may never know unless we tell them." It was, in essence, an offer of complicity; as partners, the two of us would explain the frustrations of unemployment. When he heard my proposal in those terms, the man nodded okay. Pam set the camera and we began.

"What job did you have?" I asked, and then followed with more questions.

"How long did you work there?"

"How long have you been out?"

"Who fired you?"

"How did they do it?"

"What did they say?"

"Did you see it coming?"

The man answered emotionally and, as often happens in such environments, other people asked to add a few thoughts. Before we left, every person in that unemployment line answered the same questions. In the edit room we cut them together, one after another. Instead of running a piece with bureaucrat describing statistics, we built a story with an ensemble cast. I gave the anchor most of the hard facts for his lede, leaving us with the luxury of not needing much narration. Mostly, we let people tell their stories, lending faces, feelings, and voices to the concept of ten percent unemployment in California.

Jobless
July 1991

Video shows people standing in line. We see faces. A sign reads, 'Now serving.' A tight shot shows a short pencil scribbling on a form.

IT IS ONE OF THOSE GENERIC GOVERNMENT OFFICES—A LIMBO ZONE, WHERE PEOPLE TAKE NUMBERS AND FILL OUT FORMS, USING SHORT LITTLE PENCILS WITH WORN-DOWN ENDS.

(SOT)
Wayne: "WHEN DID THIS HAPPEN?"

Man #1: "About eight months ago."

Man #2: "About nine months."

Man #3: "I was laid off yesterday."

(WAYNE ON CAMERA, STAND-UP)
AS AN INSTITUTION, THE UNEMPLOYMENT OFFICE IS A GREAT EQUALIZER. PEOPLE COME HERE FROM ALL WALKS OF LIFE. IF THEY DIDN'T HAVE ANYTHING IN COMMON BEFORE, THEY DO NOW.

(SOT)
Wayne asks Man #3: "WHAT DID THEY TELL YOU?"

Man #3: "That they were cutting back because the orders were slow and …"

Man #2: "Well the job was deleted and I didn't have any marketable skills …"

Man #4: "And then the company downsized. Manufacturing went overseas . . ."

Woman #1: "Yeah, it took ten minutes. I was out."

Man #3: "I gave four years of my can for this job. And they go, 'Goodbye!' They gave all the usual warnings and blah, blah, blah, but I am just booted out on my derriere onto the street."

Wayne asks Man #4: "HAD YOU EVER LAID PEOPLE OFF IN YOUR JOB?"

Man #4: "Yes I had. I laid off sixty-five people at one time. And it wasn't pretty. And it wasn't fun. And now I sort of feel as if I'm being paid back!"

Wayne to Man #2: "HOW MANY JOBS HAVE YOU APPLIED FOR?"

Man #2: "Twenty, maybe twenty-five or thirty …"

Man #3: "I go into Joe Smith's store and ask for an application. They look at me like they're giving it to me because they have to, but I know they're thinking they won't hire me. And they're snickering. Hey. I'm just trying to find a job …"

Man #4: "In America you are what you do. You can't go anywhere in a social situation, a party, a bar, a golf course. The first question is, what's your name and the second is what do you do?"

Woman #1: "You feel as if you don't have as much control over your life as you'd like to, or you're used to."

Man #2: "You feel despondent. You feel anger toward people who are making it. And all you want is the same chance."

THAT'S ALL ANYONE HERE WANTS . . . A CHANCE, A BREAK, AN END TO UNCERTAINTY. YOU WILL FIND IT, TONIGHT IN EVERY CITY AND TOWN IN CALIFORNIA.

Man #2: "I have to keep going. There is a better road somewhere. I know, someday, I'll find it."

AND YET, IN THIS OFFICE IN THESE TIMES, EVEN IF SOMEDAY CAME TOMORROW, IT WOULD NOT BE SOON ENOUGH.

Selecting a Principal Character

The Apartment Hunter

A few years ago, rental prices in San Francisco spiked because of low vacancy rates. Our producers read about the trend in a newspaper story. They wanted a piece for that night.

Oh, well. Sometimes, we aren't so much news reporters as news repeaters. Hopefully, when handed someone else's original work, you can find a way to advance or elaborate upon it.

"We'll need the crew back by noon," said our assignment manager. "Seriously, noon. We must have the camera." We would have two hours to get out the door, shoot a story, and return.

I saw this as a simple piece about supply and demand. We could cover the pertinent facts with two or three lines, probably in a stand-up. I thought we should emphasize tenant struggle more than numbers, but, to do so, we needed that personal angle. Where would we find it?

I considered newspaper want ads and apartment complexes, dismissed both, and began looking for a rental agency. San Francisco has dozens of them. Which of those places might offer a choice of people who might be good on television?

I called Community Rentals in the Castro district, one of San Francisco's more socially diverse neighborhoods. The man who answered the phone said, "Yes, we have clients here." With that, he and I sealed an unspoken deal. The manager would give us access to people. In return, his office would get publicity. Half an hour later, we walked through his door and found five apartment hunters.

Again, we faced the same kind of problem as in the unemployment office. Some people just don't like television news crews. They're suspicious. They find the camera intimidating. To get everyone used to our presence, I interviewed the office manager, first. "Everybody wants a perfect apartment," he said with a seen-it-all attitude. "They want to find the Victorian with hardwood floors. And, of course, they want a top unit."

"With an attractive single person living next door?"

"Or beneath them, yes."

Okay. We had one sound bite from a person who could qualify as an expert, and also possibly as a comedian. Next, we needed someone with an apartment challenge. One of the people in that room would become our main character.

Who?

It's a quandary that reporters face regularly. If they aren't looking specifically for main characters, they're at least trying to find the right people to interview. Every reporter has his own method.

It's in the Eyes

I found a key to my approach long ago, while working as a network page for ABC in Los Angeles. Among our regular assignments, we pages worked the now-iconic game show *Let's Make a Deal*. It was our job to handle the studio audiences as they lined up before tapings. The more gregarious among them would become contestants on a trading floor where, if they were lucky, host Monty Hall might deal them into a dinette set, a trip to Hawaii, or even a car.

To select its anointed few, *Let's Make a Deal* hired a staff of writer/producers who walked along the line of hopefuls, all dressed in outlandish costumes. They came as teapots, as tennis racquets, as cars, as carrots. One guy came as a corpse. His sign read, "I'm dying for a deal." Those writers, meantime, worked the crowds into greedy frenzies. They would pace, lean in close to someone and shout, "Who wants a deal?" The crowd would scream. Next, the writer might dramatically point a finger: "You!" Had we been in a church instead of a television studio, you might have mistaken those writers for faith healers.

After watching this spectacle for a few weeks, I asked the head writer, "How do you choose someone? How do you know who'll be good?"

That writer had worked television game shows for more than twenty years. "It's in their eyes," he said, as if confiding an inside secret. "It's energy. Look for the twinkle in their eyes. If the eyes talk to you, take them."

It was excellent advice. Although we don't choose people for news stories by the same criteria as game show contestants, some of the same principles apply.

Audition Your Subjects

While scanning the apartment hunters in that rental office, I remembered my writer friend and looked for eye contact, hoping for one of those twinkles. We moved quickly around the room asking questions, some on camera.

"How long have you been searching?"

"Did you believe it would be this tough?"

"Compare this with something."

"What does 'cottage' mean?"

"How do you define 'quaint'?"

Later, we used several of the answers for brief sound bites. More important, those interviews also served as auditions. They helped me discover who spoke well. Who had good energy? Who would the viewers like? With whom could I establish a rapport? Those qualities make a difference because, even in a story as simple as one about high rents, you will, in a limited way, turn your main character into a star.

One woman, Heidi Dubrot, met all the criteria. "What are you doing when you leave here?" I asked.

"Checking out a few apartments."

"Mind if we come along?"

"No problem," she said.

Moments later, Heidi, the photographer, and I went apartment hunting. Heidi explored one place, then a second, then a third. Through every phase of this dismal search, I asked questions with the camera rolling.

That night, our piece presented the straightforward facts of San Francisco's apartment crunch. More important, we made those facts relevant by framing them in Heidi's frustrating search. Ultimately, our little story about numbers told a bigger one about life. Through Heidi Dubrot, viewers not only saw and heard about how difficult it was to find an apartment in San Francisco—they experienced it.

High Rents
March 1996

(SOT)
Fingers punch telephone

SHE BEGAN THIS DAY WITH THE BEST INTENTIONS.

(SOT)
Heidi talking on phone: "I'm looking for a two-bedroom in the lower Haight area ..."

HEIDI DUBROT DOESN'T WANT THE WORLD. SHE'S SIMPLY GROWN TIRED OF MOOCHING OFF HER PARENTS.

(SOT)
Heidi on the front porch steps of an apartment

Wayne: "YOU'VE LEFT HOME BEFORE, RIGHT?"

Heidi: "Yes ... " (laughs)

AND SO, THE QUEST.

(SOT)
Heidi on phone, continuing conversation
"It was already rented?"

... WHICH BEGAT REALITY ...

(SOT)
Hangs up phone

... AND LED HER TO THIS DESPERATION CHAMBER ...
A PLACE WITH A HOPEFUL NAME.

(SOT)
Manager of rental company: "Community Rentals ... "

Wayne to a client in the rental agency: "IS THIS HELL?"

Woman: "I can't tell, yet."

Heidi looks at map

BY THE TIME THEY GET HERE, MOST APARTMENT HUNTERS NO
LONGER EXPECT TO FIND THE TAJ MAHAL.

(SOT)
Manager: "You know everybody who comes to San Francisco
wants to find the Victorian with hardwood floors. And of course
it's a top unit, lots of light, with a view of the Golden Gate Bridge
and the Bay Bridge . . . "

Wayne: "WITH AN ATTRACTIVE SINGLE PERSON LIVING NEXT
DOOR?"

Manager: "Or beneath them, yes . . . "

Shot follows Heidi as she walks

AND NOW TO THE SEARCH. BUT WITH TWO-BEDROOM
APARTMENTS AVERAGING TWELVE-HUNDRED DOLLARS
IN SAN FRANCISCO, HEIDI MIGHT HAVE BETTER LUCK
TRYING TO FIND THE GOLDEN FLEECE.

(SOT)
As Heidi talks on a pay telephone,
Wayne asks: "YOU DON'T JUDGE BOOKS BY THEIR COVERS?"

Heidi: "No."

She speaks into phone: "You don't have anything else available?"

(WAYNE ON CAMERA)
HOW BAD IS IT? WELL, EXPERTS ARE COMPARING THIS WITH THE
NEW YORK CITY APARTMENT CRUNCH OF THE 1980s.
WHY?
SUPPLY AND DEMAND, MOSTLY . . .
A ONE PERCENT VACANCY RATE. THE BAY AREA HAS MORE JOBS
THAN EVER. PEOPLE ARE MOVING HERE TO TAKE THEM. THEY'RE

MAKING GOOD MONEY, BUT NOT ENOUGH MONEY TO BUY REAL
ESTATE, SO RENT PRICES ARE RISING.

(SOT)
Wayne to Heidi: "HAVE YOU FIGURED OUT WHAT SOME OF THE
DIFFERENT WORDS MEAN? 'QUAINT,' FOR EXAMPLE?"

Heidi: "*Quaint* means older."

Wayne: "COZY MEANS?"

Heidi: "*Cozy* means small ..."

... BUT "COTTAGE"—NOW THAT'S A FINE WORD. AT EIGHT
HUNDRED DOLLARS, HEIDI REALLY GOT HER HOPES UP
FOR THIS ONE.

(SOT)
VO Heidi walks

"Maybe sunny, clean, country-like, that sort of thing."

(SOT)
She peeks into the window

"Oh God ... " (in disgust)

SHE FOUND NOBODY HOME, BUT A QUICK PEEK INSIDE
CONFIRMED THAT HANSEL AND GRETEL NEVER LIVED IN THIS
COTTAGE, AND HEIDI NEVER WILL.

(SOT)
Wayne to Heidi: "SO WHAT HAVE WE LEARNED TODAY?"

Heidi: (laughing) "I've learned I'm going to have to look some
more ... "

SITUATIONS WANTED. SINGLE FEMALE, EMPLOYED,
NON-SMOKER, STILL LIVING WITH PARENTS—
AND DESPERATELY SEEKING FREEDOM.

Not All Characters Are People

Sometimes, your best characters might not even be people, although in telling their stories, you may choose to give them human traits. Try writing a story from the perspectives of trees, cars, buildings, storms, fires, and, of course, animals.

You can't miss with animals. They're innocent. Viewers always have a soft spot for them, and so do some news managers. I learned this from a guy named Herb Dudnick, who became my nemesis and also a great teacher when he assumed the news director's job at KRON-TV in 1986.

Herb came to us from NBC News in New York, where he pioneered late-night network newscasts in the early 1980s. His *NBC News Overnight* broke the mold by being serious, yet casual. Herb helped maintain that balance by running animal segments. When Dudnick came to KRON-TV, our staff already knew he loved critters, so we assumed the new boss would be warm and fuzzy. He wasn't. Herb Dudnick had a brash New York manner that scared almost everyone.

The man did have charisma, however. On his first day, he showed up looking New York City dapper in fancy suspenders. Few people in our newsroom had worn suspenders before. It's a notable study of newsroom psychology that, the next day, about ten guys adopted the look. Unfortunately, they never noticed one important detail. Herb's suspenders attached to his pants with fashionable leather straps, while most of our impressionable staff purchased the clip-on variety.

Dudnick, we soon learned, would be a strange combination of screamer, tyrant, and mensch. He was tough on me, and I deserved it. Until Herb arrived, I thought of television news departments as existing to serve my needs, not the other way around.

Claire the Goldfish: An Exercise in "The Anvil Theory"

Dudnick brought to KRON a hard-news philosophy of owning big stories. He conducted a crash course on the concept when San Francisco's sewer system sprung a large leak. With Herb at the helm, our newsroom embraced what I call "the anvil theory of television news." We hit that story, pounded it, banged it, dented it, threw it back in the fire, turned it over, and pounded it again. The spill happened on Sunday. The city had it cleaned up by Wednesday. And Thursday? They sent me back to the sewage processing plant for yet another report about how San Franciscans could finally flush without fear.

Bang, bang, bang.

Before leaving, I noticed a big, beautiful goldfish swimming in a bowl on top of a laboratory counter. It seemed out of place. "What's with the fish?" I asked.

"That's Claire, " said lab boss Chuck Polling. "She's our mascot." Then he told her story.

Months earlier, a callous San Franciscan had, we presumed, dumped his goldfish down a toilet. Why? It doesn't matter. With a loud whoosh, Claire entered the bowels of the city sewer system.

Who knows how long she struggled? Who knows where Claire traveled or what horrors she witnessed? Who knows whether she was even a she? We did know that in San Francisco, all sewage pipes lead to the central purification plant where, before being pumped into the Pacific Ocean, material undergoes processing. For Claire, this meant certain doom. Those machines wouldn't discern the difference between a fish and a typical piece of sewage.

Polling explained how the churning, sifting and bubbling lasts eight hours. "It happens in stages," he said. Like a giant garbage disposal, the sewage plant reduces even moderate chunks of matter into tiny particles.

Poor Claire. Toward the end of her tribulations, she entered a maze of tightly wound, high-pressure pipes and fast-spinning blades known as the sludge room. The gauntlet stripped away her fins and scraped off most of her scales, but there must be a Goldfish God because Claire remained more-or-less intact. Miraculously, she passed through to the system's final stage which plopped her, along with tons of other treated sludge, into a large outdoor settling vat called the clarifying tank.

"That's where we found her," said Polling. "And that's why we named her— Claire."

The next day, Friday, offered little in the way of breaking sewer news. I pitched Claire as a kicker to our animal-loving news director. Dudnick bought the idea and, thanks to a fortunate goldfish, I found a way out of his doghouse, at least for a while.

Claire the Goldfish
Spring 1987

THIS STORY BEGINS WHERE MOST OTHERS END.

(SOT)
Shot of the city skyline with the sound of a toilet flush

AS CHUCK POLLING OF SAN FRANCISCO'S CLEAN WATER
DEPARTMENT TELLS US, IT'S A TALE OF TRIUMPH, STRUGGLE,
COURAGE, AND PERSEVERANCE . . .
THE STORY OF CLAIRE, A GOLDFISH.

(SOT)
Polling: "Her fins were torn. She was missing about a quarter of
her scales. She was missing some meat and she must have had
some kind of swim bladder damage because she was floating
crooked in the water, like that . . . "

He holds his hand upside down

CLAIRE, HE SAYS, IS THE ONLY FISH KNOWN TO HAVE SURVIVED A
TRIP THROUGH THE SAN FRANCISCO SEWER SYSTEM.

(SOT)
Shots of underground sewage

SHE PASSED THROUGH MILES OF UNDERGROUND TUNNELS
AND WATERFALLS—

THROUGH HIGH-PRESSURE PUMPING STATIONS—

AND THEN, THIS MENACING LIFTING DEVICE CALLED
ARCHIMEDES SCREW.

(SOT)
More rushing water; we look at the screw

IN ALL, CLAIRE WOULD ENDURE EIGHT HOURS OF SEWAGE
PROCESSING, INCLUDING THE SLUDGE ROOM.

(SOT)
Natural sound of pulsing pipes in the sludge room

(SOT VO)
Polling: "Well you have all these pumps in here and everything
gets pushed by little propellers."

Wayne: "CLAIRE MADE IT THROUGH SLUDGE CONTROL?"
Polling: "She was very lucky. Somehow, she passed between all
the blades of all the propellers."

. . . ONLY TO FIND HERSELF EJECTED INTO THESE HUGE
SEPARATION VATS WHERE WATER GOES ONE WAY,
AND GUNK THE OTHER. THIS IS WHERE WORK CREWS
FINALLY RESCUED HER—IN THE CLARIFYING TANK.

(SOT)
Polling: "That's why we named her."

Wayne: "CLAIRE?"

Polling: "Claire-eee-fyer is the fish's full name."

(SOT)
*We see Claire in her bowl. A finger taps on the tank. We hear him
say: "Claire . . ."*

AND THAT'S THE SOGGY SAGA OF A TOUGH LITTLE FISH WHO
BEAT THE ODDS AND BECAME A SEWER SYSTEM LEGEND.
NOW, ONE MORE QUESTION.

(SOT)
Wayne: WHAT IF SOMEBODY SEES THIS AND SAYS, "THAT'S MY
GOLDFISH AND I WANT CLAIRE BACK"?

Polling: "He'll have to prove it."

CHAPTER 3

Questions and Answers:
Interviews for Sound Bites

There is one final and most important prerequisite for developing characters in television news stories. Once you find a person and convince him to talk, he must do so openly and compellingly.

In theory, reporters should not care how their subjects come across, but don't believe it. The people in our stories speak to the viewers through us. It's our job to present them as faithfully as possible.

The perfect interview subject might be glib, funny, or deadly serious. He's insightful, honest, energetic, articulate, and conveys his thoughts in seven-second increments. But, when we're fortunate enough to interview someone who does speak in sound bites, we immediately become suspicious. It's like agreeing to teach poker to a self-proclaimed newbie who, gosh, knows nothing about playing cards, and later walks away with the pot.

Darn us reporters. We want it all. The ideal subject is savvy, but not too savvy. He's polished, but not too smooth. He's aware of the camera but doesn't play to it. In a word, he's a natural. If you encounter such a person twice in a year you're two ahead of the next guy.

As for the rest of the people you interview, don't get your hopes up. Every day brings a television news equivalent of the amateur hour.

Two Kinds of Sound Bites

When we strip away external factors, there are two kinds of sound bites.

- Sound bites presenting facts
- Sound bites with emotional content

In the most basic of factual interviews, you might speak with a police detective who only grudgingly provides the information you need. Such conversations can quickly become a version of Twenty Questions.

You ask. He replies. You catch a clue and probe again. From negative answers, you may glean useful information. Most reporters enjoy the gamesmanship in such encounters, even if the verbal jockeying never makes air. That's just as well. To viewers, it would sound ridiculous:

"Is this a murder investigation?" you might ask.

"We can't comment on that at this time."

"Are homicide detectives involved?"

"We can't comment on that, either."

"If they were not involved, could you confirm that?"

"Yes, we could confirm that, under certain circumstances."

"Is this one of those circumstances?"

"No."

"So how many homicide detectives are working this murder case?"

"Three."

Beyond the sporting aspects, however, reporters usually want more than facts from interviews. Facts, you see, are our currency. Good reporters can present them more clearly and concisely than a news maker.

There will be exceptions, and you'll recognize them when you hear them. Here's the test: *if a sound bite can explain a fact more efficiently, more clearly, with more drama, or with more authority than you, then, by all means, use it.*

Here are the words of Franklin Delano Roosevelt on December 8, 1941, after the Japanese attacked Pearl Harbor:

> *Yesterday, the Japanese also launched an attack against Malaya.*
> *Last night, Japanese forces attacked Hong Kong.*
> *Last night, Japanese forces attacked Guam.*
> *Last night, Japanese forces attacked the Philippine Islands.*

Last night, Japan attacked Wake Island.
This morning, Japan attacked Midway Island.

That's powerful stuff. Roosevelt simply stated facts. We would use such a sound bite in any broadcast, then or now.

Realistically, such large moments don't happen every day. Factual statements in routine news stories rarely have such a strong impact. Those are the times when reporters should look for sound bites expressing opinions, emotions, and reactions.

Here's a helpful general rule: *As the reporter, it is your job to present the facts of a story objectively. Use interviews and sound bites to let your subjects shade those facts subjectively.*

The Essential Question: Why?

I heard one of the best examples of a subjective sound bite from Professor Max Utsler when he taught journalism at the University of Missouri. He told the story of a state trooper who gave interviews at the scene of a fatal hit-and-run accident. To most of the reporters, the officer spoke like a typical cop. But one woman pursued a subjective line of questioning: "You look upset. Can you step outside your uniform for a moment and tell us what bothers you most about this accident?"

"In fifteen years on the job, this is the worst I've ever seen."

"Why?" she pushed.

"The little boy's shoe," said the cop. "I found it across the highway. That speeding car knocked him right out of his shoe. I'll see it for the rest of my life."

It was an emotional sound bite, one that amplified the facts. How, you might wonder, did that reporter break through the officer's thick skin and get him to talk from the heart? Simple. Her question addressed his humanity.

Having done so, she pushed it further by asking, "Why?" Isn't that the essential question? "Why" usually reveals the most about a person or a situation. If you get to "why," your viewer will already have good sense of who, what, when, where, and how.

Be warned, however, that good sound bites do not always come easily. Sometimes, you will encounter difficulties getting any kind of sound bite at all.

Overcoming An Interviewee's Discomfort

The Elephant Trainer

As soon as Patrick Harned introduced himself, I knew we had a problem. He mumbled.

He gave short, vague answers.

He barely looked at us. Instead, he lavished attention on an elephant named Shirley.

Patrick and his elephants had come to town as part of the circus. Its press relations people offered to let me ride one of the creatures in a parade, but news professionals have a disparaging description for reporters who participate in stories. We actually call it "riding the elephant." I was not about to do so literally.

We settled, instead, for a story about the elephant trainer. That's how, two hours before an evening performance, I stood in the arena parking lot, watching Patrick wash Shirley and her elephant friends.

"Don't you get tired of being around elephants all day?"

"No, not at all," said Patrick. "Elephants don't talk back. I'm a solitary person and don't much like talking to people."

Suffice it to say, Patrick didn't come from central casting. We had gone to the circus expecting a soft, upbeat story about a performer and, instead, got stuck with an introvert. Patrick Harned clammed up every time the camera came near.

"I just like elephants," he kept saying.

"Can you explain it?" I must have asked that question a dozen different ways.

"They're unique animals, and this is a unique job. How long is this story going to be? One minute? Two?"

At that rate, it might not become a story at all, so we kept after him. We spent the afternoon following Patrick around the circus, feeling like interlopers while he said more to the elephants than to us. Had I done something to offend him? In a last effort, I addressed his reticence: "Patrick, is it that you aren't comfortable with this? If so—"

He cut me off. "Not comfortable? I'm petrified."

"Of us?"

"Well, yes." And, with this admission, Patrick Harned opened up: "I'm not very good with cameras or crowds. I know that. The elephants are great but the performing part—that's hard to come by."

Patrick confessed to having a serious case of stage fright, one that extended to us. Now his weird behavior made sense, and the explanation changed our approach. Instead of doing a piece about pampered elephants, we focused on how Patrick dealt with his awkwardness in front of a crowd.

Once we understood each other, Patrick Harned shattered our preconceptions. Unlike other entertainers, applause meant little to him. He had taken the job to be with elephants. Show business only got in the way. "My bosses tell me I need to style better when performing," he said, shaking his head.

"What do you mean?"

"I don't know. That's why I have a hard time doing it."

What became our story about the shy, reluctant circus performer turned out to be much better than the one we set out to do. More important, it reminded me of a valuable lesson. When interviewing people, let them speak their minds. Help them find their comfort zones. You never know what someone will tell you, and where it may lead.

The Other Side of the Microphone

You're not likely to appreciate the art of interviewing until you experience it from the other side, with a microphone in your face. I have been interviewed several times. When the reporter asked perceptive questions and made me feel like the most important person in his world, I fared well. When he cut me off, or tried to make my answers fit his expectations, I came across badly.

Lesson learned. Let an interviewee be himself.

Disguise the Method

In Richard Ford's thoughtful novel *The Sportswriter*, his main character, Frank Bascombe, gives advice to a young intern who can't quite get the knack of interviewing. "I have a hard time asking questions," she tells him. "Mine are too complicated and no one says too much."

"You have to keep questions simple and remember to ask the same ones over and over again, sometimes in different words," replies Bascombe. "You just need to get out of their way." Even if that advice does come from a fictional character, it's absolutely true.

Accomplished interviewers work hard to make the process seem easy. They keep their questions simple. They listen. Their questions follow naturally. Then, as their subjects loosen up and answers begin to flow, those interviewers back off.

Most important, effective interviewers hide the method. They know that ordinary people are not born performers. Like Patrick Harned, they do best when they feel relaxed and natural. As a reporter, you may need to help them find that mindset. In the same way that your subject welcomes you into his home or office, make him comfortable with shooting the story. Remember, the interviewing process begins long before your camera rolls.

Imagine it from your subject's perspective. Maybe you called on short notice. He's cancelled appointments and changed plans—and maybe even his clothes. You haven't asked a question and, already, you've added stress to his day.

It worsens when you arrive late. Your subject sees a news vehicle in his driveway, and notices the neighbors walking out to look. He hadn't anticipated creating such a commotion.

As the reporter, you're oblivious to his mounting concerns. Instead, you're angry with the photographer for not driving faster, while he's miffed about having missed lunch. If you're doing the shoot alone, you will probably be in a hurry. Interviewees do not respond well to that kind of tension.

As the interview begins, your photographer turns on a bright bulb mounted atop his rig, unintentionally blinding your subject. It's the crucial moment and he freezes, becoming a human version of that deer caught in the headlights. Can you blame him?

Microphones

How then, can you make interviews less obtrusive? Begin with your microphone selection.

Try to avoid the handheld variety, particularly if your station has adorned them with fancy logos. Sticks, as we call them, work best when you're in a hurry, or in a crowd of other reporters, or shooting in environments with loud background noises—places like busy streets.

Handheld microphones clutter your artful pictures. They get in the way of intelligent conversations. How can a person feel relaxed when you continually point a microphone and take it away? You have the power. Your subject knows it.

When possible, use a wireless microphone. From a production perspective, it is easy to hide, it moves with a person, and when the interview concludes, it continues to capture close-up, natural sound.

Go so far as to help your subject attach it. In this simple but tactile way, both of you work together on a small project before the interview begins. I like to name the famous people who have previously worn that same microphone. It always makes good conversation. More important, by entering your subject's personal space, you subliminally demonstrate that you don't bite. As corny as this may sound, it works.

Additionally, as long as your subject wears that microphone, the interview continues, albeit in a more casual manner. Every question becomes progressively less threatening, allowing him or her to open up.

"What I Meant To Say…"

Keep the camera rolling for a few seconds after an interview ends. Don't be in such a hurry with that little red button. I'm not suggesting this to be shady or sneaky. In my experience, a person tends to lighten up when he thinks the heat is off. It's human nature. When you hear the words, "What I meant to say," your best sound bite will often follow.

Thirty-five Feet of Honesty

The late Ray Farkas, who produced for NBC News, turned interviewing into a science, often with visually stunning results. Early in his career, Farkas grew weary of traditional question-and-answer techniques. "As soon as you turn on the camera, a subject figuratively clears his throat and the voice drops an octave," Farkas used to say. "The whole idea is to reduce intimidation. Make a person unaware that these could be his fifteen minutes—or, more likely, his fifteen seconds—of fame."

Farkas might place the camera twenty, thirty, even forty feet away from his subject. He would shoot at long focal lengths, through foregrounds of doors and windows, across streets, and around plants. At forty feet, instead of the more conventional five feet, Farkas got what he called, "thirty-five more feet of honesty." When subjects can't see a camera, they will be less influenced or intimidated by it.

Lights, or No Lights?

For the same reason, Farkas avoided using lights when possible. "One light begets two, then three, and with each additional one, the environment becomes more artificial," he preached. "With the quality of cameras these days, we can get pictures from almost anywhere. What you gain in image quality from the lights, you lose in humanity. I want to get as close to that humanity as possible. Boost the gain switch on the camera, instead."

I do not always agree with that. As a photographer, I enjoy lighting the more formal interviews. One small soft box can look quite good. It also communicates to an interviewee that we care.

Sometimes you can work with natural sources in shooting environments. A plain bulb diffused by a lampshade or bounced off a white wall can be flattering on a subject's face. So can a fluorescent lamp sitting on a desk. When you're traveling light and hauling your own gear, finding a way to add those small touches will improve the quality of your video and your stories.

Positioning

Even when Farkas reverted to a more standard interview, he paid particular attention to body language and positioning. You would rarely see his subjects facing directly toward the camera. If they were sitting, Farkas turned their chairs by as much as ninety degrees in relation to the lens. "It changes the look. If a guy's sitting straight on, it makes a boring shot. When you rotate the chair, a person must lean in toward the camera. It's the same as being in a bar. People don't face each other on barstools. One person turns his head to the other."

Farkas added a note of caution, however, about placing an interview subject in a location as if he were a prop. "It might make a nice shot, but if a person looks or feels awkward, it defeats the purpose. The interview reflects that." As a general rule, then, *it is better to compromise the shot before you compromise a subject's psychological or personal comfort.*

Granted, Ray Farkas had more time to produce those stories than we do on a daily basis, but I still use his techniques from time to time. 'Farkasing', as his disciples call it, requires extra effort. You will like the results.

Eye Contact

People make eye contact almost every time they speak. This is doubly important when interviewing. Try to put yourself at eye level, just to the right or the left of the lens plane. Move as close to the person as possible without intruding into the frame, unless you want viewers to see you. Look directly into your subject's eyes for both questions and answers. Engage him. People will be less likely to worry about a camera if they don't have to look at it.

Keep Your Sound Bites Fresh

It's only natural that interview subjects become anxious. "What are we going to talk about? What will you ask me?" Reporters hear those questions almost every day.

Don't be too specific in your reply. "Nothing we didn't talk about on the telephone," I usually tell them, and leave it at that. Here's why. People tend to give their best answers and descriptions when they know a listener hasn't heard them before. It's human nature. Besides, no reporter wants to edit around phrases like "As I said earlier..." Keep that in mind so that you will not lose your sound bites before the camera rolls.

The late Charles Kuralt of CBS News described this as *keeping a sound bite fresh.*

Don't misunderstand. I am not suggesting you ignore someone before an interview. Quite the contrary: Establish rapport. Try to get him to open up about himself. Ask what he's done, what he enjoys, where he's been, or what he believes. With any of those four topics, you should be able to get someone talking within thirty seconds.

If you are shooting the story as well as reporting it, you have an added advantage. When subjects see me lugging gear, they often ask if they can help. I let them. My camera takes nice pictures, and also works as a very good icebreaker.

So does a small amount of personal information. For a white balance card, I often use the backside of a photo showing my daughter tasting her first chocolate milkshake. Hold something like that in front of a subject's face. Everybody relates to kids.

In short, be yourself.

Extracting Answers

Once your subjects feel relaxed and comfortable, you still need to inspire good, concise sound bites. Because you're looking for ten-second segments rather than whole conversations, answers matter more than questions. This opens up a range of interviewing strategies.

Adapt to Your Subject—Time Your Questions

As you prepare for an interview, listen carefully to your subject's speech pattern. You won't want to interrupt an answer. Nor will you want to lose a potentially good sound bite by letting a statement hang. If an answer sounds incomplete, a well-timed verbal nudge might help your subject finish it.

Read the person. Notice whether he's low-key or high-strung. Some people need sympathy. Others like to be teased. Figure out what works.

When the San Francisco Giants went to the World Series in 2002, we did a piece about fair-weather fans buying memorabilia. "The Benito Santiago jerseys are already sold out," moaned a woman who was shopping for her son. Santiago, the Giants' catcher at the time, had just won most valuable player honors in the National League Championship Series. "I absolutely must have an item with 'Santiago' written on it. Anything will do." Then, she paused. We were about to lose the conversational momentum.

"Would you settle for a map of Chile?" I quipped.

"I thought Benito Santiago was from Puerto Rico."

In response to my ridiculous question, the woman finished an exchange that fit the mood and the moment.

Challenge Your Subjects

Don't be afraid to challenge people, no matter what the circumstances. If an interview subject sounds flat, boring, or too rehearsed, play devil's advocate. With a well-placed needle at the proper time, you can become an enabler as much as an interviewer.

Try a good-natured "Aw, c'mon" sometime. Use the question as you would a corkscrew. Give it a twist, and your subject may pour himself out.

If necessary, you can always apologize later.

Ray Farkas recalled an interview about a multiple murderer. The district attorney avoided straight answers by speaking in legalese. Eventually, Farkas tried another approach. "You must have seen worse people. Deep down, is this suspect really such a bad person? C'mon."

The DA took that question as a personal challenge. He erupted, laying into the defendant. Farkas got his sound bite.

Ask Pointed Questions

Give a person an excuse to talk, and often he will. I remember the case of a professional football player and two of his friends who were accused of gang raping a woman. The victim admitted having sex with them, but only, she said, because they drugged her. After the first day's court testimony, which included stories of all-night clubs, limousines, and parties, it became clear that neither the football player, his friends, nor the young woman would ever qualify as Sunday-school role models.

Defense lawyer William Dubois played it safe when our interview began. "My client believed the woman was being cooperative," he stated. After such a colorless answer, I pressed him for something better. "Let's be honest. Your client admits to being a player with the ladies. That won't exactly make him sympathetic to a jury. What can you do to turn his image around?"

Mr. Dubois made no attempt at moral apologies. "This is not a gathering of saints," he said. "Not the plaintiff, and not the defendants. These are all people whose idea of fun is to go out to clubs, get loaded, get laid, and go to work the next day. My client is just one of the many intoxicated people who wind up in bed together at the end of the evening."

Some sound bites are too good for a general audience.

Interviewing Politicians and Public Officials

You will have some of your most challenging interviews with politicians and public officials. As a breed, they can be even more elusive than lawyers.

The most exasperating public officials remind me of that bad police robot in *Terminator II*. Remember the scene in which it chases Arnold Schwarzenegger down a hall? Arnold shoots the robot. It falls, staggers to its feet, the bullet hole heals itself, and the bad robot resumes its dogged pursuit. Many politicians and elected officials act much the same way when pressing their talking points during interviews.

Watch the national political shows. Analyze how public officials apply spin control. They have agendas, just the same as reporters. They know what they want to talk about, and also the areas they want to avoid.

The "best" of them are adept at tailoring rambling, unusable answers filled with conjunctions and asides. Just as politicians and public officials know how to make themselves quotable, they also know how to make themselves unquotable.

An Unusable Answer

During the 'Arab Spring' 2011, world gasoline prices spiked after revolutionary uprisings against the governments of several oil producing Middle East nations. The United States Department of Agriculture viewed this as a rich opportunity to promote domestic, corn-based ethanol. When rural development administrator Judith Canales visited a biofueling station in Oakland, California, my bosses asked me to cover it.

As a reporter, make it a point to ask specific questions, not easy ones. Back in the newsroom, managing editor Greg Derego and I talked about how corn is a less efficient fuel source than, say, sugarcane from Brazil. We noted that the United States placed a stiff tariff on those imports. Meantime, farmers receive federal subsidies to grow corn-based ethanol in Iowa, and presidential candidates make promises to them before the caucuses there.

Based on those facts, we wanted to ask why a nation trying to wean itself from foreign oil and reduce global warming would stick so staunchly to corn. This was not a subject the Department of Agriculture commissioner came to discuss, but Greg and I saw it as a way to add meat to the story.

Question: "If our government is truly interested in reducing our dependence on foreign oil and reducing carbon emissions, what about increasing our imports of more efficient bio sources, like sugarcane, as an alternative to corn?"

Here is the verbatim of her answer: "What we are doing is also trying to develop products in this country and so therefore corn is a part of that, is part of the solution, but corn is very quickly becoming…there is, ugh, a thirty-six billion goal per year and the corn piece to that is very quickly reaching its piece. We need the alternative source, too, which is biofuels, and, as I was stating earlier, there are algae. There is, ugh, also, ugh municipal solid waste. There is citrus agricultural waste. All of those are being looked at as alternative sources for biofuel development."

Honestly, if we could compare an answer to some of her afore-mentioned municipal solid waste, that one would qualify. I did not give up.

Follow-up question: "Okay, but this is also about keeping corn fields growing, right?

Answer: "Corn is part of the solution, but it is not the only solution."

Close enough. We used it, although the devil in me would have preferred to run her first answer.

Know Your Facts

That exchange was a good example of how, when you have command of the facts, you can keep control of an interview. Politicians respect reporters who prepare, shoot straight, and, like that bad police robot, knock them a little off-balance. As with Judith Canales, when candidates or politicians apply spin control, politely let them know they did not answer your question, and ask again. The next time, they may be less likely to mess with you.

On the other side, sometimes politicians know too much for their own good.

Before Congresswoman Nancy Pelosi became Speaker of the House, she spent more than a minute detailing a fine point of foreign policy for me in an interview. She was passionate. She was persuasive. She was not trying to be evasive. Unfortunately, while her answer would have suited a live Sunday-morning network broadcast, it would never fit into our ninety-second segment.

Clearly, Pelosi wanted to make her point, and we wanted to hear it. As I asked the question two or three ways, both of us became frustrated. Finally, I took a deep breath, turned off the camera, and said, "This is a very important point. I wish we could run all the nuances of it. At the risk of sounding shallow, how do we boil this into ten or twelve seconds?"

It was unorthodox, and it worked. Pelosi delivered.

Be Tactful: Jim Stolpa

You might remember Jim and Jennifer Stolpa and their infant son, Clayton. They're the family that, during a blizzard in 1992, tried to find a shortcut through California's Sierra Nevada. On a narrow mountain road, miles from any home or hamlet, the Stolpas got lost, and then stuck.

As the storm worsened, the couple grew weary of waiting, swaddled the baby in a sleeping bag, and set out on foot. After a day, Jennifer could go no farther. Jim used his Army survival training to build her a cave in the snow, and then pressed ahead, alone. After nine more days, he stumbled down to civilization, and then led rescuers back to his wife and son.

Their ordeal was not over. When they arrived at the hospital in Reno, Nevada, the Stolpas found a media mob waiting. The search had made them front-page news, household names, and heroes. Although Jim and Jennifer both lost toes to frostbite, young Clayton survived unharmed. At the peak of their fame, Jim and Jennifer Stolpa's story became a movie of the week.

Then they disappeared from public life.

Nine years later, we became curious and traced the couple to Milwaukee, Wisconsin, for a follow-up. The Stolpas had divorced, but remained good friends. Going in, I had one difficult question to ask. During the search, it had been only natural for some people to take the name Stolpa and precede or replace it with the word "stupid." Had Jim and Jennifer heard about that? Could I pose the question tactfully?

I hoped Jim would address it himself, and waited for an opportunity. As we recollected media coverage, I asked, "What do you imagine the world thought about you and Jennifer at that time? What do you think people said?"

"Oh, they said that we were stupid," he answered. "What we did was stupid, stupid, stupid. And it was. We've admitted it. But, after making a bad decision, we did everything right."

Jim gestured to Clayton, then nine years old. "I made it because of him," he said. "Clayton is the reason we survived. He's the proof. His little sister is the celebration of it."

That sound bite came from asking an honest question, not a tough one. Jim had heard the talk. He wanted to address the issue as much as we wanted to ask about it. Jim Stolpa was hardly stupid.

Assume Nothing: The Pizza Bandit

Off-camera interviews can be just as important as those that take place in front of a lens.

In June, 2004, we covered a sad and unfortunate use of force by the Richmond, California police. Someone had been victimizing pizza restaurants by placing orders and then holding up the delivery people. Detectives worked the case for several months and developed a profile. When it appeared that their bad guy had placed another order and was ready to strike again, they substituted a police officer for the delivery man.

As predicted, a hooded figure approached the officer from behind, held a gun to his head, and demanded money. Police surrounded the suspect. They ordered him to drop his weapon. When he refused, they shot and killed him.

That suspect, Robert Freeman, was sixteen years old.

For much of the day, we pursued the angle of police shooting and killing a juvenile. Was it preventable? Were they justified? The Richmond Police Department's public information officer spoke once, early in the morning, and then went mum until we convinced him to talk again, at 3:45 that afternoon.

"It's an unfortunate situation," Lieutenant Mike Pon said on camera.

After the interview ended, we continued talking for background information. "How many rounds were in the gun?" I asked him. Like every other reporter covering this story, I assumed the gun must have been loaded. "I suppose you might feel a little better knowing that, at least, you saved the life of one of your guys."

"I can't comment on that," said Lieutenant Pon.

"Why not? It's been more than twelve hours."

"Like I said, I can't comment on that. I can give you more on this in maybe an hour. Let me clear a couple of facts."

An hour later, the lieutenant went on camera. No, the nine-millimeter Beretta had not been loaded, nor could it have been. Sixteen-year-old Robert Freeman had used a plastic replica in that hold-up—a toy. It was the one fact that Richmond Police had not yet revealed to a sensitive community, mostly because no reporter had asked. "In the dark, this looked like a real gun," said Lieutenant Pon.

Indeed, it did. When we went on the air a few moments later, no other reporter had the information. My naïve, off-camera background question, based on an inaccurate assumption, turned the story.

Interviewing Victims

Reporters face their most difficult moments when asked to interview friends or families of victims. In the most trying of these assignments, we must put aside our sense of what feels proper, and knock on a door.

In 1988, a Napa, California, winery worker named Ramone Salcido killed his wife during a jealous, cocaine-induced rage. It didn't stop there. He also cut the throats of his three young daughters, killing two of them. Next, he drove several miles to the town of Cotati and did more of the same to his in-laws and their children.

Northern California had not seen a crime this brutal in a long time. At KRON-TV, we went to nonstop coverage. I spent the afternoon staring at yellow police tape surrounding the in-laws' house. Neighbors clustered around, energized by the excitement. Only later, when the coroner carried bloody body bags through the glare of television lights, did they comprehend the mayhem that had taken place inside.

The next morning, photographer John Laursen and I returned to the neighborhood for reactions. We did not go by choice; follow-up stories about crimes and victims feel tawdry and exploitative.

We parked on the street at noon and, unlike the day before, found that same neighborhood devoid of people. Toys lay on porches, and morning papers on driveways. Tricycles remained on curbs. It might as well have been the rapture.

Along all of Lakeview Avenue, we heard only one sound—someone practicing piano inside a house two doors down from the murders. We knocked. A woman came to the screen door. She did not open it.

"We're with NewsCenter 4." I said. "We know this is a terrible time, but we were hoping someone might tell us about the family and children down the street—what were they like?"

The woman resisted. Who wouldn't? Once we got her talking, we convinced her she had plenty to say on camera, and she stepped outside. As we pinned the microphone I realized what a telling shot John would get if the woman went back in and let the door close between us. She did. That image of her face, diffused by the screen, said more than words ever could about sadness and vulnerability. "How could this happen to little angels?" asked the woman. "If those girls could have grown wings, they would have."

As happens so often in tense environments, the first interview drew other people who also wanted to speak. Not once did we ask, "How do you feel?" Certainly, we had come to answer that question, but those specific words, "How do you feel?" make reporters look bad. Find a more tactful way to phrase them.

"What do you remember about the family?"

"How long had they lived here? "

"What did they wear to trick-or-treat last Halloween?"

With some people, we didn't need to ask anything. The mood was such that, after setting a shot, it took only a look or a nod to start them talking.

The Girl with the Red Ball

After half an hour, we had more material than we could use. Then a young girl walked up. She clutched a big red ball to her chest and, like the others, asked to speak. Her mother approved, so why not? When people want to talk, give them the opportunity. "What will you remember best about them?" I began.

"It wouldn't be a regular day if you didn't see them walking their little dog, Chiquita, up and down the street and smiling at everybody they saw," said the little girl, who seemed wise and soulful beyond her years. Her words hung there, along with the image they described. In the uncomfortable pause before I could ask another question, she kept talking. "Every movie that I see, people die in them, but I never thought about how in real life, they really die, die. Then they're just gone. You can't replace them."

By accident, my best question had been no question at all.

Interviewing Children

Art Linkletter

The girl with the ball might have been ten years old. It's worth noting her age because ten-year-olds make excellent interviews. They're just on the cusp of sophistication, old enough to articulate their ideas, yet still young enough to be cute, innocent, honest, and respectful of their elders. At ten they haven't copped an attitude yet. Keep this in mind the next time you do a segment with elementary school kids. Ask for the fifth graders.

I base my theory on both professional and personal experiences. During the 1960s, before our airwaves and cable television channels filled with titillating distractions, CBS ran a noontime program called *Art Linkletter's House Party*. He always interviewed school kids during the last minutes of his show. Linkletter was a master at it.

In 1965, *Art Linkletter's House Party* called our school, and my fifth-grade teacher, Mrs. Sherock, selected me to be interviewed. On the big day, we rode to CBS Television City in a black Cadillac limousine with fins. Mr. Linkletter met us for brief pre-interviews and, about an hour later, put us in front of a studio audience. He turned what might have been an uncomfortable experience into a fun one.

At the first writing of this book, the late Mr. Linkletter was eighty-nine years old. Except for Santa Claus, no one in the world could claim to know more about interviewing children—he had interviewed twenty-six thousand of them. Because I had something of an "in" with the man, I telephoned him to test my theory about ten-year-olds.

"It depends on what you want," said Linkletter, who described how types of answers vary with age. He compared maturity levels to foods from a buffet. "At ten, they know more. They don't have attitudes, yet. But I think younger children are more interesting because of their limited knowledge. If they don't know an answer, they may strike out wildly and say anything."

"If you had to pick one age group, what would it be?" I asked.

"Five-year-olds, because they think so directly."

Linkletter recalled asking a kindergartner if she knew her birthday. "July 15," the little girl said.

"What year?"

"Every year," she replied with conviction.

Linkletter loved the younger kids—he kept on and on about them. He recalled asking a four-year-old boy, "Do you go to Sunday school?"

"Yes," the kid replied.

"What religion are you?"

"We're either Catholic or Prostitute."

That answer, said Linkletter, drew a big laugh from the audience, and yet he didn't dare join in. "No matter what a child says, keep a straight face. Be a friend. Never let him feel as if you're making fun. You'll lose him if you do."

He gave another example of a nine-year-old boy. "What would you do if you were flying an airplane and all four engines stopped?" Linkletter asked.

"I would tell the passengers to fasten their seat belts. Then I would parachute and jump out." Although the audience roared, Linkletter says he kept a straight face. It paid off because the kid tried to reassure him. "Don't worry," he said. "I'd just be going for gas."

Meet the Child at His Level

When interviewing a child of any age, try to meet him at his level. Be wary of intimidating him with your height; you don't want to come across as an authority figure. I remember how Linkletter's show placed kids on elevated stools. He worked us close, leaning in to make absolute eye contact, much the same as I do with people today. Maybe the example came from him.

When you meet a child, be friendly, calm, and reassuring. Use a quiet voice and ask if it's all right to talk. Empower him. Expect the child to be nervous, so begin with easy questions. Ask his name and age. Once he hears his own voice, he'll gain confidence and loosen up.

Keep the interview light and upbeat. A few years ago, while doing a Thanksgiving story with some preschool students, I played dumb: "Where do turkeys come from?"

"Eggs," said one little girl.

"What kind of eggs?"

"Chickens."

"What do you do with the turkey after you've eaten it?"

"My daddy puts the turkey bones on his head," she said.

"Why would he do that?"

"He wears it like a hat!"

Choosing the Child

After deciding on an age group, you must choose the children to interview. Linkletter applied a simple and effective method. "We didn't want the model students," he said. "We wanted the troublemakers. We liked the kids with spunk." Linkletter's staff always mailed the same letter to schools. "It asked the dear teachers to give us the four children they would most like to have out of the class for a few blessed hours. The teachers would laugh and send me the rascals."

I always assumed that Mrs. Sherock sent me to Art Linkletter as some kind of reward. Now we know that it was, but not for me—for her.

Interviewing Older People and Veterans

The B-17

Mr. Linkletter finished our talk by describing the time he asked an octogenarian to give him one good reason for living to be a hundred. "There's no peer pressure," the woman replied.

If only our elders were always so easy to interview.

You may have heard the remarkable tale of Charles Brown, who piloted a B-17 during World War II. In 1943, while flying his first mission over Bremen, Germany, enemy fire knocked Brown's bomber into a high altitude death spiral. Brown had taken a bullet in the shoulder, and blacked out during the plunge. He awoke with seconds to spare, just in time to pull the plane into straight and level flight. "I still have recurring nightmares about seeing those trees out my windshield," said Charles.

His crisis was only beginning. Of the plane's four engines, just one remained running. He had lost most of the plane's tail to cannon fire, along with the plastic bombardier's bubble. As the plane flew, a bitterly cold winter wind blew through the fuselage, freezing the surviving crew members and their guns.

Having righted the plane, Brown still believed he could get it home. Then, he flew directly over a Luftwaffe fighter base. "My heart sank," said Charles.

Minutes later, an ME-109 fighter intercepted to make the kill. Its pilot, Franz Stigler, had already shot down two B-17's that day. A third would give him the Knight's Cross. As Stigler closed, however, he saw blood on the windows. He saw the motionless guns. He saw how the plane teetered to stay aloft. He moved closer and locked eyes with Charles Brown.

"What did you see in those eyes?" I asked Stigler.

"Fear."

It was December 22, three days before Christmas, and, in that moment, Franz Stigler made a personal decision. He knew the war would end someday, and how he would have to look himself in the mirror if he survived. "I thought of myself as a warrior, not a murderer."

Rather than shooting, Stigler tried to force the B-17 into landing. When Charles Brown refused, the German escorted him halfway home across the North Sea, saluting as they parted. "If he could make it back in that plane in that condition, he deserved to live," said Stigler.

Later, Charles Brown made a miracle landing at Kimbolton, England. His superiors promised the Congressional Medal of Honor, then changed their minds when Brown relentlessly praised the German pilot who spared his life. Instead, they buried his report inside top-secret files, where it remained for forty years.

Back in Germany, Stigler also kept the story to himself, for fear of being court-martialed. By the time the war ended, he had flown four-hundred eighty-seven missions, made twenty-eight kills, and was shot down seventeen times. Though it all, and after, he always wondered about that B-17.

And Charles Brown always wondered about that German pilot. Charles managed to survive twenty-six more missions, made a career in the Air Force, and spent almost five decades searching for the man who spared him.

In 1990, when the two warriors finally met, I covered their reunion for CBS News. Charles and Franz spent two days at an Army Air Corps get-together near Boston. They visited a B-17, shared beers, and discovered a soulful kinship. It often works out this way. Former enemies find they have more in common with each other than almost anyone outside their circle.

The men did not open up to us, however. We expected that. Perhaps it comes from a mindset born of sacrifices, but every World War II veteran I've interviewed was stoic and guarded, at least in the beginning. They had plenty to say, but were reluctant to say it. When talking about war, most hid their feelings with statements like, "Well, it was just tough. We did what we had to do."

That's how it went with Stigler, Brown, and the rest of Brown's crew. They talked, certainly, but did not give us the emotional kind of sound bites that we needed for this story. Steigler remained stoic. Brown took refuge in facts. Somehow, I had to capture the intensity of their encounter so many years earlier.

We began with Charles. Instead of opening with the crucial questions, I pressed him for details, hoping to trigger vivid memories.

"What was the weather like?"

"Do you remember what you had for breakfast?"

"Who was your copilot?"

"Did you bring along a good luck charm?"

Our conversation assumed a pattern of questions and answers.

"How long were you above the ball bearing factory in Bremen?"

"What does a guy worry about on his first mission?"

"What does flak sound like?"

We continued—question, answer, question, answer, question, answer—and then, as Charles Brown described the moment when his B-17 began to fall, I let the statement hang. He expected another question. When I didn't ask one, he assumed he should keep talking. In the way a roller coaster peaks and then enters free-fall, Charles Brown finally told his story with unguarded passion. His voice cracked. Tears welled in his eyes. "We flew for different sides," he said, "But still, the code, the honor was there."

As difficult as Brown had been, Stigler proved tougher still. After a similar thread of questions, the elderly German never came close to cracking.

Ultimately, we broke through with visual and tactile cues. Earlier, I had asked Brown and his surviving crew members to bring along names and photographs of their children, grandchildren, and great-grandchildren.

Near the end of our interview with Stigler, I pulled out the names and photos and, as a last resort, handed them to the stoic old pilot. "Do you know who they are?"

"I think so."

"Could you look at the pictures and read the names, please." Franz Stigler complied. He had never seen all of them together before. When he held the pictures and read the roll call of men, women, boys, and girls, a wave of emotion hit him. Those people had come into being and lived because, on a fearful afternoon three days before Christmas almost half a century earlier, he didn't pull the trigger.

The old pilot held the photographs, looking stunned. "Well, it's fate," he stammered while shaking his head. "And fate is something we have no control about."

Charles Brown and Franz Stigler, old and best friends who considered themselves brothers, died within two months of each other in 2009.

CHAPTER 4

Structure:
Beginnings, Middles, Endings, and Timelines

Young reporters ask me one question more than any others. "How can I write more creatively, especially when my bosses want two different versions of a story every day?"

First, I gently correct them on a matter of semantics. Writing a news story should be adaptive, not creative. This is a business of finding storylines and adjusting to them, not manufacturing them.

Then I give them the pragmatic answer. *Adapt a story's timeline to give it a distinct beginning, middle and ending.*

What is a timeline? Every story has three of them:

1. The order of events as they unfold
2. The order in which you record them
3. The order in which you present those events to the viewer

The third of those timelines will be the most important. It will also be where your fun and so-called creativity can begin.

Let's look at a hypothetical example: the story of Bill Johnson, an emergency dispatcher who saved a driver's life by giving Heimlich instructions to his passenger. Assume you arrive at the dispatch center to shoot a piece, and have these limited elements with which to write a script:

- Johnson at his console
- Johnson leaving work
- An interview with him
- A recording of the emergency telephone conversation
- Pictures of Interstate 80, where the emergency call originated

You do not have pictures of the car or interviews with the victim, nor with driver who made the call. How would you open the story?

Here's your first option, a straightforward linear timeline in which the story begins before the emergency call:

> IN TEN YEARS AS AN EMERGENCY DISPATCHER, BILL JOHNSON
> NEVER DEALT WITH A SITUATION LIKE THIS.
>
> (SOT)
> Emergency tape: "Help! Help! My friend is choking!"
>
> THE CALL CAME FROM A PASSENGER IN A CAR ON INTERSTATE
> 80. HIS FRIEND HAD BEEN DRIVING WHILE EATING CHICKEN
> WINGS . . .

Now, a second option that begins with recorded sound of the emergency call:

> (SOT)
> Emergency tape: "Help! Help! My friend is choking!"
>
> THE CALL CAME IN WITH URGENCY, JUST LIKE ALL THE OTHERS
> AT THIS EMERGENCY DISPATCH CENTER.
>
> (SOT)
> Bill Johnson: "The guy had maybe a minute to live . . ."

Finally, as a third option, begin the story at the end of the event timeline, and then work back. Because you arrived late and have limited elements, this would allow you to start with the latest information:

WHEN BILL JOHNSON FINISHES WORK, HE OFTEN KNOWS HE HAS HELPED TO SAVE A LIFE. BUT TONIGHT'S CALL, FROM A CAR ON INTERSTATE 80, WILL STICK WITH HIM AWHILE.

(SOT)
Emergency tape: "Help! Help! My friend is choking!"

(SOT)
Bill Johnson: "It wasn't a typical call . . ."

Of all these timelines, I prefer the last one because it gives viewers enough information to expect a happy ending, yet keeps them wondering how it came about.

Put a New Top On it

There is another benefit to manipulating timelines, especially in shops where producers ask reporters for multiple versions of stories. By changing or moving a couple of shots or sound bites, or by adding an element, a reporter can give that second story a different look. Any or all of those adjustments can alter a timeline. We call the technique "putting a new top on it."

Two Versions From the Same Material: Hurricane Gustav

When Hurricane Gustav bore down on Louisiana's Gulf Coast in 2008, it appeared to be as large and potentially devastating as Katrina, three years earlier. Gustav had already decimated Haiti, Jamaica, and Cuba as a Category 4 storm. Winds exceeded two-hundred miles per hour.

In an election year, and with so many possible consequences, KGO-TV management wanted its own crew in Louisiana. I had covered Katrina, so that made me a logical choice for Gustav. Photographer Dean Smith and I flew to Houston, Texas, and drove east from there.

Entering a hurricane zone is a little like preparing to cover the Apocalypse. Rent the biggest SUV you can find because it may become your home for several days. Purchase excess gasoline, strap the containers to the roof, and stock up on non-perishables like canned tuna, beef jerky, and Cheese Wiz. You learn a lot about a guy when hurricane shopping with him in a grocery store. Dean and I disagreed strongly about buying chunky peanut butter or creamy—chunky won.

ABC Corporate Travel found us a hotel in Lafayette, Louisiana. We used Skype to file a report for the 11 p.m. news, and then hunkered down for a few hours of uneasy sleep while waiting for Gustav to make landfall.

The station arranged for us to work out of a KTRK-TV satellite truck in Morgan City, sixty-one miles to the southeast. As Gustav roared, we made a memorable drive through wind-driven horizontal rain that stung our faces like bees, and pushed our Suburban around like a Tonka toy. Dean and I were jadedly disappointed that those winds reached only one-hundred miles an hour.

We arrived in time to watch the hurricane's leading edge wreak havoc on the city, experienced the calmness of its eye, and then braced as the second half passed through. That night, thanks to Dean's fast editing, we filed separate reports for both the 5 p.m. and 6 p.m. broadcasts.

Here are the two scripts. Notice how they use much of the same material, but we made them different by changing a few elements and manipulating their timelines.

Hurricane Gustav
5 p.m.
September 1, 2008

Video shows people huddling in the doorway of a cinder block apartment house

IF YOU CHOSE TO REMAIN IN MORGAN CITY, LOUISIANA,
THIS WAS AS GOOD A PLACE TO TAKE COVER AS ANY . . .
AN APARTMENT HOUSE FORTIFIED BY CINDER BLOCKS
AND SAND BAGS, WITH A FEW GOOD FRIENDS.

(SOT)
Sydney Chustz, Morgan City Resident:
"There ain't no running. No hiding. Can't do nothing except what we're doing, and listen to it creak."

TO BE MORE PRECISE, HURRICANE GUSTAV BANGED . . .
AS THE EYE PASSED OVER, IT HIT TWICE, ESSENTIALLY, WITH
SUSTAINED WINDS OF AT LEAST ONE-HUNDRED MILES AN HOUR.

AND YET, THE OUTRIGHT DISASTER SO MANY PEOPLE FEARED
FROM THIS STORM NEVER QUITE MATERIALIZED.

(SOT)
Woman in apartment: "I was expecting much worse."

(SOT)
Chris Cortez, Resident: "It was bad. Don't get me wrong.
Bad, but not that bad."

(WAYNE STAND-UP)
*I point to names of previous hurricanes on plywood covering
a window*

IT'S NOT AS IF MORGAN CITY HADN'T SEEN THIS BEFORE.
JUST READ THE NAMES ON THIS PLYWOOD. RESIDENTS HERE
HAVE BEEN THROUGH ANDREW, BETSY, KATRINA,
AND NOW THE LATEST FOR GUSTAV.

(SOT)
Chris Cortez, Morgan City Resident: "This comparison is a lot
stronger, bro. This is less than Katrina. It's three quarters of
Andrew."

AND STILL STRONG ENOUGH. ONE FIREMAN ESTIMATES IT WILL
TAKE THREE WEEKS BEFORE MORGAN CITY BEGINS TO LOOK
NORMAL, AGAIN, WHICH MIGHT SOUND LIKE A LONG TIME,
BUT NOT TO THESE RESIDENTS, WHO SUFFERED SO MUCH
WORSE IN THE PAST.

(SOT)
Chris Cortez: "I'm still alive and dry, and that's what counts."

Now, the 6 p.m. version. We changed the visuals of our open from the
apartment building to shots of downtown, used a different stand-up, and
expanded our narrative by elaborating on the hurricane's three acts:

Hurricane Gustav
6 p.m.
September 1, 2008

Video shows debris blowing in street

IN MORGAN CITY, LOUISIANA, THE DIFFERENCE BETWEEN
A MISS AND A DIRECT HIT IS THE FIFTY MILES BETWEEN
HERE AND BATON ROUGE.

(SOT)
Woman in apartment: "Whatever happens, happens . . ."

TODAY, IT HAPPENED TWICE AS THE EYE OF HURRICANE GUSTAV
PASSED DIRECTLY OVERHEAD.

(SOT)
Sydney Chustz, Morgan City Resident: "There ain't no running . . .
no hiding . . ."

GUSTAV'S LEADING EDGE BROUGHT SUSTAINED WINDS OF
AT LEAST 100 MILES AN HOUR, ALONG WITH A CUTTING,
HORIZONTAL RAIN.
WHAT IT DIDN'T BLOW THROUGH . . .

(SOT)
*We see the wind howling through the frame if what used to be a
neon sign*

IT BLEW OVER . . .

(SOT)
We see power lines on the ground

AND THEN, AS THE EYE PASSED ABOVE, THE CALM IN BETWEEN.

(SOT)
Wayne asks: ISN'T IT OVER?

Chris Cortez, Morgan City Resident: "No it's not over. We got another hour left, bro . . . "

(SOT)
Sydney Chustz, Morgan City Resident: "Oh it's going to get worse when the other side of the eye hits us . . . "

THEY KNOW FROM EXPERIENCE IN THIS CITY SEVEN FEET ABOVE SEA LEVEL, WHERE HURRICANE ANDREW LAID WASTE IN 1992. COMPARED WITH THOSE STORMS, MORGAN CITY RESIDENTS REGARD KATRINA, EVEN, AS AN ASTERISK.

(SOT)
Woman in apartment: "This is not our first time around the block."

(WAYNE STAND-UP)
On river's edge

THE BACK SIDE OF THE EYE HIT ABOUT 2PM. IN LESS THAN A MINUTE, CONDITIONS WENT FROM CALM TO WHAT WE HAVE HERE, AND THE WINDS ARE STILL GAINING STRENGTH.

(SOT)
Storm blows

AGAIN, MORGAN CITY HUNKERED DOWN, BUT THIS TIME, GUSTAV RESTRAINED HIMSELF. AT LEAST, IT SEEMED THAT WAY.

(SOT)
Sydney Chustz: "You got to sit and wait. Sit and wait, dude, that's all you can do . . . "

OLD WISDOM IN AN OLD TOWN THAT HAS BEEN THROUGH HURRICANES BEFORE, AND PROBABLY WILL, AGAIN.

(SOT)
Chris Cortez: "I'm alive and dry. That's what counts."

Choosing Your Structural Timeline

So now you see how even a simple story can present multiple structural options. Before you decide which to use, ask yourself the following questions:

Is it hard news or a feature?

The harder the news story, the more quickly you must get to the point.

Which is more compelling, the facts, or the way those facts developed— or possibly the video?

Try to open with your strongest material. In a feature, that may mean romancing the open a little to let the piece develop.

What is your focus?

During shooting, did you capture a key moment—something memorable, funny, touching, or poignant? Can you build your story either to or from such a moment for maximum impact?

How much time do you have?

You cannot put as much structural nuance into a ninety-second story as you would into a longer piece. Shorter stories usually require you to write along a straighter line.

Will anchors introduce the piece from the studio, or will you front it from the field in a live shot?

To accommodate your time live on camera, insert packages generally run a little shorter. In such circumstances, consider saving a couple of details for use in the live transitions.

Weigh these factors before you write the piece. Soon, you will develop an instinct for making such decisions. With time and experience, it becomes second nature.

The Almost-Perfect Crash

In 1984, the Federal Aviation Administration experimented with a gelatinous jet-fuel additive called Anti-misting Kerosene. In theory, if a plane crashed, the AMK in its tanks would prevent the fuel from spraying and exploding.

To test it, the FAA and NASA rigged an old, four-engine Boeing 720 airliner for remote control fight. Scientists planned to load the plane's tanks with the new fuel and then to crash it. They even gave the exercise one of those fancy acronyms—CID, for Controlled Impact Demonstration—and invited members of the press to Edwards Air Force Base, in California's Mojave Desert, where they would watch.

Before dawn, and with typical military efficiency, the FAA shepherded more than a hundred reporters through a maze of high-security dirt roads, and delivered us to a mountaintop overlooking the test area. Once there, we spent several hours waiting and shivering.

To help us produce our stories, NASA and the FAA handed out videotape of the preparations. The reel included pictures of technicians strapping doomed test dummies into airline seats before their final, fateful rides.

At long last, the remotely controlled plane took off, circled the valley, and positioned for its final approach. At impact, it would twist and careen into a steel structure designed to rip the wing tanks, spray fuel, and create sparks. Under such conditions, an airliner loaded with regular fuel would explode easily.

This plane wasn't supposed to.

What we saw from that mountain, however, played out like a slow-motion nightmare. As planned, the airliner descended, dipped its left wing, and slapped to the ground in a cloud of dust. The jet twisted into the wing-ripping structure, its fuel spilled out and—kaboom! That airplane blew into smithereens. So much for Anti-misting Kerosene. We felt the rumbling shockwaves from two miles away. The fireball made spectacular video. NASA cameras captured it from several angles, both outside and inside the plane. Those test dummies never had a chance. (You can see the crash at www.dfrc.nasa.gov/gallery/photo/CID.)

As I sat down to write this story, the material presented several structural possibilities. It seemed that we should use as much of the spectacular crash video as possible. Rather than writing a linear timeline, I opted for a structure in which we showed different versions of the fireball at the beginning, in the middle, and at the end.

The script begins late along the event timeline, only a few seconds before impact. We open with a point-of-view angle of the plane approaching a NASA camera mounted atop the wing-ripper. Viewers see the plane wobble and dive, clearly about to auger in. Here is the first line:

IT WAS AN ALMOST PERFECT LANDING . . .

As the jet pancakes into the ground and blows up, we let the natural sound play full. That sets the scene. Here are the other elements, in the order we used them:

- The preparations, including dummy installations
- The takeoff
- Historical footage of other fatal crashes
- Shots of the test dummies at impact
- Reactions from the scientists
- More crash pictures, this time from a camera mounted on the plane's tail
- A stand-up bridge, summarizing the day's events
- One final, well-cut crash sequence

For a last line, I made an observation about how perfect tests sometimes lead to imperfect results.

Fundamentals of Narrative Structure

In even the earliest days of language, our ancestors sat around campfires and told stories. They might have described the day's hunt—how they awoke early, crossed the river, found tracks, closed on the prey, made the kill, and returned home with dinner. If you examine the essentials of that one sentence, you'll notice how it begins, has a middle, an ending, characters, tension, resolution, and tells a story.

The biggest difference between those old days and now is that our campfire has evolved into television and the Internet. Instead of a few people gathered around, our audience numbers in the tens of thousands, if not millions. But here's the tradeoff: When we tell those stories, we no longer see those people directly. Sometimes we forget they even exist.

Sell the Story: Set A Scene

When you tell a story to a friend, how do you begin? If you're like most people, you probably sell it a little. You engage his interest and take it from there. Try to do the same in a news story. Set a scene with a line or two, or possibly three. As with that crash test in the desert, a scene set does not need to be elaborate.

Here is an opening line from January 2010, when a seaside cliff collapsed beneath apartment units in Pacifica, California:

> IN AS LONG AS IT TOOK FOR ANOTHER CHUNK OF SANDSTONE
> TO TUMBLE EIGHTY FEET, THE CLIFFSIDE APARTMENT DWELLERS
> OF PACIFICA CHANGED STATUS, THIS MORNING,
> FROM RESIDENTS TO REFUGEES.

That scene set is straightforward and factual, much like the top of journalism's classic inverted pyramid. In one sentence, it provides the who, what, when, and where, and promises the why. Stylistically, it has rhythm. The words 'residents' and 'refugees' both begin with same 'R' sound, and have contrasting meanings. When you put all of those subtleties together, the line works.

Make A Scene Set Sizzle

Play With the Words

One of my favorite scene sets for a general news story involved San Francisco's then-gregarious newspaper publisher Phil Bronstein, who was married to actress Sharon Stone. Bronstein loved reptiles so much that in the summer of 2001, his wife made a large donation to the Los Angeles Zoo. In gratitude, zoo officials granted the celebrity couple a special tour inside a cage containing a ten-foot-long Komodo dragon, the most rare and ferocious of carnivorous lizards.

Before Bronstein entered that cage, zookeepers asked him to remove his shoes and socks. He did, much to the delight of the Komodo dragon, which chose to dine on a section of Bronstein's foot.

Although the Komodo mauling took place in Los Angeles, we gave it big play in San Francisco. Thankfully, several Los Angeles stations covered the attack and shared their video. From our perspective, most of those stories missed the spirit of it. One version began with a tight shot of the lizard's gaping jaws and razor-sharp teeth:

> AT THE LOS ANGELES ZOO, OFFICIALS SAY THEY
> ARE PUZZLED HOW THIS RARE KOMODO DRAGON
> ATTACKED A SAN FRANCISCO NEWSPAPER PUBLISHER
> LAST NIGHT.

That writing was safe and serviceable, but hardly sizzling or enticing. The reporter might as well have been describing a press conference.

Here is my opening line, using the same video:

> THIS IS THE MOUTH . . .
> THAT MUNCHED ON THE BIG TOE . . .
> THAT IS ATTACHED TO THE RIGHT FOOT . . .
> OF THE MAN WHO IS LEGALLY ATTACHED TO
> ACTRESS SHARON STONE.

Which sets a scene better?

Which establishes the proper mood? Don't merely cram facts into a story. Use those facts. Weave them.

Scene Sets Are Narrative

Good storytelling engages viewers. We refer to our scripts as "tracks," but we really mean narration, which derives from the word "narrative" and implies, in turn, a relationship between the storyteller and his audience.

It harks back to that campfire and the hunt. In the oral tradition, a good storyteller keeps listeners hanging on every word. But, in television news, reporters rarely achieve such success. They forget the storytelling part.

David Busse, a photographer at KABC-TV in Los Angeles, recalls working a story about a missing three-year-old boy. When investigators began to suspect that someone had abducted and killed him, they spent two days searching a landfill for his body. Just before deadline time on the second day, authorities allowed a pool camera to get close-up shots of workers sifting through the mountains of trash. "They weren't really gripping pictures," said Busse. "Unless the words to accompany them made them gripping."

Most of the reporters wrote leads that went something like this:

> MORE THAN ONE-HUNDRED WORKERS CONTINUED THE
> SEARCH OF MIRAMAR LANDFILL LOOKING FOR ANY SIGNS
> OF A MISSING THREE YEAR-OLD.

Busse, however, has a way of bringing out the best in a reporter. Jaie Avila's lead line spoke to the mood and the moment:

> THE ONLY THING WORSE THAN THE WORK WAS THE THOUGHT
> OF WHAT THEY MIGHT FIND.

Both opens were factually correct. Which will stay with you?

You might even be provocative when writing a quick scene set. I got away with one in 2008, when doing a history of the Point Montara Lighthouse, south of San Francisco. At just thirty feet tall, no one took it seriously. Then I learned how, decades earlier, the United States Coast Guard had moved it three-thousand miles from Cape Cod, Massachusetts. Hence Point Montara's stubby uniqueness. No other lighthouse has stood sentry over two oceans:

> IT SOUNDS SHALLOW, BUT REMAINS UNFORTUNATELY TRUE,
> THAT WHEN LIGHTHOUSES MAKE FIRST IMPRESSIONS,
> SIZE DOES MATTER.

Lead Viewers into the Story

Here is the open to a segment about San Francisco's annual cable-car bell-ringing championships. Note the quick timeline jumps—from the morning, to two days earlier, later that afternoon—and how the tracks invite viewers to make their own discoveries. In the first sequence, they see the defending champion as he arrives at the contest:

> WHEN BYRON COBB FINALLY SHOWED AT FISHERMAN'S WHARF
> TODAY, IT WASN'T SO MUCH AN ARRIVAL AS AN ENTRANCE.

(SOT)
Guys greet Byron. They slap hands:
"How's it going, baby?"
"Bring it on!"

SUCH IS THE BURDEN OF EXPECTATIONS,
AND ALSO THE ROLE OF A CHAMPION,
BECAUSE MEN WITH TITLES ALSO
HAVE TARGETS ON THEIR BACKS.

(SOT)
File tape from two days earlier: a cable car passes, ringing bell

ALONG CALIFORNIA STREET, BYRON'S RIVALS EYE AND
LISTEN TO HIM 364 DAYS A YEAR. THEN, ON THE 365th,
THEY TRY TO BEAT HIM.

Based on that open, would you want to see who wins the contest?

Setting the Scene In A Longer Story

In 1992, photographer Pam Partee and I traveled Route 66 and stopped in what remained of Chambers, Arizona. There, we profiled a die-hard desert recluse named Nyal Rockwell, who owned a wrecking business and roadhouse called Rocky's. He had moved to Chambers in the 1950s when "the Old Road," as they call it, still carried traffic.

Rocky's did brisk business for more than a decade, but, when the federal government replaced Route 66 with Interstate 40, life along that corridor changed. As part of the new highway deal, the feds promised to build an off-ramp into Chambers. Alas, they never delivered—not to Nyal Rockwell's satisfaction, anyway.

"How far is it from the off-ramp to here?" I asked as we walked along a chain link fence at the back of his property.

"Five miles down and five miles back," Rockwell answered. "Ten miles round trip."

And yet, from that fence, we could feel the wind generated by traffic whooshing past on Interstate 40, less than twenty feet away. For Nyal Rockwell, those cars might as well have been in another galaxy.

By the time of our visit, Interstate 40 had turned Chambers into a ghost town, and Nyal Rockwell into an angry, stubborn man still waiting for his off-ramp. Aside from his sickly, loyal wife and a collection of rusting classic cars with fins, Nyal had Rocky's, and little else. He clung to it.

The piece opens with shots of the abandoned highway, accompanied by lonely music from Ry Cooder's *Paris, Texas,* soundtrack. We show the remnants of a derelict church, and then cut to a tight shot of a rotting sign out front. Termites crawl across the plywood. You can barely make out the meeting times. We use that sign, and others, as a theme for the piece. Our scene set also serves as a prologue:

ACCORDING TO THE SIGN, THERE WILL BE WORSHIP AT THE
CHAMBERS PENTECOSTAL CHURCH THIS SUNDAY.
FROM THE LOOK OF THINGS, ONLY TERMITES WILL ATTEND.

Music bump, with pictures of an old gas station

NOT FAR AWAY, ANOTHER SIGN SAYS THEY STILL SELL GAS FOR
THIRTY-EIGHT CENTS A GALLON.

Another music bump as we dissolve to a shot of peeling signs along the road

BUT, ON ROUTE 66, SIGNS MAY BE DECEIVING. THEY HAVE A WAY
OF POINTING TO THE PAST, NOT THE FUTURE.

We see Nyal Rockwell holding a metal road sign

(SOT)
Nyal: "Can you read that? National Old Trails Road, it says."
We dissolve to a compression shot of a dusty dirt road

NEAR CHAMBERS, THE NATIONAL OLD TRAILS ROAD IS A DIRT
PATH BUMPING OUT OF THE DESERT.
IT IS THE TRAIL THAT BEGAT ROUTE 66, THAT BEGAT
INTERSTATE 40, THAT BEGAT THE SAD ENDING OF NYAL
ROCKWELL'S WRECKING BUSINESS AND ROADHOUSE.

For what it's worth, I could work another forty years and never write a better open to a feature story. It delivers viewers into a place and a time, and establishes a mood.

Using Bookended Structure to Craft A Package

Joey's Scrapbook

Here's a trade secret—with a proper beginning and ending, the middle of a story will usually take care of itself. You will always find it easier to write a piece if, before leaving a location, you already know how it will start and finish. Think of this as planning your entrance and exit routes.

I remember the piece we did about a Memorial Day luncheon at Jack's Grill in San Francisco. Management wanted to honor the families of Vietnam veterans killed in action. They anticipated more than a hundred people. Fewer than twenty showed.

It did not look like much of a story, but those people had sacrificed loved ones. It would be bad form to rush out of there.

We interviewed a few family members and started to leave. Then I spotted an elderly woman, Gloria Dougherty, holding tightly to a scrapbook. On a hunch, I asked her about it, and she began to talk. Those pages told the full life story of her son, Joey Artavia. She showed us his birth certificate, his death certificate, and most everything in between.

Mrs. Dougherty had deep, sad eyes. She clutched that book as if Joey himself might still be inside. From one short interview, she gave us three very good sound bites and came across as a strong character. In order to make this a complete story, however, it needed structural framing—a beginning and an ending.

"Where are you going after this?" I asked Mrs. Dougherty.

"Joey's grave."

"May we come along?"

Mr. and Mrs. Dougherty agreed.

By then, photographer Doug Laughlin and I began to worry about an approaching deadline, so we split up. I returned to the station and logged tape. Doug took his camera to the cemetery and waited at telephoto distance. When Mr. and Mrs. Dougherty appeared, he made a poignant, beautiful shot. His raw video never left the headstone as the couple walked into frame, kneeled, laid flowers, and wept. The only sound came from a briskly blowing wind.

These words open the piece over that video:

IF YOU ARE FORTUNATE, YOU OBSERVE MEMORIAL DAY
FROM A DISTANCE. YOU HAVE NO CEMETERY TO VISIT,
NO LOVED ONE TO REMEMBER. YOU WOULD NOT BE LIKE
GLORIA AND VICTOR DOUGHERTY, WHO SPENT THIS HOLIDAY
WITH A HEADSTONE AND BLACK AND WHITE PICTURES.

As the story develops, we look into the scrapbook and tell an abbreviated version of Joey Artavia's life story. To broaden events at the restaurant, we include sound bites and pictures from some of the other families who were also present. At about the ninety-second mark, we return to Joey's story, and then to our opening shot of Mr. and Mrs. Dougherty at the grave:

SUCH IS THE PAIN OF LOSS, OF WONDERING, OF SACRIFICE,
OF FEELING CHEATED. THIS IS THE DAY OF NAMES AND FACES . . .
OF THOSE WHO SUFFERED AND PASSED . . .
OF THOSE WHO LIVE ON AND GROW OLD.

(SOT)
The wind blows. Mr. and Mrs. Dougherty lift their heads, rise, and leave. Only the headstone remains in the shot.

IN MEMORY, JOEY ARTAVIA OF MISSION HIGH SCHOOL,
WILL ALWAYS BE NINETEEN.

On the timeline, this story begins and ends with our last shot of the day, in the cemetery. The piece works because we used that one moment to create a bookended structural framework. Again, it was not creative as much as adaptive.

Using Sound Bites to Open or Close a Piece

A colleague and I had a spirited discussion after she opened a story with so-called "can't miss" sound of her main character breaking into tears. She reasoned she should use the moment right off the top, before a line of track, because it was the strongest element in her piece.

"It might have worked better, later," I suggested to my friend.

"But the woman was absolutely distraught. And, we had other strong sound."

"I still think you wasted it at the top."

"Tell me why," she insisted.

"Because without a line of track to set it up, viewers knew nothing about her. How can they care about someone they haven't met, yet?"

"The sound bite makes them want to care," she argued.

"True, it does get a viewer's attention," I agreed. "But, at that point in your story, the sound bite only objectifies her emotion. I think you needed to introduce her first, to make the moment more meaningful."

Such are the subjective mysteries of using sound to open or sometimes close a television news story. There is no hard-fast rule, but here is the one I follow:

> *When you use a sound bite at either the beginning*
> *or the end of a story, set it up with a line of track.*

In an open, use a preceding line to introduce the moment or the character. In a close, that preceding line of track should signal the story's conclusion. Essentially, it becomes the last line. If sound follows, it must build on or strengthen that last thought.

Build A Strong Ending

Now to the most important part of a story. People remember endings. What would a joke be without the punch line? Ever watch an Olympic gymnastic competition? What do the announcers often say? "He needs to nail the landing."

Reporters do, too.

No matter how good the rest of your material may be, a weak ending guarantees a weak piece, while a strong one virtually assures success. Let's look at some ways to leave a lasting final impression.

Refer to the Beginning

In "Rocky's" we found our ending by referring back to the beginning, with a subtle reference to the opening pictures along Route 66:

> AND NYAL ROCKWELL WILL STAY, HE SAYS, BECAUSE, AFTER ALL
> THE YEARS AND ALL THE TROUBLES, THIS IS STILL HOME. FOUR-

HUNDRED ACRES, CUT OFF FROM THE HIGHWAY, ON A STRETCH
OF ROAD NO ONE TRAVELS ANYMORE.

Hold Back a Fact

Never underestimate the power of revealing a surprise twist. Move your facts around, or add one that puts the story in a different light.

The late Paul Harvey used this technique quite effectively for a segment he called, "The Rest of the Story." Try it when you find yourself in a storytelling bind. Save a strong or surprise fact for the end.

We did that in a segment about "the David," a violin that once belonged to the great Jascha Heifetz. When he died in 1987, he willed his instrument to the Fine Arts Museums of San Francisco, stipulating that it remain in the city and be played by a worthy musician.

"The David" may be the most famous musical instrument in the world. It is a relic from the golden era of violin making. Joseph Guarnerius del Gesu, who built "the David" in 1742, took the secrets of its dark, singular sound to his grave.

The Fine Arts Museums waited several years before choosing a recipient. In a quiet backstage practice room during the summer of 2002, curators finally gave "the David" to Alexander Barantschik, concertmaster of the San Francisco Symphony Orchestra. As our camera watched, Barantschik opened the case. It looked as if Heifetz had just been there. Barantschik found the violinist's chin piece, some twisted, broken strings, and a few scribbled notes. He was humbled and awestruck. "It's impossible to think that part of his soul is not inside."

As Barantschik tuned the instrument, it came slowly back to life.

"What is the difference between this violin and others," I asked.

"It has an amazing complexity of sound," said Barantschik. "If you were to compare it with a painting, it has a hundred colors, not fifty; colors within colors within colors. It's unforgiving. If you hit the wrong spot, this violin lets you know. And the audience knows. They'll say it used to sound better."

Talk about challenges. Alexander Barantschik received a violin more famous than he—a piece of history that might allow him to create his own. Having spent four years with the London Symphony Orchestra, he already enjoyed world renown. "The David" would enhance it.

Barantschik cradled the instrument as he carried it onto the empty stage of Louise Davies Symphony Hall. He played for himself, for us, for the empty seats, and mostly for the violin. It seemed we were watching the first moments of courtship in an arranged marriage.

When writing the closing line for that scene, I pulled information from a sound bite that had been too long to use in the piece. Barantschik's life and work had led to this moment:

> WHEN GROWING UP IN RUSSIA AS THE SON OF A
> FACTORY WORKER, ALEXANDER BARANTSCHIK WOULD
> LISTEN TO MUSIC AS HE WENT TO SLEEP.
> "THE DAVID" IS THE FIRST VIOLIN HE EVER HEARD—
> THE ONE THAT ALWAYS PLAYED IN HIS MIND.
> NOW, WITH THAT INSTRUMENT IS IN HIS HANDS,
> HE MUST LIVE UP TO IT.

End with Humor

When appropriate, humor can be an excellent way to wrap a piece—just make certain it's actually funny. Nothing thuds louder than a dud joke, especially at the end of a story.

Here's a last line from a piece about an obsessive man who amassed tens of thousands of miniature liquor bottles. Before we left, it dawned on me that all of those little bottles remained sealed and full. "I am a reformed alcoholic," he declared. "I collected all of those bottles after I stopped drinking." It is another example of giving a story a twist by holding back a fact until the end:

> HE GOT HIS LIFE OUT OF THE BOTTLE.
> NOW, HE CAN'T GET THE BOTTLES OUT OF HIS LIFE.

More Complicated Timelines

I could easily write another two thousand words with more examples of structures and timelines. There are so many of them.

For example, I divided a story about Oregon's famous exploding dead whale into chapters. It begins in the present with *The Place*, flashes back twenty-five years and tells the story through, *The Victims*, *The Whale*, *The Event*, returns to present day with, *25 Years Later*, and concludes with a surprise ending entitled, *Fin*. Technically, that's a bookended structure divided into chapters, I suppose.

On another occasion, I used a merging "Y" structure in a story about a racing mule named Black Ruby. That piece begins with the owners comically chasing the elusive mule around their ranch. It cuts almost immediately to another scene, weeks later at the track, where that same couple prepares Black Ruby for a major race. My script alternates from ranch scenes, where I tell the backstory, to the track, where the race draws ever nearer. Eventually, those two timelines merge into one epic moment at the finish line.

If you wonder whether complicated structures like those are beyond you, don't worry. They aren't. In most cases, they just kind of happen from discovering what fits and flows during the shooting, writing, or editing. Once you grasp the timelines concept and try it a few times, you will begin to use it naturally, and your writing will improve.

There is one caveat, however. *Remain faithful to the truth—the original context of your material. Again, journalism is about adapting and adjusting, not creating.*

In Summary

So, what should you take away from this long and important chapter?

Three words. Tell a story.

There should be more to news reporting than cramming facts into the formulated track, sound bite, track, stand-up, format to which we've grown accustomed. People relate to facts when we integrate them into stories. That is why I wrote this book in an anecdotal style. If you remember the stories, I'm hoping the lessons will stick, as well.

Using structure is a lot like building a house. If you lay a strong foundation on solid ground, it will support a variety of forms above. Structural timelines can be your most important tools for writing adaptively, or creatively, or whatever you want to call it, even under deadline pressure.

Structure will get you through the tough times.

CHAPTER 5

Universal Appeal

Have you ever wondered why some television news people move into better jobs while others go nowhere? I gained a good sense of it in 1992 after spending a day with Bob Jordan, who was then the news director at KING-TV in Seattle. He had come to San Francisco and the office of Don Fitzpatrick, an industry icon who collected tapes of every single news talent in every market in the country. Jordan was hoping to hire a reporter. It was an eye-opening experience.

"I tell people we run a glorified video dating service for television newscasters," said Fitzpatrick. "What news directors get here is a first look, kind of like what they would get in a singles bar."

His office contained thousands of reels that categorized talent by market size, sex, ethnicity, and job descriptions. Don Fitzpatrick and Associates provided the ultimate one-stop reference library for television news anchors, reporters, sportscasters, and weather people. News directors like Bob Jordan could fly in and search through the electronic ether, hoping to find those singular traits that, when combined, form an elusive quality in talent known only as *it*.

"*It* is three-dimensional," Fitzpatrick tried to explain.

"Looks, voice, charisma," continued Jordan. "When they don't have *it*, it's real easy to spot *it*."

"You know *it* when you see *it*, added Don. "But you can't describe *it*."

As comedic as their description sounds, these guys were deadly serious. Jordan had a quick hook for resume tapes. Some reporters lasted less than ten seconds before their reels joined a growing pile of rejects.

"While I was in the middle of a stand-up," voiced one reporter as an event happened in the background . . .

". . . Uh-huh. He becomes the news," Jordan broke in. "Spare me! Spare me!"

Slam—another tape hit the floor.

"I don't do anything here that people don't do at home with their remote controls," said Jordan. "They go up and down the dial, and they don't stop until they find someone they like. When I put someone on television, I want the viewer to pay attention to them, and to what they're saying. Not on their hair. Not on their jewelry."

As if on cue, the next tape applicant did a stand-up with a live boa constrictor around her neck. Jordan just laughed. "Bag the snake, honey."

Slam!

It was intimidating as hell.

When you try to land that first job or hope to move to a better one, this is the arena in which you and your work will compete. It's a tough crowd and a meritocracy. Rules change with every viewing, based on the preferences of individual news directors. They all want something slightly different. If you know in advance who will be looking at your reel, disc, or web page, find out what that person likes. It stands to reason that if a prospective employer relates to your stories, he will also relate to you.

My boss at KGO, Kevin Keeshan, makes it easy. When he places an advertisement for a reporter, Kevin asks applicants to send three enterprise stories along with proof that they generated those pieces on their own. If the cover letter doesn't match Kevin's criteria, he never even looks at the reel. Keeshan abhors desk feeders. "I want people who break stories. In the context of people looking for work, I would hope they know how to follow directions."

If Kevin likes your work, he's likely to call your competition and ask what they think of you. Next, Kevin Keeshan might call you and ask for your last two stories, whatever they were.

With a potential boss like Keeshan or anyone else, how do you make a good impression? Well, in addition to fitting a news director's criteria for looks, voice, presentation, and content, you must engage him. That won't be easy. Hence the need for an intangible I call *universal appeal.*

"Nobody ever calls back," one reporter complained to me a few years ago. His name was Brian Kuebler, a relative rookie who had broken a big story in his first serious market, Memphis, Tennessee. After all the praise he heard from colleagues and competition alike, Brian used that story as the first example on his reel.

It was a mistake. As impressive as the story had been, it failed to resonate with people from other cities. Why? Simple. While Brian had done a stellar job, 'getting it' required too much local knowledge for anyone outside Memphis. Put simply, the piece did not have enough *universal appeal*.

I have seen a plague of such efforts when looking at resume tapes and Emmy Award submissions. Viewers in other markets, whether they be news directors or judges, rarely give an inside strike to a stranger. Remember, they have not seen his work every day. He has not established a track record with them. Nor has he become an acquired taste. First impressions begin early and last a long time. Simple mistakes make bad first impressions, and lead to fast rejections.

An introductory letter or précis has never won a person a job or earned an Emmy, while misspellings, grammatical errors, and boastful claims have certainly lost a few of both. You will have a difficult time creating *universal appeal* if you begin by making a fool of yourself. And yes—I'm speaking from experience here.

Later, I explained my theory of universal appeal to Brian, who has never lacked confidence. "It's easy for you," he argued. "You work in a major market. Every story is interesting in San Francisco."

Not so. In a major market like San Francisco, we have a higher bar for "selling" stories because our viewers live in a larger, more diverse region. Capable reporters bridge geography and other factors, and make those stories appealing to everyone.

Brian Kuebler understands that much better, now. Within a couple of years, he moved from Memphis to an investigative reporting job in Baltimore. His work becomes more *universal* and award winning with every year.

Universal Appeal In Stories From Small or Medium Markets

When I moved from Louisville to my first major market television station, KDFW-TV in Dallas, the reel consisted of relatively small, "chicken salad" stories that made the most from limited reporting opportunities. One segment showed the wild crowd at a rock concert. Another followed a labor march. The third was an economic piece about an unemployed factory worker. The fourth showed viewers how to find cheap parts for old cars in a junkyard.

All of those pieces shared one characteristic. They had *universal appeal*. At twenty-six years old and less than eight months into my first, full-time reporting job, I had somehow learned the innate skill of telling large stories through smaller ones, and smaller stories through larger ones.

The Rock Concert

I looked back at the rock concert story on that old reel to see if it held up after thirty years. It did, and the reason why was obvious. The piece is a freak show. It begins with Jehovah's Witnesses trying to save the souls of resistant young concertgoers. "God gave us free choice," says a kid, "And I choose to go to the concert."

Inside the stadium, he joins an overflow crowd of rowdy fans. It's hot and muggy. Many of those fans walk through ankle deep puddles of beer. Fights break out. Some kids get so high on marijuana that they stick campaign-style band buttons into their bare, bloody chests. "The girls think it's sexy," says one nearly incoherent devotee as he impales himself.

Later, the story shows overzealous fans climbing a fence and charging "REO Speedwagon" on the stage. Security men tackle those fans and heave them back over the fence, into the crowd from where they came. As I wrote in the script:

> WHEN SOME FANS MOVED TOO CLOSE,
> SECURITY MEN HELPED THEM FIND NEW SEATS.

The report ends with those same security people escorting photographer Kerry McGee and me out of the venue. Our offense? We shot video of a passed-out woman, and asked about her care.

In retrospect, I don't know if the story produced *universal appeal* or *universal revulsion*, but it must have had a *universal something*. Unlike every unsuccessful demo reel before it, the one with "Summer Jam, 1980," led to offers from stations in Baltimore and Milwaukee, besides the job I took in Dallas.

Why Dallas? My college girlfriend lived there, it was a good station, and the move brought me closer to home in California, in that order.

Look for *universal appeal* in every story you do, and not just for the sake of finding a better job or winning an award. Those are mere by-products. Finding *universal appeal* is just plain good journalism. Such broadening will help any kind of story. Of those, crime stories will pose some of your biggest challenges.

The Barricaded Man

In July 2003, a Berkeley, California man got into an argument with his girlfriend, pulled a gun, ran her out of the house, and barricaded himself inside. To your life, my life, or most anyone else's life, this distracting little drama meant nothing. It amounted to a bubble in what author Jack London used to call, "the human stew."

In that Berkeley neighborhood, however, the barricaded man created a minor-major inconvenience. Police closed streets. They evacuated twelve people from homes and apartments.

My assignment, that day, was to file a report if or when the shooting began. Our managers had little interest in any outcome less exciting than that.

I arrived as the drama entered its twenty-fourth hour. SWAT teams remained under cover behind power poles, cars, and the corners of buildings. Meantime, residents and businesses tried to carry on normally. I remember being struck by the sight of restaurant customers casually slurping their lunchtime soup behind a large picture window. For them, the barricaded man had simply become part of the landscape. Even the news crews looked comfortable. The most blatant of them, a guy from a rival station, lounged in the middle of the closed street beneath a large, festive beach umbrella.

To me, however, those visual juxtapositions seemed more than a little odd, especially when I spotted a large billboard advertising the action movie, '*SWAT*.'

It was just too ironic. Maybe this barricaded man wouldn't ripple the cosmos anywhere else, but he sure did in this small section of Berkeley. And, we all live in neighborhoods. That was my hook.

Ever hear of *universal appeal*?

Besides, the station assigned two crews to the story, a rare opportunity. I bounced between them, shooting story elements and interviews with anyone who looked interesting. In the quirky city of Berkeley, they're everywhere. "Do some yoga. Meditate. Eat organic," one woman proposed as a solution to the barricaded man's issues.

In Amsterdam Art Supply, we discovered the strangest sight, yet. Owner Rene Minneboo had stacked reams of paper on the floor of his office, turned them into a bunker, and taken refuge inside while continuing to work. "There are guys with guns out there," he said conspiratorially.

It was all too real, or maybe surreal. When the suspect, Anthony Arrington, Jr., eventually surrendered, news photographer John Griffin got a good shot of police handcuffing him on the sidewalk. Then we tracked down the suspect's father for a quick question. "What are you going to say to him when you get alone with him?" I asked.

"That will be between him and me," the father said with elusive honesty.

As the standoff ended, I knew we would need a closing sequence, and asked both photographers to show police ripping away their yellow police tape.

Last, we made an unusual stand-up in which I stood among the remaining onlookers and spoke to a camera across the street, through passing traffic. It would give us a transition to the arrest sequence.

Only one challenge remained—selling this production to underwhelmed managers back at the station. "He surrendered. Nothing happened," they reasoned.

"No. Everything happened," I argued. *When a reporter makes a strong, impassioned pitch, good producers should listen.* Thank goodness KGO has a few of those. They agreed to run a short package that became one of my all-time favorites.

Barricaded Man
July 2003

Video begins with shots of SWAT teams crossing street behind police tape

IN BERKELEY, IT TOOK JUST ONE MAN AND A FEW HUNDRED FEET OF POLICE TAPE TO STOP AN ENTIRE NEIGHBORHOOD.

(SOT)
Woman in car: "Is he making some kind of demand, claim?"

THE EPISODE BEGAN AT AROUND NOON, YESTERDAY.

(SOT)
Male witness: "We watched him shoot out the window. You could see his hands. You could see his face. You could see the gun."

Video shows SWAT team members hiding, then the flashing lights of police cars, and last, a billboard for the movie, 'SWAT'

AND WITH THAT, FOUR SQUARE BLOCKS BETWEEN TENTH AND HEARST ASSUMED THE LOOK OF A MOVIE. REALITY CLASHED WITH FICTION, THOUGH IN THIS CASE, IT WAS NOT NEARLY AS ACTION-PACKED. POLICE DID EVACUATE TWELVE NEIGHBORS, INCLUDING MARKEESHA WILLIAMS, IN HER PAJAMAS.

(SOT)
Markeesha Williams: "I stay right across the hall. I'm in D. They be in C. The police had to take us out the windows."

Video shows police, followed by people eating lunch inside a restaurant, and lastly, that rival station's crew camped out beneath an umbrella

THEN THE WAIT BEGAN.
THROUGH THE NIGHT, INTO THE MORNING,
PAST THE LUNCH HOUR.
BY THEN,
THIS STAND-OFF HAD BECOME PART OF THE LANDSCAPE.

(SOT)
Sensitive Berkeley man: "People are unemployed. People are desperate."

Less sensitive Berkeley woman: "Do some yoga. Meditate. Eat organic."

Video shows interior of art supply store. Next, we show Rene Minneboo sitting low on the floor of his office with big boxes surrounding him. The final shot in this sequence looks outside through blinds on his window.

... ALTHOUGH AT AMSTERDAM ART SUPPLY, THEY COULD HAVE USED A LITTLE PATIENCE. OWNER RENE MINNEBOO SPENT MOST OF THE DAY ON THE FLOOR OF HIS OFFICE BEHIND BUNKERS MADE OF PAPERWORK. HE WORRIED ABOUT BULLETS FLYING IN HIS WINDOW.

(SOT)
Rene Minneboo: "There's a lot of guys sitting out there with guns. We can't see them."

(WAYNE STAND-UP)
I stand across the street among a crowd of onlookers. The camera pushes in slowly

IN ALL, THE STAND-OFF WOULD CONTINUE FOR TWENTY-FIVE AND A HALF HOURS. A MARATHON. BUT FINALLY ...

Video shows police arresting suspect

... ANTHONY ARRINGTON, JR, GAVE HIMSELF UP. HE NOW FACES SEVERAL FELONY FIREARMS CHARGES, PLUS ANOTHER FOR A PROBATION VIOLATION. HIS FATHER, WHO HAD NOT SLEPT, EXPRESSED PRAISE FOR POLICE AND RELIEF FOR HIS SON, BUT HE STILL DOESN'T KNOW WHAT SET HIM OFF.

(SOT)
Wayne to father: "What are you going to say to him when you get alone with him?"

Anthony Arrington, Sr.: "That will be between him and me."

Video shows police tape coming down in multiple locations

IN A REAL LIFE DRAMA, NOTHING BEATS A QUIET ENDING.

Do It Right Because It's the Right Thing to Do

At day's end, our report about the barricaded man succeeded because we took an event of minimal importance to most viewers, and made it compelling. That's the beauty of giving a story *universal appeal*. Other news professionals might call it *viewer benefit* or *take-away* value. Those are mere names.

I feel obligated to mention that our efforts paid off with an Emmy® Award for that story, which appeared in a reporting composite. Winning an Emmy never occurred to me when shooting that piece. Like every other day, I wanted only to do the best possible job.

Imagine that—a thumb-sucking little story about a guy with a gun who locked himself in a house, and somewhere, in a city far, far away, a group of cynical judges liked it.

Even though almost nothing happened.

Part Three

PRAGMATICS

CHAPTER 6

The Facts of Life in Television News

Here's my definition of the ideal job in television news. Reporters do only the stories they choose. They have the best crews standing by at their personal disposal. Money is not an issue. Reporters take as long as they need to work on a piece, and as long as they need to tell it.

Dream on.

I made those demands, in jest, to a boss recently. It felt good to get them off my chest. Her response was hysterical, and unprintable.

Now, reality.

The glitz wears off quickly in any form of journalism—usually during your first job, when you realize you can't write checks for both the car and the rent in the same pay period. Typically, you will achieve this insight after an unusually exasperating day. What? Jobs in television news can be exasperating?

Absolutely. Every newsroom begins each morning with blank scripts and hours of live broadcasting to fill. Our industry demands speed, and almost always at the cost of perfection. If you insist on being a purist, you may not last long in this business. Our bosses don't pay us for doing the flawless story. Instead, they settle for the best story possible within limitations. It's only a matter of time until that truth will collide with your idealism. Television news reporters excel by making the best of difficult situations. It's work, and as in any business, work is an exercise in problem solving.

Adapting to Desperate Moments

The Bubble Gum Test

If I ever teach a journalism class, students will have a busy first day. We'll go outside. I will point at a piece of gum on the sidewalk and give them half an hour to write a story about it.

Here's one possible approach:

> THERE IS A PIECE OF GUM ON THE SIDEWALK. IT CAME FROM
> A SHINY, CLEAN WRAPPER. THEN, SOMEONE UNFOLDED IT,
> CHEWED IT, ENJOYED IT, AND FINALLY, WITHOUT WARNING OR
> EXPLANATION, SPIT IT OUT. THAT GUM HAS BEEN STUCK ON
> THE SIDEWALK FOR SEVERAL WEEKS, NOW, FORGOTTEN AND
> FORLORN. IT TURNS GOOEY IN THE DAY, AND ROCK HARD AT
> NIGHT. NO ONE CARES. WHEN THE GUM STICKS TO A SHOE, THE
> OWNER JUST SCRAPES IT AWAY . . . ONE MORE MANIFESTATION
> OF OUR DISPOSABLE SOCIETY.

Once the students had written those stories, they would not be finished. News people know all-too-well that, if we filed such a script, somebody in the newsroom might demand a harder angle. So, here's a second treatment; a mockery of television news at its most sensational:

> WE HAVE LATE-BREAKING NEWS. THERE IS A PIECE OF GUM ON
> THE SIDEWALK, AND IT DOES HAVE LOCAL CONNECTIONS.
> WE DON'T KNOW WHO PUT IT THERE, OR WHY, BUT WE'RE
> HEARING OF PEOPLE STEPPING ON THIS GUM,
> AND FOULING THEIR SHOES WITH IT.
>
> NOW, THIS JUST IN. WE HAVE REPORTS OF TWO OR POSSIBLY
> THREE MORE PIECES OF GUM NEARBY. DETAILS REMAIN
> SKETCHY. WE DO NOT KNOW IF THESE NEW PIECES ARE THE
> SAME FLAVOR, OR FROM THE SAME PACK, OR RELATED IN ANY
> WAY. BUT WE CAN CONFIRM AN APPARENT PATTERN,
> AND THE VERY REAL POSSIBILITY OF A SERIAL GUM-SPITTER
> OPERATING IN THE NEIGHBORHOOD.

Ridiculous as that material might seem, reporters have had to do more with less. While such a story would certainly never appear in a newscast, the exercise has merit. It stands to reason that, if a person can turn a piece of gum into a story, then he probably has the mind set to handle whatever zany challenge comes his way. And in our business, it will.

On your most trying days, equipment will break, a story won't work out, or the desk will change plans. Without warning, you will need to scramble and find something else. Learn to take those aggravating or desperate moments, keep a straight face, and adapt.

My career has been rife with such days.

First Day of First Grade

Photographer Johnny Kabasakalis and I still talk about the time we covered a little girl's first day in the first grade. Her name was Jenna Copeland, and because she was the daughter of his best friend, we thought she would make a perfect subject. Johnny spent the night at his buddy's house. He began shooting as soon as she awoke.

All went well until I arrived a bit later. Jenna took one look at my bald head, ran away, and would not allow me to come near. Still, our producers expected a package. What's a reporter to do? I couldn't exactly call the station and announce, "Sorry, no story. Our little girl thinks I'm the bogeyman."

Johnny saved us with innovative thinking. He suggested that, instead of trying to interview the girl, we should use her as a mobile human microphone stand. It made sense. Jenna was only five years old. She had no idea what a wireless microphone was or could do. Johnny rigged Jenna, kept his distance, and we watched her go. That microphone gave us access to intimate sound and a different kind of piece, written from a child's perspective. If not for the difficulties, we would never have thought to try it.

The First "Hybrid" Car

In the mid-1980s, General Motors collaborated with Toyota to build a car at a factory in Fremont, California, about forty-five minutes south of San Francisco. Ultimately, that car became the Geo, but, at the time, the companies treated their joint project as top secret. They said only that the new vehicle would combine the best elements of a Chevrolet Nova and a Toyota Corolla.

KRON-TV photographer George Griswold and I went to cover the car's grand debut. Unfortunately, the desk misread the press release and sent us a day early. The security-minded factory wouldn't allow us past the gate, and when we telephoned the newsroom with our bad news, no one took responsibility. The producers still wanted a piece. "Get reactions or something," they suggested.

Reactions? To what?

That left the "or something" part. George and I hadn't a clue what to do, so we drove in circles through the neighborhood, bemoaning our bad luck and the desk's questionable judgment. Then George, who has always had a brilliant, free-thinking mind, noticed an automobile wrecking yard.

"Isn't that an old Corolla?" George asked.

I caught his drift immediately. "Isn't that other car a Nova?"

"Ugh huh. I also see a car crusher," George chuckled. We entered the wrecking yard and engaged the owner's sense of humor. Would he use his machine to crush the Nova and Corolla together?

"Sure," said the owner, who helped us produce an irreverent story about how the new car might look if the American and Japanese teams did not work well together.

A Life in Television News: My Background

I am a mature family man living out the career ambitions of a less experienced nineteen-year-old. Yes, that is how old I was when I decided to become a television news reporter. Close to forty years later, some of the bloom has faded, yet I don't regret a single moment. This can be a wonderful job. It grants a license to pursue your interests, witness history, see the world, meet people, and ask questions.

Clearly, I love news reporting enough to want to see it done well. That is why I wrote this book. Every word comes from the heart. Given our industry's trend toward bottom lines and deadlines, I worry that narrative, visual storytelling may become impractical or obsolete. Such work requires time and a financial commitment, which not all our corporate masters seem willing or able to provide.

The Speech: "It's Not Like the Good Old Days . . ."

Reporting is a craft that feels more like a calling. When we choose this career, however, most of us don't consider the long-term consequences of how it might affect our lives. That wide-eyed energy you feel at twenty tends to diminish by fifty. Hopefully, by then you will have learned enough to work smarter and wiser, but no less harder.

When I was nineteen, I had the advantage of having grown up around both television production and performing. My mother, Alicia Krug Freedman, danced the "Ballet Laurey" role in Agnes DeMille's original Broadway production of *Oklahoma!* She met my father, Mike Freedman, while he was working on ABC's *Paul Whiteman Revue.*

Dad began with the network in 1948, and ultimately directed and produced for ABC Sports. He also made history as the first photographer to conceive and then use a live, handheld electronic camera that they named the 'Creepy Peepie.' Mike Freedman was a "video journalist" long before anyone came up with the name. He was the first to take pictures on the sideline of a football game; the first to go mobile from the floor of a political convention; the first to carry a live camera into a rodeo pit; the first to go underwater. Many sports fans indirectly remember my dad for a 1977 football game between Michigan and Ohio State. After a fumble, Ohio State coach Woody Hayes threw a tantrum on the sidelines, and attacked the first person he saw. That was Dad, who had the shot—live. When Woody slugged Mike Freedman's camera, he also assaulted a national television audience.

"I felt sorry for him," Dad said of Woody. He considered the matter closed.

Suffice it to say, my pop was a smart guy who knew the business. He once told me, "Son, if you want to make a consistent living in television, work in the news. They'll never cancel the news." He was right, as fathers usually are.

Dad dispensed that advice in 1974, the golden age of our industry. By then I was a college student who had already caught his journalism bug. Six years earlier, in the ninth grade, I had started my first regular column for what became *The Los Angeles Daily News*, and kept it going through high school.

In 1974, I was studying political science at UCLA and had a full-time job in the KABC-TV newsroom. There, I used razor blades and scotch tape to cut and paste rolls of teleprompter copy for, as the station announcer read excitedly every night, "Jerry Dunphy, Christine Lund, Dr. George, Stu Nahan with sports, and the rest of the Eyewitness News Team!"

That invigorating environment convinced me to become a reporter. It looked, dare I say, noble and prestigious, but, when I declared my intentions to the trusted newsroom veterans, they frowned, shook their heads, and tried to set me straight. "TV news is going to hell," they warned gravely. "It's not like the good old days."

Is anything?

Naturally, their good old days were different from my good old days, which will be different from this generation's good old days—but not that different.

For proof, look no further than a former editor in the KGO-TV news department, Elsa Trexler, who kept a file of directives, complaints, memorandums, and company newsletters. One day, she shared them with other staff members. Those memos were close to thirty years old at the time, but if you updated the names and looked only at the subject matter, they would be similar to staff emails of today. Those memos prove that while technologies have changed, newsrooms and news people remain more or less the same.

"Has television news gone to hell?" I asked Elsa.

"No more than usual," she smiled.

So now, when young people say they want a life in the business, I make the same speech those KABC-TV veterans gave me, hoping to save starry-eyed hopefuls from their own extravagant delusions. They listen. They nod as if they understand, but warnings can never substitute for experience. Many of those young people will try. Most will fail. All will learn the hard way. At best, maybe in another forty years, those who persevere and succeed can warn another generation about how television news in whatever form it becomes will be going to hell then, too.

Darwin

Succeeding in journalism, and especially television news, is just as Darwinian as the rest of the world. Our business culls out the weak. The fit adapt and survive.

As long as there are commercials to sell, we will work in a form of journalism that caters to people with short attention spans. Most news professionals are not proud of that, nor do they happily admit to it, for fear of guilt by association. Quite the contrary—when describing television news to outsiders, we prefer to make it sound like brain surgery.

Sorry. It isn't.

Television News Isn't Just a Living—It's a Lifestyle

If you want to be a television news reporter, expect to pay a price for your success. This is more of a lifestyle than a job. In the first years of a career, you will probably become a nomad, moving up to better positions in city after city. While you won't starve, do not expect to earn more than a basic living wage. Even with an advanced college degree, you will watch people who never graduated from high school make more money and drive nicer cars and live in bigger houses and have more time off.

Get used to it. The civilians will always have more time off. But television news people have more fun. At least, we did in the good old days.

Accept that this industry may inhibit your having a normal personal life. Expect to feel as if you spend more energy observing other people's problems, struggles, and triumphs than your own.

At times, the job will require twelve-hour days, six or seven days a week, including holidays. If you have a family, plan to miss many of your kid's soccer or Little League games. Forget about coaching. When 6 p.m. comes around, you will probably be tethered to a live signal instead of relaxing at home. As you become older, this will matter.

In a typical week, a major market reporter will easily log five hundred miles on the road, if not more. On a typical day, you will not have time to sit down for a civilized meal. Consequently, we journalists have become experts at scarfing lunches in moving cars, sometimes while steering with our knees. We don't chew. We inhale. This is why some of us have terrible table manners. Just ask my wife.

Our chronic traits include massive egocentrism, insecurity, self-importance, and countless other forms of social maladjustment. In short, we are utterly charming. The only good news is that we feel right at home among our coworkers. Newsrooms, you see, are like dysfunctional families. We're three-dimensional people stuck in a two-dimensional medium.

If this sounds familiar, promise yourself to seek help early and often. A good therapist can work wonders. A patient and understanding spouse is essential.

Dealing with Management

In any newsroom, reporters must please managers who may change their minds several times a day. Those managers have the best intentions. Still, they have been known to make questionable decisions when understaffed and trying to predict the whims of viewers wielding remote controls or computer touch pads.

"I know it isn't really news," a boss once confided about a story, "but this is one of those days. Just give it the look and feel of news." As a reporter and an employee, it will be in your best interest to make even the most wishful of these management decisions look good.

Clearly, reporters and managers do not always agree. While we work together on the same team, we may have different priorities and strategies. In the field, reporters and crews fight for the quality of their stories. In the newsroom, managers and producers juggle broadcast rundowns, live trucks, editors, and overtime to build the best possible broadcast. From this conflict, there will always be tension. Journalism is a profit-oriented industry with limited resources. As a reporter, you will be one of them.

Scavenger Hunts

You might compare news reporting to scavenger hunting. We scramble, hustle, and, at the end of the day, compare our work with that of the competition. If you don't feel comfortable putting yourself and your reputation on the line, in public, find another career.

Being a reporter means performing miracles daily, tirelessly, year after year, for as long as you work, wherever you work, and making those miracles look easy. Brilliance with one story does not carry over to the next. You must prove yourself with every new assignment. In newsrooms, institutional equity rarely exists.

The Right Stuff for Reporters

At nineteen years old, I was ignorant of those realities. I blindly assumed I had what it took to be a good reporter. If you'd asked me for a description of what "it" was, I couldn't have told you. Now, I can.

Good reporters are curious.

They want to know everything. To quote the late Dick Schaap, "For a journalist, there is no such thing as useless knowledge. Every fact from every discipline has the potential to brighten style or strengthen substance. Journalism is a profession where practitioners should know everything and pretend to know nothing."

Good reporters learn to find and recognize stories.

They can grasp the complexities of issues or events, and then simplify them. Good reporters keep open minds. They present all sides of a story without bias.

Good reporters write succinctly, accurately, and emotively.

Yes, reporters write, much to the surprise of many viewers. The good writers among us understand and apply the principles that make stories work. They do not waste a viewer's time. In my opinion, effective reporters write in a narrative style. They have the ability to make any story interesting to just about anyone. In addition to writing in broadcast form, they also write in print style for the Internet and for all other multimedia outlets. As an aside, I have noticed that while a site like Twitter teaches brevity, it butchers grammar.

Good reporters manage time.

This is a business of time and distance management. Wherever they go, whatever they do, no matter what the demands, successful reporters meet deadlines and finish stories within prescribed time limits, often with seconds to spare, and preferably with more. Good reporters write fast. In the most stressful situations, they scribble stories a paragraph and sound bite at a time, handing them off to an editor who cuts them on the fly.

Good reporters are researchers and detectives.

They know how and where to locate people. They read those people quickly, gain their trust, ask provocative questions, and elicit memorable answers.

Good reporters are diplomats.

They negotiate constantly—with management, with crews, with the people in their stories, or those who make them available.

Good reporters speak clearly, conversationally, spontaneously, knowledgeably, and with energy.

Because they do so many live shots, they're equally comfortable talking to a camera or a person. They know their material. You will appreciate having those abilities the first time your notes blow away in a windstorm just before a live shot, or when a teleprompter goes haywire while you're live and in mid-sentence.

Good reporters develop a specialty.

Good reporters carve niches and rely on them throughout their careers. They may become experts at breaking news, general assignment, consumerism, weather, science, politics, features, or whatever. No matter what his specialty, a valuable reporter also has the bandwidth and willingness to do any kind of story well.

Good reporters find their own voices and audiences.

They're confident, with distinctive styles and points of view. The more they appear, the more their audiences learn to know them, to trust them, and sometimes, to give them tips. As those reporters break stories and develop a following, they become more valuable to their bosses.

Good reporters have thick skins.

Increasing numbers of Americans fail to appreciate the role of a free press in our society, and the rules that guide journalists. If your objective, diligent work fails to match their subjective, strong opinions, they will make you out to be the villain. When viewers call, email, or write, take their complaints respectfully. Surprise them by responding politely. You might even win a few of them over.

Good reporters learn to alter their styles and formats, reflecting the desires of changing management teams.

Don't be surprised when a newsroom's philosophical universe suddenly flips, and what used to be the right way suddenly becomes wrong. It's fairly easy to please the boss who hired you. The test will be to satisfy that new boss who replaces the old one, sometimes while trying to maintain your self-respect. As a general rule for long-term survival, it's a good idea to make your boss happy before your make yourself happy. You may love that last story you produced, but if it caused problems for management, they will make you pay.

Good reporters who survive in this business learn to reinvent themselves.

My own career odyssey provides a good example. I always wanted to report, but in 1979, to get a proverbial foot in the door, I took my first full-time job out of The University of Missouri master's program as a photographer and part-time reporter for WLKY-TV in Louisville, Kentucky. There, I shot, processed, and spliced 16mm film, schlepped eighty pounds of camera, deck, lights, and batteries for video, and cut my own stories.

After ten months, a friend and former classmate, David Busse, helped me land a job across town at WAVE-TV as a general assignment reporter. Within a year, I moved to KDFW-TV in Dallas, Texas, for another general reporting job.

Ten months later and just two years out of school, KRON-TV hired me in San Francisco, where I eventually transitioned from general news reporting to long-form features. That professional persona lasted the better part of two decades and led to a dream job at CBS News, producing and reporting national feature stories for *CBS This Morning*. But, nothing lasts forever. The network suffered cutbacks, I adapted back to daily news at KGO-TV in San Francisco, earned a reputation as the station's "fireman" for breaking news, developed a new specialty in science reporting, and have now come full-circle. In April 2010, the station gave me a video camera. Once again, I shoot and edit many of my own stories. Based on that history, let's add another qualification.

Good reporters know how to shoot and edit their own video.

The new generation of reporters is as comfortable with a small camera in hand as previous ones were with pens and notepads. Now, a well-rounded reporter knows sound, lighting, composition, shoots in sequences, and edits to a clean, professional standard. The lines between who does what job have blurred in our business. Even if that reporter is fortunate enough to work with a photographer, becoming technically and visually literate will make him better.

As fair warning, being a reporter who also shoots and edits may lead to schizophrenic conflicts. My inner reporter gets frustrated by my inner photographer when he makes technical mistakes. Meantime, my inner photographer resents my inner reporter for rushing him. Both of them get angry at my inner editor when he omits a shot, or cuts a line.

"Leave me alone, you egomaniacs," barks my inner editor in defense of himself. "Why is the video blue? And why can't 'the talent' read without stumbling?"

The Makings of Good Stories and Good Reporters Remain Timeless

Through all those years and incarnations, I have learned one other consistent truth. The "makings" of good stories and effective reporting do not change. What worked in the past still works now, and will in the future.

My friend, the same David Busse, has been a news photographer at KABC-TV in Los Angeles for more than thirty years. He could do any job in this business, including station management. David is a sage and solid old-school guy. I asked what makes a good reporter in his eyes.

"I've worked with some great reporters and many average ones," Busse said. "Trust me, the difference between great and average is not measured in market size or salary. It's not a result of educational background or upbringing.

- Great reporters are great team players with photographers, producers, and other reporters in the newsroom.
- In the field, they keep their heads in the story of the day. They do not lock themselves in the vehicle and gab on the phone or send text messages of little or no reference to the job at hand.
- Great reporters arrive at a story prepared.
- Great reporters think in three dimensions. They see the video, write the script, and understand how to communicate by merging the two."

It Takes More Than Good Looks

In keeping with the title of this book, and contrary to what you might have heard, *it takes more than good looks* to succeed as a reporter, although good looks certainly help.

If you are not particularly good looking, take heart in the fact that most reporters will spend at last eighty percent of their time off-camera. Survivors in our business rely upon how they sound more than how they look. As long as a reporter is presentable and distinctive, he can last in the job, provided he masters the non-glamorous skills first.

Now, if after reading any of this you have reservations about a career in television news reporting, put the rest of this book down, congratulate yourself for exercising good judgment, and back away slowly. Seriously. Enjoy your nice, normal life.

Conversely, if you are willing to be a foot soldier and cannot imagine yourself doing anything else for a living, then keep reading. Welcome to our insane asylum. You just committed yourself.

CHAPTER 7

Getting Ahead: Create Your Own Luck

In the summer of 2001, baseball star Cal Ripken Jr. made his farewell retirement tour through every American League city, and received the royal treatment. Teams declared days in his honor. They orchestrated gushy ceremonies, bestowing praise and gifts.

Ripken had earned baseball's affection during a sixteen-year stretch in which he broke Lou Gehrig's supposedly unapproachable record for playing in consecutive games. Equally important, Ripken did it at a time when the public perceived professional athletes as spoiled and overpaid. Because of Ripken's work ethic, average people connected with him.

For the baseball star, Oakland meant another stop, another tribute. For local media, it created a whirl of reporters trying to chronicle every step of the great man's last playing visit. As one of those reporters, I knew it would mean a tough day.

Sure enough, when photographer Dave Pera and I arrived at the stadium, we found a Broadway-size cast of news crews already there, along with a cadre of marketing people establishing ground rules. "You can take pictures, but no interviews," said one of them. I remember thinking that reporters have had better access to some presidential candidates.

At noon, when Ripken emerged from the dugout, security men formed a protective circle. As he ran down the right field line to stretch, at least a dozen photographers moved with him, running backwards, forwards, and sideways. If one of them had tripped, it would have caused a chain-reaction pileup.

Ripken, meanwhile, ignored their commotion, but not his fans on the first base side of the field. After finishing his warm-ups, he walked toward them. Eager, excited people leaned out, offering memorabilia for him to sign: baseballs, pictures, bats, even themselves. Ripken tried to please everyone. In the midst of a pressing, demanding crowd, he remained humble and gracious, as if this were his first time.

If only the security men had been as accommodating. You'd have thought they were the Secret Service. They kept cameras so far away and blocked so many angles that we could not even see Ripken's face. This posed a problem. If we couldn't really see the man and they wouldn't let us interview him, how would we make this piece?

Look the Other Way: Watch the Watchers

Sometimes you take what an environment gives you. With Ripken, I felt we needed to turn away from the action, and shoot reactions instead. Maybe that sounds counterintuitive, but it's an old-school journalism trick. After you get enough pictures of a fire, an accident, or anything that draws a crowd, watch the watchers. Often, you will capture telling images and sound.

In the stadium that day, no one obstructed our view of the fans when Dave pointed his camera at them, and none of those fans noticed. As Cal Ripken passed, their expressions reflected him. You would have thought the kids were in the presence of a superhero. And the grown men? They looked like starstruck boys.

To Distinguish Your Work, Find an Unusual Angle

To succeed as a reporter, your stories must stand out against the competition. Sometimes, this requires taking a gamble. In sports, they call it having a "heads-up" attitude. Work within the rules, be aware of your surroundings, and anticipate. When you see an opportunity, make the play. Do something special.

When Ripken and the gaggle moved on, Dave Pera and I hung back and approached a fan named Herb Saxton, who proudly held a freshly autographed baseball. Saxton, in his twenties, grinned as if he'd just won the lottery, "There is nothing like being here or shaking his hand. No money could buy this. You can't give me five hundred dollars for this right now."

"What does Cal Ripken have that nobody else has?"

"Ripken has dignity," answered Saxton.

It was a start.

Don't Always Follow the Crowd

At such times, my competitive juices take over. The more someone or an agency tries to orchestrate or limit news coverage of an event, the more it makes me want to change their "script". Our bosses do not pay us to be extensions of public relations machines, human microphone stands, or to do stories just like the next guy.

As Ripken moved toward home plate to begin the ceremony, the other crews set their tripods in a semicircle—the pack mentality in action. By playing it safe, they aired similar stories. And, they missed some telling images.

Dave and I shot the ceremony too, but, instead of locking down in one spot, we moved around to get different, more interesting angles. I expected the formal affair would be staid and predictable, and it was, so after getting the requisite pictures we turned away to observe the other ballplayers. In the Athletics dugout, they paid reverential attention. By contrast, Ripken's Orioles teammates exuded boredom. They had seen these tributes before.

"Let's stay on the Orioles side of home plate," I suggested to Dave. Ripken had brought his wife and children along. They stood by, watching. If we couldn't speak with the man himself, I hoped maybe a member of his family would talk, and approached Cal's wife, Kelly.

"No, I don't mind reporters. They're more interested in him," she said, nodding to her husband.

"Would you mind if we ask you a couple of questions on camera?"

"Why not?" Kelly Ripken described Cal as an ordinary guy who never received this kind of superstar treatment at home.

"Does he do the dishes?" I asked.

"No."

After the interview, we stayed nearby. *When you get a good spot, never give it up until someone asks you to leave.* I was thinking that Ripken might pass his wife when returning to the dugout. We might finally see him up close. Realistically, we couldn't hope for more.

The ceremony ended and Ripken did move toward us. Even better, he stopped next to his wife. Just like that, Cal Ripken Jr. and I stood shoulder to shoulder, with nary a security man or any other television crew anywhere nearby. Ripken turned to me and nodded.

"Congratulations," I said to Ripken. "This must be nice."

"It is. Thank you," Cal Ripken replied just as casually. We shook hands, he saw the microphone, and then, in the tone of two guys having an ordinary conversation, I asked a couple of easy questions. The security people looked irritated, but they also knew better than to interrupt Cal Ripken Jr. What he said didn't matter. What did matter is that he said it to us, and only us.

Ripken and I are about the same age and size, yet somehow, in reliving the moment, he has grown about six inches taller.

As the game began, a sports reporter from a competing station wandered over. "You lucky dog," he marveled. "You lucky, lucky, lucky dog."

Perhaps he's right. Maybe we did luck out. Then again, maybe we *made* our luck by working harder, against the flow, and then applying a strategy that worked better than expected.

It certainly put me in a positive frame of mind for writing the story:

Cal Ripken's Last Game in Oakland
August 2001

Cal Ripken runs onto the field as the press follows

FOR CAL RIPKEN JR., ROAD TRIPS BRING A
DIFFERENT KIND OF PRESSURE NOW.
HE FEELS IT WITH EVERY MOVE, EVERY STEP, EVERY BREATH,
IN FRONT OF EVERY CROWD, IN EVERY TOWN.

(SOT)
Ripken: "It's getting more emotional. I'm thinking of taking this thing off . . ."

BY THAT, HE MEANS THE NUMBER EIGHT. IT WAS EVERYWHERE AT THE COLISEUM TODAY.

ON BASES . . .

IN BATTING CIRCLES . . .

ON PHOTOS . . .

THERE HAS BEEN A CAL RIPKEN DAY IN EVERY AMERICAN LEAGUE CITY IN THIS, HIS FAREWELL SEASON. HIS WIFE, KELLY HAS BEEN PRESENT FOR EACH OF THEM .

(SOT)
Wayne asks Kelly: "IS HE AS PERFECT AS HE SEEMS?"

Kelly: "I don't know anyone who's perfect."

Wayne: "DOES HE DO THE DISHES?"

Kelly: "No."

BUT, AS A BASEBALL PLAYER AND MERE MORTAL, CAL RIPKEN SET HIMSELF APART BY PLAYING IN 2,632 STRAIGHT GAMES.

FOR SIXTEEN YEARS BEGINNING IN 1982, HE NEVER MISSED A DAY OF WORK…

NEVER COPPED AN ATTITUDE…

NEVER CHANGED TEAMS…

(STAND-UP)
CAL RIPKEN'S STREAK ENDED IN 1998, AND, IN THE TIME SINCE, ITS LEGEND HAS GROWN. WHEN PEOPLE TALK ABOUT HIM, THEY USE WORDS LIKE CONSISTENCY…

LONGEVITY…

LOYALTY…

CAL RIPKEN NEVER TOOK THE JOB OR THE GAME FOR GRANTED.

(SOT)
Wayne: "WHAT DO YOU THINK THESE FANS SEE IN YOU?"

Ripken: "Someone who loves the game. Who does his best, I suppose."

BEFORE TODAY'S GAME, CAL RIPKEN SPENT A FEW MINUTES GIVING LIFETIME MEMORIES TO SOME OF THE PEOPLE WHO IDOLIZE HIM. WATCH THEIR FACES.

YOUNG BOYS SAW HIM AS A SUPERHERO.
GROWN MEN FELT LIKE YOUNGSTERS AGAIN.

AMONG THEM, HERB SAXTON, WHO HELD A BALL RIPKEN HAD JUST SIGNED.

(SOT)
Herb Saxton, a fan: "There is nothing like being here or shaking his hand. No money could buy this. You can't give me five hundred dollars for this right now."

Wayne: "WHAT'S DOES CAL RIPKEN HAVE THAT NOBODY ELSE HAS?"

Herb: "Ripken has dignity."

DIGNITY—A SIMPLE DESCRIPTION WE DON'T OFTEN HEAR IN REFERENCE TO PRO ATHLETES, ANYMORE.

IN OAKLAND TODAY, IT FIT. TO HEAR A FAN SAY CAL RIPKEN JR. HAS DIGNITY MAY BE THE BIGGEST TRIBUTE OF THEM ALL.

Fisherman's Luck

News people can be a jealous, petty lot. Out of frustration or insecurity they belittle their competition, and even their colleagues.

"How did he get that job?"

"How did she get that story?"

"Can you believe the luck of that guy?"

The good fortune that follows from luck, however, is not entirely accidental. If, early in my career, someone offered an option to be either lucky or good, I would have chosen the former. Now, I know better. Luck makes a difference only when you've prepared to take advantage of it.

It reminds me of the first time my father took me fishing. Being a typical kid, I spent most of my energy baiting the hook and casting the line. Meantime, Dad caught all the fish. That didn't make sense. I was working harder.

"Nobody ever caught a fish without his hook in the water," Dad said. "Fisherman's luck has a lot to do with knowing where the fish are, keeping your hook wet, and being ready when the first one bites." In Hemingway's *Old Man and the Sea*, the fisherman, Santiago, had a similar attitude. He kept his gear ready for "the big one."

Put that philosophy into practice, and you may be surprised by how preparing for good luck improves the odds of it happening. Journalism is no exception. Keep a pen in your pocket, your mobile device charged, and your camera ready to switch on and shoot. "Big ones" don't wait.

Local Knowledge

On November 12, 2002, Iraq's parliament rejected a United Nations weapons inspections resolution, pushing our nation closer to a possible war. The next day, KGO-TV's assignment desk received a tip that former president Bill Clinton was playing a round of golf at San Francisco's Olympic Club. Our assistant news director, Tracey Watkowski, broke me off another assignment to track him down. We were hoping Clinton would comment about the crisis.

The Olympic Club is an exclusive establishment. When I telephoned to ask for confirmation and admission, the head professional politely referred us to the general manager, who was "unavailable," according to his receptionist. I did not give up. He wasn't the only source, just a source who couldn't talk. We needed someone with less at stake. I called back and asked for the desk in the pro shop, where assistants answer the phone. *You can get plenty of tips on stories by speaking with lower level administrative assistants, bellmen, waiters, and parking attendants, among others. People with the least amount of power often turn out to be very good sources. They love to tell what they know.*

"I hear Clinton already teed off," I prompted the kid who picked up.

"Sure did," he volunteered. "Nine forty-five on the Lake course."

This meant Clinton had been golfing for almost three hours. I calculated he would be approaching the tenth or eleventh hole by then. Having played Olympic, I knew the thirteenth runs along the course's edge next to a chain link fence, a creek, and about fifty feet of woods on city land, next to a road.

Photographer Doug Laughlin and I parked our truck, slashed through the wilderness, and waited. A few minutes later, two Secret Service men appeared, followed by the former president's foursome. Mr. Clinton looked surprised to see us. He waved.

We waved back.

Clinton finished the hole. We motioned for him to come over. "Sir, how about a word with a couple of bushwhackers?"

He laughed at the pun, walked twenty-five feet out of his way down a bank, and answered a question about Iraq. "We knew President Hussein was homicidal, but not suicidal, " said the ex-president. "I hope there won't be a conflict, but if he doesn't let the inspectors in, there will be."

Clinton gave that interview over a fence and across the creek from fifteen feet away. Our sound and lighting were not perfect, but Doug and I didn't worry. Clinton made our day, our week, and our month. We scored an exclusive one-on-one with a former president who then moved to the next tee, hit a bad shot, and took a mulligan.

Yes, we saw that through the clearing, too.

Clinton in the Woods
November 2002

IT'S NOT EVERY DAY THAT FORMER PRESIDENT BILL CLINTON COMES TO TOWN, AND EVEN LESS LIKELY THAT HE'LL INVITE REPORTERS TO WATCH HIM PLAY GOLF.

(SOT)
Clinton swings

AS USUAL, THE SECRET SERVICE PROTECTED HIM.

AS EXPECTED, OLYMPIC CLUB MANAGEMENT KEPT THE PRESS OFF ITS PROPERTY.

BUT, THERE IS A CLEARING BY THE FENCE ALONG THE THIRTEENTH HOLE.

(SOT)
Wayne: "SIR . . . HOW ABOUT A WORD . . ."

ON A MORNING WHEN THE FORMER PRESIDENT CLEARLY WANTED TO RELAX, HE LEFT HIS FOURSOME TO COMMENT ON THE IRAQI PARLIAMENT'S REJECTION OF THE UNITED NATIONS WEAPONS INSPECTIONS RESOLUTION .

(SOT)
Clinton: "Well, now they're asking for a conflict. The inevitable conclusion is they have chemical and biological weapons and they don't want to give up."

BASED ON THAT RESPONSE, MR. CLINTON APPEARS TO BE AS KEENLY INTERESTED IN WORLD AFFAIRS AS EVER.

WHEN ASKED TO TRANSLATE THE LANGUAGE OF DIPLOMACY, CLINTON SOUNDED LIKE A STATESMAN, NOT A POLITICIAN.

(SOT)
Clinton: "My guess is they're still playing games. I cannot believe they really want a conflict because before, President Hussein was always homicidal, but not suicidal. I hope there won't be a conflict, but if he doesn't let the inspectors in, there will be."

SUCH IS THE LIFE OF A FORMER PRESIDENT.

BILL CLINTON WENT FROM BEING A PRIVATE CITIZEN, TO A

PLAYER ON THE WORLD STAGE, THEN BACK TO HIS ROUND
OF GOLF . . . AND ALL IN TWO MINUTES.

We used a secret weapon in getting Bill Clinton. It's called local knowledge. As a reporter in any market, apply your local knowledge to the job every day. Do you know the radio frequencies of your fire department, police, and airport? Do you have good working relationships with the people who run them? Do you have a reliable reputation overall? People speak to, and take chances with, reporters they trust.

At the scene of a murder, do you know the detectives by sight and name? Are you familiar with the routines and protocols of an investigation? If so, you'll also recognize when police will remove the body. If you've worked with the coroner before, he might tell you his exit route in advance. With such information, you can place your camera to get just the right angle.

After finishing a piece, do you file information in a computer? Do you cross-reference names, telephone numbers, job descriptions, and areas of expertise? That kind of data adds up and begins to pay off quickly.

When checking documents in the local courthouse, talk up the clerks. Get to know their names. Leave business cards with them. Ask them to call when they see or hear something interesting. Clerks don't miss much, you know.

How often do you call sources or people from previous stories, just to chat? If you made one extra call a day, they would total five in a week. With that many hooks in the water, you have a good chance of catching something.

Set Your Own Standards

When evaluating your performance, be your own best critic. Set higher standards for yourself than those of your competitors and coworkers.

In your first job, especially, do not fixate about days off, vacations, and setting down roots. You will never again learn so much about your craft in such a short period of time. If you aren't excited about going to work every day, regardless of the hours, consider another career.

As in any field, it takes a dedicated effort to improve. Find reporters you admire. Study their stories. Model your own pieces to reflect your career aspirations. *Your reel should look like, and have the quality of, the place you want to go, not the one in which you work.*

When the workday ends, don't be in such a hurry to rush out the door. If you made mistakes with a piece, or ran out of time and couldn't finish it the way you wanted, return to the edit room and get it right just because you can. You will not be as likely to repeat errors after you correct them.

Learn to Love the Process

People go into television news for many reasons—excitement, commitment, vanity, and fame, among others. The ones who last usually say they've learned to love the process. On bad days, the process gets them through.

Even if you don't like an assignment, always give it your best effort. That's part of the process. Your worst stories reveal as much about you as your best ones, and probably more.

If life is about the journey, reporting is about the doing. Commit to high standards in every phase of a piece; from making the phone calls, to prepping for your interviews, to asking the right questions, to getting the sound, lighting and video right if you're shooting, to logging your shots and sound, to writing the script, to voicing the copy, to scrutinizing the edits. One or two frames, pictures, facts, words or phrases can, in a lucky situation, advance your career by leaps and bounds.

That's the process.

The Right Place at an Unfortunate Time

"On the Street, Lost and Forgotten"

In 1982, KRON-TV's managing editor, Doug Caldwell, took a risk with photographer Todd Hanks, editor George Griswold, and me. We were new to the staff, and yet he assigned us a series about homelessness on San Francisco's streets. Why Todd? Why George? Why me? Maybe he figured we were young, single, and hungry enough to regard working all night as fun.

We threw ourselves into the project, and linked up with a group of city-roaming winos who became recurring central characters in the stories. Their unofficial spokesman was a scruffy guy they called Rubidub, who earned the name "because I used to drink rubbing alcohol. Whenever we open a new bottle, we always pour a little out for the brothers."

"The brothers?"

"Yeah," added Rubidub's buddy, Norman Bushard. "We toast the brothers who died in the war, on the streets, and in the penitentiary." Norman spoke in a thick working-class accent and always wore a soiled navy blue stocking cap. He had a weepy left eye. From that side of his face, Norman always appeared to be crying. From the right side, however, he looked scowling and mean.

Rubidub, legally named Robert Brennan, had fought in Vietnam. He wore a full beard with matted, shoulder-length hair, and saw the world through a pair of large, cracked glasses held together by a thick wad of surgical tape. The man looked half-blind and completely deranged. "After the divorce, I hit the streets," he explained. "It's the life I want to lead. It's freedom."

It took only a whiff to notice that Rubidub rarely bathed. He must have had six years of dirt caked into the folds of his neck. You've never met a louder, more obnoxious, and sometimes articulate drunk. Nor would you want to.

Todd, George, and I spent so many days and nights with these men that we began to wonder if we were covering this story or becoming part of it. We watched the winos get arrested and, just as quickly, released. San Francisco did not have an effective system for dealing with its drunken homeless, and they, in turn, couldn't plan beyond their next bottles. The gang slept in bushes, under freeways, or in quiet alleys, and proclaimed their lifestyle to be grand.

It took us two weeks to produce three long pieces, and we had fallen behind. With only one more day to shoot, "On the Street: Lost and Forgotten," as we called it, still needed an ending. Todd, George, and I considered watching a homeless person's funeral at sea. The Neptune Society told us none were pending.

Since nobody had a better idea, Todd suggested another visit to the Tenderloin district, where we had spent most of our time. Maybe we would run across Rubidub and Norman, and could ask some tough questions about where their lifestyle might lead.

This time, however, as Todd, George, and I drove through the neighborhood, we couldn't find the winos. They had disappeared. Hours passed. Sunset approached. We began to lose hope. "It's not happening," said Todd.

"Let's keep trying," I insisted. Keep that hook in the water.

Out of desperation, I threw up a wild prayer. "Help us find an ending."

We parked the car. We sat in silence. Moments later, we either got lucky, or else received divine intervention. Rubidub, Norman, and maybe ten members of their gang strolled around the corner and greeted us. They were cold sober, for once, and able to speak rationally on camera.

"Do you worry about dying?" I asked Bushard.

"No, no, no. I don't care. I don't care about dying at all," he said bitterly.

Bushard and the others talked tough, defending their drinking and their homeless lifestyle.

Rubidub, soft-spoken and sensitive in sobriety, described the wife, kids, and mortgage he'd left behind. "If I die right now, so be it. That's dead and stinkin', man. Nobody gets out of life alive."

We recorded forty minutes of such bold talk. When I ran out of questions, Todd asked a few more. As a reporter, I never had a problem with that, nor he with my framing an occasional shot. Todd, George, and I worked collaboratively, as a team. We shared ideas in the field, in the writing, and also when editing. This project belonged to all of us.

Todd must have asked the guys six or seven questions. Whatever the number, he kept us there long enough to witness a sad and extraordinary climax to our weeks on the street.

Earlier in the conversation, a wino named Melvin Schmidt had stood up and stumbled away. We didn't much notice at the time. Schmitty, as they called him, was the old man of the group, He had been barely coherent in interviews. "I'm down for the count," he once told us on camera.

That statement would be prophetic.

We ended our heart-to-heart with the winos only after Todd's camera battery ran low. As we thanked the gang and began packing up, an ambulance approached with siren blaring, and stopped just around the corner. There we found Schmitty on his back, staring blankly at the sky, dead, with an empty bottle of Night Train wine in his hand.

Todd squeezed just enough juice from his battery to record the winos as they discovered Schmitty and broke into tears. Five minutes earlier, those same guys had spoken boldly about defying death. Strange how, while they did so, death made its own play just a few steps away.

"Dammit! Oh, Schmitty, man, please don't go," pleaded Buschard. Todd kept hoping the battery would last a little longer. Thankfully, in that era before cell phones, we had brought along a radio. George used it to make a frantic call for fresh batteries. KRON-TV photographer Chuck Hastings heard us from two blocks away and came to our rescue.

It was another of many breaks that day. In retrospect, we captured this remarkable scene because earlier, when our prospects for finding the story seemed most bleak, we stayed with it, waiting for fortunes to turn.

I cannot explain why all this happened in front of a camera. Luck, certainly, had nothing to do with it. Schmitty would have died whether we'd been there or not. Still, it was upsetting to watch and difficult to report. I'm probably trite and self-absorbed in believing that the timing of his death served a greater purpose. Maybe it just feels better that way.

Or maybe Rubidub summed the event more succinctly with this comment: "At least he died drunk."

CHAPTER 8

When You Have No Time:
Hamburger Helpers for Television News

Perhaps you've seen *Iron Chef*, a Japanese television show in which two culinary masters, a champion and a challenger, have one hour in which to create gourmet meals from identical but limited ingredients.

"Why do you like this show?" my wife once asked.

"Because I do the same thing."

"But you hardly cook."

True, but television reporters can relate to those chefs and their challenges because we are their short-order journalistic equivalents. Like the Iron Chefs, reporters work with limited ingredients and tight deadlines, and almost always deliver.

Let's be realistic about the job. Most major-market television stations cover large geographic areas with a relatively small number of crews. Unless reporters shoot a story themselves, they may wait several hours for an available camera. Either way, they commonly spend more time driving to and from an assignment than shooting or editing. We're like quick-strike teams, traveling fast and light.

The next time you find yourself in a hurry, try a few of the following suggestions. If you can't be an Iron Chef, become an Iron Reporter.

Add Dimension To Your Characters

How often have you heard someone described like this in a story?

MABEL THORPE HAS WORKED IN THIS POTATO CHIP FACTORY
FOR THE LAST TWENTY YEARS . . .

How much does that line really tell you about Mabel? And yet, many reporters automatically use age or years to characterize someone, overlooking how just one more thoughtfully chosen fact might add substance and depth:

... THAT'S A LONG TIME TO WATCH CHIPS ON A CONVEYOR BELT, BUT NOT TO MABEL. BY SITTING HERE, SHE EARNED ENOUGH MONEY TO PUT A SON THROUGH MEDICAL SCHOOL.

And now you know Mabel better. When she speaks, you have a sense of where she's coming from. Her words carry more weight.

Find the Details—Write Outside of the Frame

Mabel's son is an example of how, even when we don't have perfect sound or pictures, we can expand a story by adding small details from outside the visual frame.

Read the work of Edna Buchanan, whose crime reporting for the *Miami Herald* won a Pulitzer Prize for general news reporting in 1986. She was the queen of details. In her book *The Corpse Had a Familiar Face*, Buchanan describes how, if a wife killed her husband while he watched television, she would go so far as to ask the name of the program.

> "Police say she bludgeoned her husband to death with a frying
> pan as he sat in an easy chair in the living room. The TV was on
> channel 5. It was 7:15 p.m. He had been watching *Family Feud*."

Those kinds of details—the frying pan, the time, the channel, and the irony of the show's name—give texture to the story. Edna Buchanan could never know enough. She would ask what a deceased was wearing, and even what the coroner found in his pockets. In the case of one murdered politician, she learned he had been found wearing a dress.

Such particulars enhance any form of journalism. They can be especially valuable in television news when you run short of time to shoot or to tell.

Richmond Explosion

In 1999, a plastics recycling company blew up in Richmond, California, northeast of San Francisco. The blast spewed debris and toxic fumes downwind. Here's the first line of that piece. I wrote both inside and outside of the frame by describing how it looked, smelled, and sounded:

> EVEN WITHOUT THE RAIN, RICHMOND STREETS
> WOULD HAVE BEEN EMPTY THIS MORNING.
> IT TOOK ONLY ONE LOOK AT THE RISING SMOKE . . .
> ONE ACRID WHIFF AND THE SOUND OF HELICOPTERS. . . .
> IT TOOK ONLY ONE OR TWO PIECES OF BURNED PLASTIC.
> THEY CLUNG TO TELEPHONE LINES AND FLUTTERED DOWN
> LIKE FALLOUT FROM A POLYMER-FILLED SKY.

That was a hectic morning. The station dispatched crews from everywhere, or so it seemed. As soon as I linked up with photographer Ron Guintini, the assignment desk ordered us to find a local resident, and tell his or her story. We picked the first person we saw. Gleena Allen, a single mother of three, was sitting in a parked car with the windows rolled up. She agreed to let us follow her home:

> . . . TO THE HOUSE SHE GREW UP IN, JUST TWO BLOCKS
> DOWNWIND FROM THE EXPLOSION.

There, Gleena introduced us to her children and then to her hunchbacked seventy-six-year-old grandmother, Willie, who barely looked up while frying salt pork on the kitchen stove. The elderly woman told us she suffered from heart and lung problems, and that the explosion made her feel worse. "I smell it here inside this house," she said. "Can't hardly breathe."

"Can you describe the smell?"

"It's like a knife handle burning on a stove."

Next, we moved to the living room and asked the oldest daughter, Leticia, about her experience with the explosion. "It shook the whole house, like an earthquake," she told us.

Fifteen minutes later, the family packed their car and left for an aunt's house. We followed and would eventually shoot more, even though we had already gathered several good details to use in the narrative track:

BY ELEVEN A.M. THE FAMILY DECIDED THEY'D HAD ENOUGH . . .

(SOT)
Gleena tells kids: "Get your shoes. We're out of here."

THEY LEFT THE SALT PORK SITTING ON THE STOVE.

THEY LEFT THE DISHES IN THE SINK.

THEY LEFT THE HOUSE AND TOOK OFF FOR
CLEANER AIR AT AUNT VERNA'S HOUSE.
BUT AUNT VERNA LIVES JUST TWO MILES AWAY.

Give a Story New Looks by Changing the Scene

From start to finish, the story took less than one hour to shoot. We made it visually interesting by showing several different locations, including the street, the house, and Aunt Verna's place. At each of them, Ron Guintini had collected quick sequences and details.

On the street, he shot the sky, the power lines, and the family car.

In the house he shot the salt pork in the frying pan, dirty dishes in the sink, and latched windows in the living room.

At Aunt Verna's, he took pictures from outside and inside the apartment.

By visiting so many places and showing so many elements, the piece never repeated a scene. It moved fast, even at more than two and a half minutes.

Shoot Wisely and Efficiently, In Sequences

When working in multiple locations as we did that day, do not overshoot. Generally, you shouldn't need more than ninety seconds of set-up video from any one scene, unless you plan to dwell there in the piece.

This is doubly important for those of us who shoot our own stories under daily deadline pressures. Ninety seconds should allow you to get a basic sequence with wide, medium, tight, and cutaway shots. If you have more time, go for style points with a couple of extreme close-ups to use as natural sound, transitions, or as moments. Whatever you do, always get that wide shot first. When you're "running and gunning," a basic wide shot can set up a location, person, or sound bite, even if it isn't pretty.

When you finally do get around to asking the questions, maintain that same discipline. Keep interviews short and to the point. Know what you need, listen for it, and move on.

Use Photographs and File Video to Expand the Time Frame

Many times when producing a story, I ask for photographs, even from a wallet, because they tell more about a person or his family. This also works with home movies or file video. Any of them expand a time frame by showing how someone has aged or changed. They add another layer of those important visual elements.

Once, we faced a short deadline while doing a story about Carla Picci, a teenage girl struck by lightning on her right arm. After a brief hospital stay, doctors sent her home where, like a typical sixteen-year-old, she worried only about tryouts for the softball team, three days hence. "I want to make the squad," she told us, "but my arm hurts."

How could we visualize her apprehension? Carla found a photograph of herself posing in a softball uniform. We stuck that picture to the refrigerator, rolled a few seconds of video, and used it in the piece. No, this wasn't as optimal as seeing Carla actually play, but it did provide a visual reference, and showed her in another setting.

Again, we gave the piece an additional look.

Change the Background During Interviews

In the early 1990s, Yuba City, California, earned *Money* magazine's distinction of being America's worst place to live. The day of the announcement, KGO-TV chartered a plane and sent us north. Unfortunately we got a late start. After landing, renting a car, and rolling into town, we had all of thirty minutes in which to shoot the story and return to the airport, so we made the most of what we could get. For our wide shot of the town, we used an aerial from the plane. Later, we pointed our camera out the car window for driving shots down the main street.

Thirty minutes to shoot—that's cutting it close, and we still needed reactions from local citizens. As time ticked away, we stopped outside a shopping center and grabbed interviews in the parking lot. From what viewers saw, we might as well have spoken with people in four different locations.

How? North, south, east, and west. In four directions we could see four different views; the shopping center, the mountains, the main street through town, and a stand of trees. *By facing people in four different directions, we changed the backgrounds four times.*

I use that technique quite often, even when not in a hurry. It makes good television. If you know you'll need more than one sound bite from a person, rotate or move him during casual interviews. By altering the background even slightly, you subtly change the scene and keep the visuals more interesting.

"This way, it looks like we spent more time with you." I usually say. That almost always gets a laugh.

Change the Light and Camera Angles

In the early 1990s, KGO-TV newsroom staff members began receiving yellow three-by-five cards in the mail from Leon Lukaszewski, one of our viewers. His messages politely, but firmly corrected our grammar. "Your copy in the segment April 8 suffered from an elementary case of singular, plural conflict," Lukaszewski once wrote.

Who was this guy?

I made a call and learned that our self-appointed grammar policeman had retired after twenty-three years of copy editing the *Los Angeles Times*. Once an editor, always an editor, Leon Lukaszewski couldn't leave it alone, and took it out on the media. Leon kept a pencil and paper in his hand whenever he watched television, intending to prevent what he called contagious diseases of the English language. "What happens is some moron comes up with an expression," said Lukaszewski. "And I wonder how he can get away with it. And soon everyone else in town is getting away with it."

Leon Lukaszewski made a wonderful character.

Shooting this story challenged us because most of it took place in one small room of Leon's house. Thankfully, photographer Cathy Cavey is an expert at working with light and angles. She made the piece work. First, she took the camera outside to shoot Lukaszewski through a window.

Inside, Cathy used natural light coming from that same window for one sequence, then the fluorescent lamp on his desk for another. Later, she pointed her own tungsten light at a wall, and used the reflection. Cathy even turned the room lights out when Mr. Lukaszewski watched television, letting the glow of the screen illuminate him. Why? Light from different sources varies in textures, and so does its look.

Additionally, Cathy changed the physical level of her camera, shooting high, low, around doorways, and through openings.

In actual size, Leon Lukaszewskiís room might have been ten by twelve feet. You would never have known it by the time Cathy Cavey finished shooting.

Hamburger Helpers Make Good Television

These "hamburger helpers" are, in fact, tried-and-true examples of television field production. In your role as a story producer, remember that they add more than speed. They make good television, particularly for longer segments. You will need them. Ninety seconds worth of elements can rarely support two or three compelling minutes. *Longer stories require more interviews, more characters, more changes of scenery, and more depth.*

The Fountain Fire

We used several of these hurry-up techniques while covering the remnants of a forest fire in northern California. Photographer Clyde Powell and I flew in by helicopter with orders to get quick pictures and sound, and then do two simple live shots. The assignment editor told us specifically, "Don't bother with a package. We already have too much news."

Clyde and I arrived in the fire zone with just enough time to visit a Red Cross shelter. There, we interviewed a woman who had lost her mobile home in the fire. She told how her son and daughter, who lived two doors away, had also lost their homes. "It just wiped our family out," said the woman.

That charred mobile home park lay between us and our live-shot location. We stopped en route, took pictures, and used those shots, along with her interview, during our live segments.

Except for the helicopter ride, it had been a relatively simple day. That changed as we headed for home. Minutes before our chopper would lift off, the assignment editor sent a message. "Your satellite window is at 9:00," he said. "Keep the package to less than two minutes."

"What window? What package? Nobody said anything about a package." Not to us, anyway. But the station had hired a new and zealous producer for the late broadcast, and he ordered an update on the fire. Nothing would dissuade him, even after we explained how both the flames and sun had almost disappeared behind opposite mountain ridges. The producer didn't care. He had created a slot in his rundown and he expected us to fill it.

Be the Solution, Not the Problem

Both Clyde and I had been in the business long enough to know that it rarely pays to fight managers, producers, or the desk. Save your energy for the assignment. Be the solution, not the problem.

We sat down on a couple of tree stumps, shook our heads, and muttered some unprintable words. We hadn't a clue about what to do.

Within five minutes a couple of minivans, packed with kids and belongings, pulled up. An exhausted-looking woman, Lynn Doro, slammed a door and trudged toward us. "Do you know the way to Buzzard's Roost?" she asked.

"No," I answered. "How would you like to be on television?"

Examine my reasoning. Lynn Doro was somehow involved with the fire. *Find a person, tell a story.* Remember my mantra? If we couldn't cover the big story, at least we could tell a small one about Lynn and her family. With a tight deadline, that would be more than enough.

Lynn Doro, meanwhile, just wanted to get home. "On the day of the fire, as we left our house at Buzzard's Roost, the flames were moving as fast as our car was," she said. After four days of running, and with the roads still closed, she and her husband, Bill, wanted to find a find a back way in.

"I was told we can't cut through. But maybe we can use our knowledge of the back roads," Bill hoped.

Lynn gave us an interview at that first location. Then she and her family climbed back into those minivans to see if a roadblock had opened. Clyde hauled his gear into one of the vans and rode with them. It was a really smart move. The Doros didn't travel more than a mile, but by using a ten-second shot from inside their moving van, we gave viewers a sense of sharing space, spending time, and journeying with them. *This extra element added a sense of intimacy.*

When the family stopped again at the roadblock, we took more pictures and asked more questions. Now we had seen them in three locations, which gave us the beginnings of a narrative.

So, what could we do next to expand the story's context? Well, we had that interview with the woman from the Red Cross center. And what about those burned mobile homes? We used those elements in the middle of the package, adding overview, depth, and giving the story five different looks.

To close the piece, we returned to the Doro family as they pulled into yet another location, a campground, where they would spend at least one more night away from home. In total, Clyde and I spent less than half an hour with them. The story ran two minutes, using ten minutes of raw video from six locations.

Better yet, we'd cobbled together enough ingredients for a complete story with a beginning, middle, ending, main characters, interesting visuals, and a quest:

The Fountain Fire
September 1992

WE MET HER DURING ONE OF THOSE IN-BETWEEN PERIODS.
WITH THE SUN FALLING BEHIND ONE RIDGELINE
AND A HOTSPOT RISING ON THE OTHER,
LYNN DORO WANTED TO GET HER FAMILY HOME
AFTER THREE DAYS OF RUNNING.

(SOT)
Lynn: "On the day of the fire, as we left our house at Buzzard's Roost, the flames were moving as fast as our car was . . ."

SO TONIGHT, HUSBAND BILL TOOK THE DOGS IN ONE CAR,
AND LYNN TOOK THE KIDS IN ANOTHER,
SEARCHING FOR A WAY THROUGH THE FIRE ZONE.
THEY RAN INTO ONE ROADBLOCK AFTER ANOTHER.

(SOT)
Bill: "I was told we can't cut through. But maybe we can use our knowledge of the back roads to find a way in now."

IT HAS BEEN THIS WAY FOR MANY LOCAL FAMILIES.
WHEN THE FOUNTAIN FIRE BROKE OUT LAST THURSDAY,
PEOPLE GRABBED WHAT FEW ITEMS THEY COULD.
THEY'VE BEEN MOVING EVER SINCE. AND YET, BY SOME
STANDARDS, THE DOROS ARE LUCKY. THE FOUNTAIN FIRE
HAS DESTROYED 308 HOMES SO FAR. EVACUATION CENTERS
HAVE FILLED WITH WIPED-OUT FAMILIES.

(SOT)
Woman in the Red Cross center: "When the fire came through,

it just wiped our family out. It got me, my son, my daughter. Everything's gone."

(SOT)
Doors slam as we see Lynn and Bill climb out of their cars again, now in a parking lot

WHEN WE SAID GOODBYE TO LYNN AND BILL TONIGHT, THEY WERE STILL IN LIMBO. THE LAST THEY HEARD, THEIR HOUSE REMAINED STANDING, BUT THERE WERE FLAMES IN THE AREA.

GOOD NEWS . . .

BAD NEWS . . .

NO NEWS, REALLY . . .

(SOT)
Lynn: "This is like being chased. I feel as if I've been chased by this fire since an hour after it started."

Bill: "This is four days now. Four days of not sleeping through the night . . ."

Lynn: "Maybe we should find a motel and get some rest."

Bill: "Yeah, a bath and shower would be good. Then maybe we can go to a movie and forget about all this until tomorrow, when we'll try it all again."

Less Can Be More

The Lottery Winner

If you have not, yet, covered a multi-million dollar lottery winner receiving a big cardboard check, give it time. You will. It baffles me that recipients appear before the press, disclose their lucky numbers, and announce to the world what they plan to do with the money.

The events are always interesting, however, even if somewhat predictable. A few years ago, one winner held out for a couple of days before going public, and then held her press conference at 4:00 p.m. Our 5:00 p.m. producer wanted a full package and a live shot.

Photographer Jose Reyes and I were not happy about doing a quick, non-visual story about people sitting at a desk in front of a lottery banner, so we began to fantasize. "Just once, could one of those people be drunk, or outrageous, or something?" I asked Jose.

Our wish came true. We soon learned that our lottery winner waited so long to come forward because she had become happily inebriated. She remained in that condition when she arrived at the press conference. The woman's comments were fall-down funny. She delivered them in perfect sound bite increments.

The press conference ended with thirty minutes remaining until our live shot. We could have tried to write and edit a conventional story, but that would have been risky. Instead, I opted to pick the best sound bites and bump them together.

"What about jump cuts?" asked Jose.

We worked around that problem by shooting the side of our white van, and then inserted the video in five-frame white flashes between each cut. It was simple, minimal, and effective. I led into the video by telling how much our recipient had won, and noted that while we had covered many lottery press conferences, none had been as entertaining. I led into the clip by reciting her winning numbers. As the following sound bites show, less can sometimes be more:

Lottery Winner
2002

Lottery Winner: "I read them three times, didn't believe it. Ran into the house, told my boyfriend. He was just getting out of the shower, and said, 'Read these numbers to me.' He read them to me, we looked at each other and said, 'Holy (Bleep)'.
Ooops. I'm sorry! Ha ha Ha!"

(WHITE FLASH)
Lottery Winner: "I haven't stopped laughing. I told him, 'How am I

going to go to work? All I'm going to do is go, ha ha ha, you want what, when?' Ha-Ha-Ha! Ha-ha! I'm sorry. It's just been pretty damn funny all day! Ha-Ha-Ha!"

(WHITE FLASH)
Wayne question: "WILL YOU BE HAVING A LISTED NUMBER?"

Lottery Winner, Giggling: "I won't even be around. I'll be in Europe. If you can find me, catch me." (Giggles uncontrollably).

(WHITE FLASH)
Wayne question: "WHAT DO YOU GET FROM COMING OUT HERE AND TELLING THE WORLD YOU WON THE LOTTERY?"

Lottery Winner: "Just, you know what? Ha-ha, I won the lottery!!!!"
She almost falls out of her chair from laughing

"I'm sorry. That's how I feel right now."

Television News Versus Orthodontics

An intern in our newsroom stopped by for a chat recently. She'd just turned down a scholarship and career in orthodontics to pursue reporting. "Are you sure you want to do that?" I asked. As an orthodontist, each of her projects would last a lifetime, not ninety seconds. Better still, patients would expect her to do the best possible job, without taking shortcuts. "Don't you see the luxury in that? Television news, whether broadcast or on the internet cannot approach such a standard."

"Teeth bore me," confessed the intern.

Television news reporting will always involve compromise, to a degree. That doesn't mean we need to sell out in making it. Quite the contrary; knowing the ideal sets a standard. By understanding what a story lacks, you may be able to make up for it some other way. "We can't let the ideal stand in the way of the good," I told the intern. "If that bothers you . . ."

She finished my sentence: ". . . then become an orthodontist."

CHAPTER 9

Thread Stories Around Spontaneous Moments

I f aliens visited Earth and landed among the tailgate parties before an Oakland Raiders home game, they would take one look, run back to their space ship, and never return.

"Earthlings are menacing and dangerous," the aliens might report. They would have found themselves among goblins, ghouls, and monsters, all dressed in silver and black—a beer-frothing, meat-eating, garlic-spewing mob. No doubt, every professional football team has its own cadre of devoted, bizarre fans, but for sheer spectacle nothing compares with the costumed, maniacal misfits of the Raider Nation.

For generations, its citizens gathered in tribal clans, staking out territories in the Oakland Coliseum's massive parking lot. No one ever drew official boundaries or markings, but to Raider fans, those sections of concrete were sacred turf.

"Yeah, like this is our light pole," gestured Raider fan Rick Sanders one summer afternoon. "D-24. That's us."

At least, it used to be until stadium management resurfaced the lot, repainted the lines into smaller spaces, and changed the policy. Where before, fans could park anywhere they wanted, the new system funneled cars into sections. "It's a matter of safety and efficiency," explained a Coliseum spokeswoman.

"They want to turn us into sheep," countered Sanders. "I'm mad. I'm teed off."

Tensions escalated in the weeks leading up to the team's first home game.

Coliseum management refused to compromise. Raider fans threatened blatant disobedience.

Local news stories don't get much better than this.

On game day, cars lined up hours in advance. Some of them came in convoys, hoping to break the rules by parking together in their usual spaces, but when the lots opened, they never had the chance. Coliseum parking attendants waved flags, blew whistles, and herded them like cattle through a series of metal gates into tight little compliant rows.

Raider fans, who take pride in their renegade image, took this as the ultimate insult. "Nobody's happy," whined Rick Borba, who we found in the parking lot, guarding his old spot with crossed arms and defiance on his face. After six seasons of beers and barbecuing there, Borba insisted on making a last stand. "We're loyal fans, and this is how they treat us?"

When we finished the interview, photographer Jack Fraser shot a few more pictures of Borba. As he did so, another man came running. His approach ruined the sequence, but Fraser had the good sense to keep rolling as the newcomer shouted, "Rick, you got a casualty! Your wife just hit another car!" Rick still wore the microphone, so we followed as he investigated the damage.

Sure enough, a Coliseum parking attendant had taken his directives a little too seriously, and ordered Mrs. Borba to pull into a space already occupied by another car's open door. She was furious in describing the incident to us. "He said, 'Pull forward.' And I go, 'I don't want to hit that car's door.' And he said, 'Pull forward!' I kept refusing. But he made me drive into the door!"

Mrs. Borba was pretty darn passionate. I considered, for an instant, whether we should pin the microphone on her, but that would have interrupted the moment. The shotgun microphone atop Jack's camera worked well enough. *Whatever we might have lost in clarity, we more than made up with spontaneity.*

Next we heard from David DeLoach, who owned the car Mrs. Borba had hit. He gestured to the frazzled attendant and told us a similar story. "He told the lady to pull up. She didn't want to. He insisted, and then she ran into my door. Can you believe this?"

The parking attendant said nothing. He merely stood there, withholding comment, looking frazzled.

Mrs. Borba had made only a small dent—hardly serious damage, but the event served as a catalyst in uniting all parties against Coliseum management.

For us, this was news on a serving plate—a minor drama inside the bigger one. *If on good days you identify a main character, then on the better ones you also find a narrative thread to weave through the story.* This one practically wrote itself.

We followed up by interviewing Coliseum general manager Mark Kaufman, who defended his new policy. Lastly, we took a few more pictures of other cars in the parking lot. The entire story required twelve minutes of raw video. We didn't need more. Why waste time?

Spontaneous Ignition in a News Story

Our Raiders parking piece demonstrates how spontaneous moments can bring energy, and sometimes structure, to television news stories. Most cases won't be as obvious as that fender bender, but if you keep an open mind and look for possibilities, you'll notice that they present themselves quite often.

This goes to the philosophy that when we cover news events, we also try to capture them. Stand back and look around. Like strings, story lines lead through all kinds of events. Follow them. The pictures and sound need not always be perfect. Viewers like to be witnesses, seeing their news fresh, as it happens.

Crash, Bang, "Go Raiders!"
August 2001

(SOT)
Parking attendants wave flags to direct cars

THEY'RE PLAYING FLAG FOOTBALL AT THE NETWORK ASSOCIATES COLISEUM TONIGHT, AND THE RAIDER NATION DOESN'T LIKE THE GAME .

(SOT)
Rick Borba: "Nobody's happy."

FATEFUL WORDS FROM RICK BORBA AS HE STUBBORNLY STAKED OUT A WHAT USED TO BE HIS OLD PARKING SPACE, AND WAITED FOR FRIENDS WHO HAD ALREADY "BUMPED" INTO EACH OTHER.

(SOT)
A friend approaches Borba, shouting: "Rick, you got a casualty. Your wife just hit a car!"

ON AN AFTERNOON WHEN RAIDER FANS ALREADY FELT MALIGNED BY BEING FORCED TO PARK BETWEEN THE LINES, THIS WAS MADE-TO-THEIR-ORDER—A WRECK IN THE PARKING LOT, THREE MINUTES INTO THE NEW SEASON AND NEW RULES.

ALL PARTIES INVOLVED BLAME AN OVERZEALOUS PARKING ASSISTANT.

(SOT)
Mrs. Borba: "He said, 'Pull forward.' And I go, 'I don't want to hit that car's door,' and he said, 'Pull forward!' I kept refusing. But he made me drive into the door."

(SOT)
David DeLoach, damaged car's owner: "He told the lady to pull up. She didn't want to. He insisted, and then she ran into my door."

(SOT)
Wayne to Rick Borba: "WHO'S RESPONSIBLE?"

Borba: "The parking guy. It sure wasn't my wife."

INDIRECTLY, THEY BLAME, NOT THE ATTENDANT BUT THIS MAN, MARK KAUFMAN, THE COLISEUM'S NEW GENERAL MANAGER. HE CHANGED THE PARKING POLICY.

(SOT)
Mark Kaufman: "Well they don't like me because I'm doing my job. If you look at the situation right now, it's safe."

KAUFMAN RAISED RATES, RESTRIPED THE PAVEMENT, BEGAN TELLING PEOPLE WHERE TO PARK, AND PUT AN END TO TRADITIONAL TAILGATING TURF. HE CALLS IT A LIABILITY.

(SOT)
Kaufman: "You had people racing across the parking lot in vehicles, and they were driving through areas with people sitting in lawn chairs. They were competing for parking spaces. It was dangerous."

(SOT)
Rick Borba examines the wreck: "Look at how this door opens across the damn parking line. There's no room. This is ridiculous."

THERE'S A POPULAR BOOK ON THE RACKS RIGHT NOW, ABOUT DEALING WITH CHANGE.

IT'S CALLED "WHO MOVED MY CHEESE?"

IF THIS CONTINUES, OAKLAND RAIDER FANS MAY WANT TO DO SOME READING . . .

(SOT)
Disconsolate fan sitting on a bumper with a beer in hand: "And this isn't even the regular season, man. It ain't gonna work!"

Postscript

It's worth noting that, one hour after the fender bender, Rick Borba, his wife, and David DeLoach had exchanged barbecue recipes, hoisted a few beers, and become pals.

They left the rest to their insurance companies.

CHAPTER 10

Using Comparison, Contrast, and Opposites as Storytelling Devices

I f you ever visit Moscow, leave plenty of time to explore its subway system, the Metro. Each station is an elaborate and individual work of art, with walls and floors made of granites and semiprecious stones. Moscow Metro stations are like hybrids of underground palaces, basilicas, and fortresses. Joseph Stalin envisioned them as grand tributes to socialism. They also doubled as bomb shelters.

One of the stations, Revolution Square, has a theme of utopian murals and bigger-than-life bronze statues. While waiting for a train, you stand next to imposing forms of the Mother, the Father, the Doctor, the Scientist, the Farmer, or other proud-looking heroes of the working class.

KGO-TV sent me to Moscow in the winter of 1992 for a series of stories about Russia's transition to a free-market economy. It was a difficult project, so I was grateful to receive help from Maxim Tkachenko, a local producer, and Sergey Gorychev, a freelance photographer. When on foreign assignment, it's always good to partner with people who know the landscape. We call them "fixers." Together, Maxim, Sergey, and I worked a series of exhausting yet exhilarating sixteen-hour days.

Maxim is one of the finest journalists with whom I have ever worked. He went on to report for many years at CNN. In five days of shooting, Maxim gave me a guided tour of his country's economic struggles. We looked at religion, employment, gay rights, deserted villages, and people who wanted desperately to leave the country because inflation had rendered the ruble almost worthless. Average Russians spent hours waiting to purchase items that we Americans take for granted. For toothbrushes or vodka, a line might extend outside and into the cold. For milk or chicken, it would stretch around a corner.

After our last scheduled shoot, Maxim and I celebrated by hitting a few of his favorite Moscow nightspots. Details are fuzzy because we drank plenty of vodka. I do remember how we walked it off by circling Red Square in a gentle midnight snowstorm, and that I never felt the cold. It was a wonderful experience—one made possible by reporting for a living.

On our way back to the Hotel Savoy, we passed through the Revolution Square station once again. This time, with all that vodka in me, inspiration struck. I saw those statues in contrast with the flesh-and-blood citizens standing beneath them. The real people looked exhausted and demoralized while the statues, in their noble, idealistic poses, struck me as being impostors.

The moment inspired one last piece in which we used the statues and people as counterpoints:

The Metro
January 1992

Change in hand

FIFTEEN KOPECS.
IN AMERICAN MONEY, THEY'RE WORTH A LITTLE MORE THAN ONE-TENTH OF AN ABE LINCOLN PENNY, BUT IN MOSCOW . . .

(SOT)
Coins into slot

FIFTEEN KOPECS WILL STILL BUY A TICKET TO UTOPIA . . .

(SOT)
People on escalator

THIS IS THE MOSCOW METRO . . .
A SUBTERRANEAN WORLD WITH A TRANSIENT
POPULATION OF EIGHT MILLION PEOPLE A DAY.
THEY COME, THEY GO . . . AT FORTY-FIVE SECOND INTERVALS.

(SOT)
Train arrival

(STAND-UP)
CRITICS CALL THE METRO THE ONE PRODUCT OF COMMUNISM
THAT REALLY WORKED. THEY SAY THAT, IF AN OUTSIDER
CAME HERE AND SAW ONLY THIS, HE MIGHT CONCLUDE THE
COMMUNISTS HAD BUILT A PERFECT WORLD.

(SOT)
Subway car door closes

STALIN ENVISIONED THE METRO AS A GRAND MONUMENT TO
SOCIALISM. EVERY STATION IS LIKE A PALACE OR ART MUSEUM,
BUT WITH DIFFERENT THEMES . . .

GLASS . . .

MURALS . . .

AND IN REVOLUTION SQUARE—STATUES.

THIS IS THE MOST HAUNTING STATION OF THEM ALL.

(SOT)
Young man in his mid-20s: "These are my grandparents.
My parents. They believed in what they were doing. And finally
they found out their ideals were an illusion . . . nothing.
This is a station of tragedy, frankly. This is a big tragedy."

BUT HIS ANCESTORS ARE STILL HERE AND BIGGER THAN LIFE—
NOBLE FIGURES OF THE WORKING CLASS, CAST IN BRONZE
WITH STRENGTH AND ENERGY.

THE DOCTOR . . .

THE FARMER . . .

THE ENGINEER . . .

(SOT)
First Russian male: "It's sad, really. Sad. Sad that the people who
made these people believed in what they were doing, and yet
they were betrayed. They were betrayed by themselves, by their
very own ideals. This is sad."

THE STATUES NEVER MOVE. THEY NEVER CHANGE EXPRESSION.
THEY'RE FROZEN IN A WORLD OF FAITH AND PURPOSE,
BUT IT IS NOT THE WORLD OF TODAY.

(SOT)
Old woman: "I am a pensioner. An invalid. I worked forty-two years
and now I can hardly buy bread. The system has fallen apart."

(SOT)
Older man: "Even in childhood, these statues didn't have a place
in my world. I was in prison a long time. I served in labor camp."

THROUGHOUT HISTORY AND CULTURES, MEN HAVE USED
STATUES TO PORTRAY IDEALS AND INSPIRE FUTURE GENERATIONS.

IT'S THE HOPE THAT LIFE WILL IMITATE ART.

NOT HERE, NOT ANY LONGER. . .

IN RUSSIA, TIMES HAVE CHANGED.

(SOT)
Train goes away

1 + 1 = 3: The Theory of Opposites

Our essay in Revolution Square used comparison, contrast, and opposites as a narrative tool. Reporters utilize the technique every day, although in simpler forms. It's as basic as getting two sides of a story.

Sometimes, you can build an entire story around opposites. Or, you might use them for references. During a heat wave in San Francisco in September 2000, I made the most of opposites two different ways on consecutive days.

The city had endured ninety-degree temperatures for more than a week. Such numbers might not sound severe to the rest of the country, but along the Pacific coast of northern California, yes, that's hot. We call that time of year our Indian Summer, and this one had lasted so long that we'd begun to run out of story ideas. A guy can cover only so many ice cream factories, blacktop pavement crews, heatstroke victims, and threats of electrical brownouts.

On the ninth day, while shooting yet another general story about heat, I spotted a group of young, drop-dead gorgeous people in front of a coffee shop. Despite the ninety-degree heat they wore furs, scarves, leathers, sweaters, parkas, and full-length coats. Huh?

They were fashion models doing a photo shoot for the winter collection on, of all days, that day, the hottest of the year. This was a made-to-order reference contrast. Across the street and all around, regular people were sticky, miserable, and wearing as little as possible. Those poor beautiful models, dressed for winter, were not allowed to sweat.

By including them, we rounded out our piece. Unfortunately, however, a reporter cannot rest on his laurels. As soon as that story aired, our executive producer at the time, Dennis Milligan, began pestering me: "What do you have for tomorrow?"

If You Steal an Idea, Take It from Yourself

Indian Summer

I had nothing, except a crazy idea. Twenty years earlier, while working in Louisville, Kentucky, I'd done a heat wave story by inter-cutting scenes from a blizzard the preceding winter. If memory serves, it was the first time I had stumbled upon the concept of using opposites as a storytelling device. When Dennis posed his question, that Louisville piece came to mind.

"We'll do a rain story," I said.

Dennis didn't see the humor. "It's not raining tomorrow. It's going to be ninety-eight."

"Trust me."

Milligan did—barely. If a reporter establishes a pattern of coming through for his bosses, they will begin to give him some leeway, especially when those bosses don't have a better idea. Dennis didn't. Nobody did.

Two decades after the Louisville piece, San Francisco had just endured a wet El Niño winter. I followed my old recipe, went to the archives, and pulled file tape of mud, flooding, and people complaining about the rain.

My new hot day story began with shots of heat waves, and people moaning about the high temperatures..

"It feels like Phoenix," says one.

"You sweat all the time," adds another.

Having established their misery, we cut to a shot of me driving. I turned to the camera and asked viewers if they would want to trade summer for winter. The camera nodded, "Yes," by moving up and down. Like a magician, I snapped my fingers and, on the sound, we cut to a shot of rain pelting that very same windshield six months earlier. With that visual gimmick, we transported viewers back to a wet winter, and put the heat wave in a different perspective.

Indian Summer
September 2000

WE CALL IT INDIAN SUMMER, AND WHILE THE NAME MAY NOT BE POLITICALLY CORRECT, HERE IT IS, AGAIN, RIGHT ON TIME.

(SOT)
Shirtless man on the street: "The Native American people do not own this time of year. It's for all of us."

A TIME TO SEEK SHADE . . . TO SAVOR OR PERHAPS EVEN SUFFER BENEATH SWELTERING, SUNBURST SKIES.

(SOT)
Woman in shade: "It feels like Phoenix."

Second woman: "You sweat all the time."

Third woman: "It's so hot you can't sleep."

(SOT)
Wayne driving car

I'M NOT A BIG FAN OF HOT DAYS LIKE THIS, EITHER. ARE YOU?

Camera shakes back and forth: "NO"

EVER THINK WISTFULLY OF WINTER?
WISH YOU COULD GO BACK?

Camera nods: "YES"

SURE?

Camera nods: "YES"

OK . . .

Wayne snaps fingers

(SOT)
Cut to shot from winter, looking out the front of a windshield in a driving rain storm

WHOA! WHAT HAPPENED?

(SOT)
Man in file tape during rain storm: "It was quite an adrenaline rush."

ACTUALLY, IT'S A DELUGE. WELCOME BACK TO THE LAND OF
LA NIÑA, THE HELL OF EL NIÑO—THE WETTER SIDE OF WINTER.
OR HAD YOU FORGOTTEN?

(SOT)
File of woman downtown woman in rain

Wayne to woman: "YOUR HAIR IS REACTING REALLY WELL TO THIS."

Woman: "You mean my frizz?"

WE MEAN, YOU ASKED FOR IT. YOU'VE TRADED HEAT WAVES ON
PAVEMENT FOR THE WINTER STORM VARIETY, AND GREEN GRASS
FOR MOUNTAINS OF MUD.

YOU'RE BACK IN THE AIRPORT NOW, THE VICTIM OF ANOTHER
WEATHER DELAY.

(SOT)
Man in airport during weather delay: "The travel agent should
have warned us."

NO, YOU SHOULD HAVE REMEMBERED HOW, LAST WINTER,
WE SUFFERED THROUGH MORE THAN ONE HUNDRED
CONSECUTIVE DAYS OF RAIN.

(SOT)
File of construction worker in rain: "Today I need my weather
boots. My back is soaked."

(SOT)
Frizzy-haired woman: "I'm sick of this. It's like the seven plagues.
It's Biblical . . . "

AND YOU ASKED FOR IT.

(SOT)
Wayne, on camera, snaps fingers

BUT ENOUGH, ALREADY. TWO MONTHS FROM NOW, IT WILL BE
COLD, WET, WINDY, AND WE WILL BE WISHING FOR BEAUTIFUL
WEATHER LIKE THIS. SO, LET'S ENJOY IT WHILE WE HAVE IT . . .
EVERY SINGLE SWEATY SECOND.

Opposites work because they illuminate the true natures of pictures, people, places, and events. To appreciate black, you need to know white. It's the same with good and evil, communism and autocracy, hot and cold, or any other subject you might deem appropriate.

Comparison and contrast is just another of those reporter tricks; one to keep in mind for a rainy day—or maybe a hot one.

CHAPTER 11

Stand-Ups

Every year, a new group of interns and production assistants comes to work in our news department. Predictably, some of them will say they want to report, and then request the staff's help in preparing so-called résumé DVD's. Long before these interns ask about what makes a story, or how to conduct interviews, or write, or edit, most will mention the need to "shoot a few stand-ups," as if they imagine that's a reporter's foremost job qualification. In watching these youngsters, one gets a feeling they want to work *in* television for the thrill of getting *on* television.

Someone needs to tell these wannabes they have it backwards.

Being on television should be a by-product of reporting, not the ultimate goal. The rest of the job comes first. Television news reporting should not be about the presenters.

Stand-Up Basics

Reporters do stand-ups for a number of reasons:

1. Stand-ups help reporters describe what they can't otherwise show, including the past, the future, or concepts.
2. Stand-ups provide an extra production element. When a reporter has a visually challenging story, every new scene helps keep a piece moving.

3. With a well-placed stand-up, a reporter can turn a storyline in a different direction.
4. Stand-ups can help reporters confide, or make an aside, or take a break from the main body of a piece.

Natural Looking Stand-Ups Do Not Happen Naturally

It's natural for young reporters to struggle when learning to speak to a camera. They ask similar questions.

"How do I act?"

"What should I do?"

"What do I say?"

"When do I say it?"

Those are normal concerns. Though the years, I have developed a number of techniques and guidelines. Maybe they will also help you.

When NOT to Do a Stand-Up

Although it is difficult to learn how and when to use a stand-up, it's equally important to learn when not to do one. We reporters may worship the sights and sounds of ourselves on television, but we tend to forget that we're still just talking heads—and, often, obtrusive ones. A stand-up in the wrong place or with the wrong tone can hurt a piece. Reporters make these mistakes at every professional level.

A few years ago, I sat on an awards panel and judged features from a top-three market. One entry profiled a high-school girl who played on the varsity football team, won the title of homecoming queen, and then kicked a winning field goal, all in the same night. Panel members loved this piece until the last few seconds. Then, instead of finishing with a classic shot of the girl walking off the field, the reporter ruined our reverie with a stand-up close.

What could he have been thinking? The report had been about her, not him. This is a classic example of how a stand-up can ruin a story as easily as it helps one.

Stand-Up Bridges

We do not see many stand-up opens these days, but some of us still do stand-up closes, often habitually. Stand-up closes tend to detract from central characters or narrative storylines, unless they never existed. Do a stand-up close only when you do not have other options.

Generally, it's good practice to do a stand-up bridge in the first half of a story. Why? The later you appear in a piece, the greater your risk of intruding, although this isn't a hard-and-fast rule. When I put a bridge in the second half of a story, it often reveals a twist.

Contemplate Fit and Flow

Anticipate how a stand-up will suit the rest of the piece. Does it fit into the pacing, or distract from it? Should you add movement, or simply stand and talk? Weigh the story's content, mood, and rhythm. Be natural on camera, not forced.

If your news director asks you to walk and point at something or hold it up, do so for the benefit of your viewers. For example, when you kneel down and pick up dry leaves that might be clogging a storm drain, finish the move by showing them to the camera, up close, in front of the lens. Speak to and treat the camera as if it were a person.

Behave in a Stand-Up as You Would in Real Life

Your appearance on camera should come across as being part of a conversation. A reporter loses credibility when he tries too hard in a stand-up. If you look as if you're performing, viewers will sense it.

Don't talk to the camera with your subjects supposedly ignoring you in the background. Everyone knows they aren't.

Don't sling a jacket over your shoulder to affect a look because, well, it looks affected.

Most important, do not try to fool viewers by forcing yourself into unnatural situations, or by faking it. Several years ago, an NBC News correspondent broadcast live while paddling a canoe during a flood. As she spoke, two men strolled through the frame directly in front of her. That water was barely ankle deep.

"Canoe Girl," as she became known, later explained that the strong current had forced her close to shore. It also came out that her producer purchased the canoe to use as a prop.

He had it delivered.

Note Your Composition in the Frame

Note where your interview subjects appear in the picture. Are they facing screen right or screen left? Are they big or small? If you will be leading into or following an interviewee's sound bite with a stand-up, try to juxtapose your head or body into a different part of the frame, and at a different size. Good composition makes cleaner edits.

If you shoot your own stories, I'm willing to bet that more of your interviews face screen left than screen right. There is a simple reason for that. Blame the manufacturers, who put viewfinders on the left sides of cameras to accommodate a right-eyed world. Compensate by doing more of your stand-ups from the left side, facing the opposite direction, screen right. The odds may work in your favor, sometime, when you cut a stand-up against a talking head.

Use a Wireless Microphone

Unless you're working in a loud environment and need the superior sound qualities of a stick microphone, wear a lapel microphone instead. It frees your hands, allowing you to gesture, lean on, or touch something. You'll feel more comfortable and communicate more effectively.

Make certain to mount that mic on whatever side of your body will be facing the camera, be it right, left, or front. Microphones produce their clearest sound when you speak toward them, not away from them. Follow the same practice with people you interview, as well.

Find Friendly Light

Nobody looks good in direct sunlight. It casts dark, harsh shadows. Sunlight makes you scrunch your face. Try to find open shade, or else a location where your photographer can put a scrim or a fill light on you.

If you cannot avoid the sun, minimize your time on camera. Find a reason to do the stand-up in a wide shot, and keep moving. One method might be to establish a presence at the scene, say a few words, point to something, and have the camera follow.

Such a move will be impossible for those of us who shoot our own stories. There are other options, however. If you use the same camera every day, and if it offers multiple presets, ask one of the engineers in your station to set it for faces in bright daylight. In my camera we decreased the contrast while increasing the black and chroma levels. This adjustment makes other people look better in bright sunlight, too.

Why Are You Walking and Talking?

Before he died too young, former NBC News correspondent Bob Elliott returned to Portland, Maine, where he worked several years as a feature reporter and social commentator. Bob liked to poke fun at everyday life. In stories, Bob used himself and a revolving cast of characters, including his friends, his wife, and his soft-spoken father. Viewers particularly loved the senior Elliott. They were upset when he decided he'd spent enough winters in Maine, and announced he was moving to southern Florida.

Before the old man left town, Bob reprised his father's television "career." In that piece, the elder Elliott tells how he plans to land a better gig in Miami, a much larger market. Bob warns his dad that he'll need to make a résumé tape.

The segment has a wonderful scene in which Bob tries to teach his dad how to do a stand-up: "Walk, Dad. Just walk and talk."

"Why do reporters walk when they talk?" his father asks.

"I don't know. They just do. They do it too much. Now walk. But start walking before you start talking."

Bob was correct. People *do* walk and talk too much in stand-ups, and it shows. Why are they walking? Where are they going?

If you must have movement, try an alternative. Stand in one spot. Have the camera push in to you. This is more dignified than walking. A tightening shot adds importance to whatever you're saying.

Conversely, I caution you against having the camera pull back during a stand-up. Even when a widening shot reveals something, it can kill a story's momentum. Why should viewers pay attention to a visually shrinking reporter? It's the equivalent of trying to listen to someone when he's backing away.

Use the Medium

Not every stand-up must originate in the field. When appropriate, you might work with an electronic chroma-key, the same technology we use to insert maps behind weather forecasters.

Let's say you need to explain the moving parts of an airliner's tail section. Obviously, you can't go to the airport, climb a ladder, and do the stand-up there, but you can use the chroma-key to insert a close-up picture behind you as you do a walk-around in the studio. Point to the parts of that tail as a weather forecaster would to a storm front.

I have also used chroma-keys to give a 'tour' on the surface of Mars, insert myself into an award winning film by Pixar, and to 'stand' on a country road during the Civil War.

Work With Your Art Department

If you're working a fact-heavy, non-visual story, split the screen and make a list. Have the photographer frame you in the right-hand side of his screen, leaving room for postproduction graphics to appear on the left. As you run down the list on camera, have each item appear as a bullet point, to which you nod or refer.

Why should you be on the right and the words on the left? Simple. That's how people read—from the left.

You Need Not Speak Directly to the Viewer

Try a stand-up which includes the viewers, even though you never speak directly to the camera.

Photographer Scott Arthur tried this technique when we visited a secret room atop San Francisco's Transamerica Pyramid. It's a tiny glass lookout barely big enough for two people and one very bright beacon. To get there, a person must climb more than two hundred steps, and then a precarious-looking ladder.

We began our segment in the express elevator. As it beeped upward through the floors, viewers saw chief building engineer Mike Bellafronte and me staring straight ahead. Here is the narration:

> BY ELEVATOR STANDARDS, THIS PUSHES THE ENVELOPE FOR LONG HAULS. HOW ELSE WOULD YOU EXPLAIN TWO MEN OBSERVING PROTOCOL BY MINDING THEIR OWN BUSINESS, IN THEIR OWN SPACE, AS TIME DRAGS BY IN A SMALL, UPWARDLY MOBILE BOX?
>
> (WAYNE ON CAMERA)
> Wayne turns to Bellafronte and, with the camera looking over Bellafronte's shoulder toward him, asks:
>
> "WHY DON'T PEOPLE SPEAK TO EACH OTHER IN ELEVATORS?"
>
> Mike: "It's not proper elevator etiquette."

Although I addressed my question to Mike, it also included Scott's camera and the viewers, who might as well have been riding with us. And who, at one time or another, hasn't asked that question of himself?

A One-Word Stand-Up

Several years ago, KGO-TV photographer Cathy Cavey and I traveled to Carvers, Nevada, a tiny cluster of businesses in the desert. Their owner had put all of them up for sale. Essentially, that meant he was selling the entire town.

Our route took us along Highway 50, which Nevadans describe as "the loneliest highway in America." After about a hundred miles, Cathy asked, "When do we get there?"

"Hours," I replied, in a bored and sarcastic tone, and that gave us an idea. We would do a stand-up consisting of one word. Here's how it worked, surrounded by the narration leading in and out:

> TO GET TO CARVERS, WE RENTED A CAR AND THEN
> DROVE, AND DROVE, AND DROVE, FOR . . .
>
> (WAYNE ON CAMERA)
> Wayne turns from the steering wheel and says: "HOURS . . . "
>
> . . . ABOUT FOUR HOURS AND TWO HUNDRED FIFTY MILES
> SOUTHEAST OF RENO. OUT THROUGH THE MOONSCAPE . . .
>
> OUT PAST THE SAND DUNES . . .
>
> OUT WHERE OLD BEER BOTTLES CRACK IN THE SUN . . .
>
> OUT TO WHERE WINDMILLS HAVE BULLET HOLES . . .
>
> AND STOP SIGNS MUST WAVE FOR YOUR ATTENTION.

With one short word, we set up a sequence of cool pictures that visualized a very long trip.

Write Into and Out of Your Stand-Up As You Would Any Other Piece of Sound

Look again at that one-word stand-up. Notice how the narration leads to me on camera. I fill in the blank by saying, "Hours," and then the narration resumes, all in one thought. Treat a stand-up as you would any other sound bite. Transitions shouldn't call attention to themselves.

Stay in the Moment

A few years ago, the desk sent photographer Randy Davis and me to cover Tiger Woods as he played in his first AT&T golf tournament. Woods had just turned professional and, because he had Kevin Costner for his partner, the crowd swelled, making it almost impossible to get a good shot of either man.

We decided our best option would be to turn that negative into a positive. Just before the stand-up, I wrote to pictures of the difficult viewing conditions:

> . . . TO BE MORE PRECISE, YOU DON'T SEE THEIR SHOTS
> AS MUCH AS LISTEN FOR THEM. THAT LITTLE DOT
> DOWN THERE IS THE YOUNG MR. WOODS
> AS HE MISSES A PUTT . . .
>
> (SOT)
> The crowd loudly sighs: "Augh."
>
> . . . AND NOW, KEVIN COSTNER TEES OFF. HE MAY "DANCE WITH
> WOLVES," BUT HE ALSO SLICES INTO THE WOODS . . .
>
> (SOT)
> Costner hits a horrendous shot. The crowd moans: "Oooooh."
>
> . . . CLEARLY, ONE OF LIFE'S GREAT TRAGEDIES . . .

Here we cut to my stand-up. Randy wanted me to walk through the gallery, but the crowd would not cooperate. I couldn't finish a sentence without someone stepping in front of the camera, so we turned that to our advantage. In a long-lens shot surrounded by people, I said:

(STAND-UP)
IT'S HARD TO BELIEVE, BUT WE SPENT ABOUT AN HOUR TRYING
TO GET JUST ONE GOOD SHOT OF THAT GROUP, AND...

At that moment a golf cart stopped and blocked Randy's shot. I kept talking and ad-libbed:

(STAND-UP CONTINUES)
... UGH ... AND ... OH WELL.
MAYBE WE'LL HAVE BETTER LUCK BY TRYING TO GET PICTURES
OF SOMEONE ELSE.

We never planned for that golf cart to stop between us, but it helped show the difficulties of getting from place to place. Randy and I had worked together long enough that he knew to keep the camera rolling. That ad-lib worked better than any stand-up we might have scripted.

Adapt to Your Environment

The 360-Degree Stand-Up

As you do more stand-ups, you will begin to recognize the visual and editorial possibilities in every story and location.

Again with Cathy Cavey behind the lens, we covered the aftermath of a warehouse fire. This one was unusual because, before the place burned, its tenant, a guy named Stephen, had collected dozens of old pianos, and mounted them from floor to ceiling. Moreover, he placed those pianos in chronological, clockwise order, from oldest to newest, as an artistic statement. It made an eerily unusual sight.

As I stood in one spot, Cathy made a clockwise, 360-degree pan around the room. I disappeared from the left side of the screen, and reappeared in the right. Here are the words:

(STAND-UP)
YOU CAN'T TELL FROM THE CHARRED REMNANTS, BUT THOSE
PIANOS ARE STACKED IN CHRONOLOGICAL ORDER. THAT'S
1865 OVER THERE, THE END OF THE CIVIL WAR. AND IF YOU

MOVE CLOCKWISE AROUND THE ROOM, YOU CAN TRACE MORE HISTORY AS YOU WOULD WITH THE RINGS OF A TREE, OR THE NUMBERS ON A CLOCK FACE. NOW WE'RE PASSING THE TURN OF THE CENTURY. THERE'S WORLD WAR ONE, AND BEHIND ME HERE—1930. IT'S THE NEWEST PIANO STEVEN KEPT. HE SAYS THAT'S WHEN THEY STOPPED MAKING GOOD ONES.

James Dean

The James Dean Memorial near Cholame, along California's central coast, is a peculiar place. It sits in front of a small post office just below Polonio Pass on Route 46, not far from where the movie star died in his 1955 Porsche Spyder. All day, every day, tourists drive miles out of their way to stop at the spot and take pictures. Most of them can't even explain why. It's just something to do.

Lilly Grant, who ran that post office, insisted she isn't a James Dean fan, but, because of the many questions she has fielded from curious people, she probably knows more about his death than anyone else on Earth. "I can't see what his fans saw in him," Lilly confided.

She did, however, like telling stories about him. For the most exuberant visitors, Lilly would even pull out her police photographs of the accident scene. "Some of these people ask about James Dean's last coke bottle," said Lilly, with a wry laugh.

"What coke bottle?"

"He's supposed to have stopped for a coke a few minutes before he died," she explained. "They think the bottle flew from the car, and wonder if anybody found it."

Around sunset, photographer Clyde Powell and I went to do a stand-up at the accident site. We tried a few takes, describing what happened there so many years before. As the sun dropped lower, I began to squint, and realized that, when James Dean came down that road in similar conditions, he probably squinted, too.

I changed a few words and choreographed a move with Clyde. From my starting point, I walked past him as he moved backward to a second position from which his camera "squinted" into the sun to see me. Then we reversed that move and finished where we started:

(STAND-UP)
Position 1: looking up road as I walk toward the sun

BY NOW THE STORY OF WHAT HAPPENED HERE HAS BECOME
PART OF THE LEGEND. JAMES DEAN CAME DOWN THIS HILL
DOING PERHAPS EIGHTY MILES AN HOUR IN HIS SMALL
PORSCHE CONVERTIBLE. HE PASSED ONE CAR.
THEN A SECOND CAR BLOCKED HIM IN.

Position 2: camera squints into sunset as I speak with sun behind me

AT THAT MOMENT, HE MIGHT HAVE BEEN BLINDED BY THE SUN
SETTING BEYOND THOSE COASTAL HILLS . . .

Position 3: Clyde and I reverse positions again

BY THE TIME HE COULD SEE AGAIN, IT WOULD HAVE BEEN
TOO LATE TO AVOID A THIRD CAR MAKING A LEFT TURN
IN THE INTERSECTION AHEAD.

Clyde and I didn't recognize it at the time, but that was a darn near perfect stand-up.

We described something we couldn't show—an automobile accident.

We gave the details of what happened.

We used movement.

Better still, we put viewers into James Dean's place by showing them what he saw in his last conscious seconds. Stand-ups don't get much better than that.

CHAPTER 12

Face Time: Going Live

Regular viewers don't know this, but some of the most entertaining television news never makes air. Oh, it's available, all right, but, unless you're one of the gang in transmission or have a special satellite receiver at home, you will miss the show.

It isn't a program. It hasn't an official name, channel, or time slot. It stars any reporter with access to a camera, a dish, and a satellite window. If you're curious about a reporter's true nature, observe him in the moments just before he takes his cue from an anchor. How does he handle the pressure? Is he in a good mood, or sniping at the crew? It's always worth a chuckle to watch some snarling grouse who, seconds before going live, miraculously changes his demeanor from black cloud to teevee perky.

For a time, I collected some of these performances. Our transmission people monitored satellite feeds and recorded reporters standing in adverse conditions—blizzards, hurricanes, and swamps populated by bloodthirsty mosquitoes. That's what we do, right? It's part of the unwritten job description. At the first hint of bad weather, management sends us into the elements with orders to stand there, absorbing nature's abuse like experimental test strips. "Thanks," the anchors inevitably say. "You're a trooper."

More than once, while doubling as a human rain gauge, I have been tempted to cut loose and tell viewers the truth. "Yes, this is how ridiculous you, too, could look if you chose television news reporting for a career."

Actually, I have said those words, but never on air, merely when waiting, and only to a satellite thousands of miles above, along with whomever might be watching below. More than once I have dared phantom viewers to guess my location. "Here's my telephone number. Go ahead and dial—it's on vibrate. Reach out and tickle me. If you name the place and story, we'll send you a plastic promotional Circle 7."

Some guy actually called from Connecticut. He only missed by three time zones and a sunset that, for us, hadn't happened, yet. I believe he had been drinking.

We sent him a plastic promotional Circle 7, anyway.

Frankly, unless a reporter has a deep-seated craving for face time, doing a live shot usually complicates an assignment. Live shots often shorten deadlines and frazzle reporters, who must race from the site of a story, back to the station for editing, and then return to the location. Or else they remain at the scene, spending the day in a small truck that gets hot in summer and cold in winter. In terms of square footage, Apollo astronauts had more room.

Live Shots Are Here to Stay

If you get the impression that live shots are not my favorite part of the job, you're correct. Reporters used to craft narrative stories with pictures and sound. Now they stand and talk, often over cherry picked wallpaper video. Stations and news networks settle for this because it gives them their best bang for a dollar. Live shots cost less and fill more time than a carefully honed package. Live crews often spend entire days in one spot, filing report after report, hour after hour. Instead of showing the news, they tell it. What fun is that?

Live shots appear in newscasts almost automatically, nowadays. Managers and producers insist that having a live reporter adds pacing and production values. Often, they are correct. Sometimes, they are wrong.

Inevitably, certain live shot assignments may not make any sense to you. It won't help to argue. For the sake of your career, just smile and do the job. Understand that sometimes, your producers have undisclosed reasons or pressures.

"Level with me," I once asked our noon producer. "Why do you need this live shot so badly?"

"I need you to go live because we're short of writers," she confessed. "Just stand there and tell us what you know. I don't have enough people to work the copy or edit video."

She was honest. I respect that.

The Positives

In fairness, however, a live shot can have a place and purpose. Used properly, it allows a reporter to do his job more effectively.

If news has just broken or continues developing, reporters can go live to provide viewers with new information. If an assignment is lean in terms of visuals or people, or if a reporter couldn't physically cover every aspect of a story, or if he arrived late, the live shot allows him to fill in the blanks. He can tell viewers what he knows, or with whom he just spoke, and give other pertinent details. When circumstances come together, nothing in our business beats a strong live shot.

My Best Live Shot Ever

Yosemite Rescue

The best live shot I have done, so far, happened by virtue of preparation and luck. In October, 2004, a surprise and particularly bitter early season storm moved into California's Yosemite National Park. Keith Lober, who runs the Yosemite Search and Rescue team, described the onslaught as being so strong that it sounded as if someone had turned a fire hose on his roof. When that freezing rain turned to snow, it might as well have been a January blizzard.

There were some thirty rock climbers on the vertical, sheer granite face of El Capitan, that night. For them, the ferocious storm led quickly to a battle of life or death thousands of feet above the Yosemite Valley floor.

Climbers from around the world make pilgrimages to El Capitan for its rigorous and technical challenges. It is more than a one-day ascent, requiring those hearty souls to spend nights in porta-ledge tents, dangling from taught lines with nothing but thin air separating them from certain doom far below.

As the storm hit, fifty-mile per hour winds battered those tents against El Capitan's unforgiving wall. Icy rain cascaded from the summit, beating down upon them as miniature waterfalls.

Two Japanese climbers died that night. Several others remained drenched, injured, starving, and stranded. The rescue effort was dramatic. When it attracted national attention, KGO sent me to Yosemite with photographer Paul Zarro.

If not for the spectacular scenery, our assignment had all the trappings of a typical stakeout. Curiosity seekers outnumbered rescuers, who retreated into daily briefings mode. Paul and I peered at the action far above. We struggled to snag interviews with any pertinent people, when we could get them to talk.

Shortly before my six o'clock live shot on the second day, a rescuer stopped by to fill some time. I pointed at one particular tent high up the cliff, and remarked that the men inside had another cold night ahead of them.

"There's not a lot we can do, right now," said the rescuer. "We could hover the helicopter and try to rappel supplies over, but that's risky in these winds and fog."

"Will your people try?"

"I doubt it. We've never tried it on El Capitan," he said. "You never know, though. Keep your eyes open."

That rescuer must have known more than told us. Just before my live shot, a helicopter appeared out of the fog and hovered next to that fragile, hanging tent. I ditched my original plans, adapted to the moment, and ad-libbed.

After anchor Pete Wilson tossed to me, I updated the situation while Paul, who knew his camera well, executed a perfectly smooth, double extended zoom from me on the ground to that helicopter and tent up the cliff. He never lost focus, and then reversed the move when our live shot ended.

Here is the verbatim, including the package:

Yosemite Rescue
October 17, 2004

(ANCHOR PETE WILSON)
. . . MORE ON AN EFFORT THAT HAS ALREADY SEEN THE DEATHS OF TWO CLIMBERS. WAYNE???

(WAYNE ON CAMERA)
AND PETE, RIGHT NOW IT IS VERY DRAMATIC. LET'S TAKE A QUICK SHOT, RIGHT UP THE MOUNTAIN. YOU'RE
LOOKING AT ABOUT 25-HUNDRED FEET ABOVE THE VALLEY FLOOR. THAT IS A RANGER SERVICE HELICOPTER. THEY ARE DROPPING SUPPLIES TO TWO MEN WHO ARE STILL IN A TENT ON THE SIDE OF THE CLIFF TONIGHT. THESE ARE TWO MEN WHO WILL COME OUT TOMORROW. THIS IS A TECHNIQUE RARELY TRIED. THEY HAVE NEVER ATTEMPTED IT BEFORE. INSIDE THAT WHITE POUCH ARE A SLEEPING BAG, CLOTHING, AND SUPPLIES

TO HELP THEM GET THROUGH THE NIGHT. JUST FOR THE RECORD, THE TALLY, NOW, IS FIVE PEOPLE DOWN OFF THE MOUNTAIN. THREE OF THEM ARE SAFE. TWO OF THEM ARE DEAD. AND TWO MORE, THESE TWO, STILL ON THE FACE OF EL CAPITAN.

Insert Package

Video shows rescuers pulling bodies from a helicopter

UNTIL THE BODIES OF TWO JAPANESE CLIMBERS CAME DOWN THIS AFTERNOON, THE REALITY SEEMED SO DISTANT. THIS MAN AND WOMAN DIED JUST TWO-HUNDRED AND FIFTY FEET FROM THE SUMMIT.

(SOT)
Keith Lober, Rescuer: "They may not have been aware that the route was entirely one they could retreat from."

Shots of El Capitan and rescue efforts

THE CRISIS ON EL CAPITAN BEGAN WITH A SUDDEN AND BRUTAL STORM EARLIER THIS WEEK. COLD WINDS AND RAIN BATTERED SEVEN PEOPLE. DAVE TURNER WAS THE FIRST TO BE RESCUED YESTERDAY. HE SAYS HE LEARNED A LESSON.

(SOT)
Dave Turner, Rescued Climber: "Maybe I won't do much different but, ugh, at least I'll be more aware that it can hit the fan."

Video shows a wide shot of El Capitan, and people peering through binoculars. We see more shots of rescuers
FROM BELOW, TODAY, IT WAS A LOT LIKE WATCHING ANTS. SPECTATORS PEERED THROUGH BINOCULARS AT THIS ON AGAIN, OFF AGAIN, THEN ON AGAIN EFFORT TO REACH OTHER DISTRESSED CLIMBERS. VOLUNTEERS RAPELLED DOWN, AND HELPED THEM UP.

(SOT)
Chopper lands with more rescued climbers
Rescued climbers turn away from cameras

THESE TWO RESCUED CLIMBERS SAID NOTHING
WHEN THEY FINALLY REACHED THE VALLEY FLOOR
AFTER A SIX HOUR RESCUE EFFORT.
THEIR SAVIORS NEVER EXPECTED SUCH A DIFFICULT TASK.

(SOT)
Rescuer: "Our guys have been getting lowered into icy cold
water, and sleeping out there for more days than they thought,
so, it has been tough duty up there."

*Shot of tents hanging of cliff as seen from a helicopter earlier
that day*

BUT, AMONG RESCUE CREWS, EL CAPITAN REPRESENTS A
MECCA. THERE ARE FEW TOUGHER PLACES. IF IT TAKES GREAT
SKILL TO CLIMB THIS PLACE, IMAGINE WHAT IT TAKES TO SAVE
MEN FROM IT.

WAYNE LIVE over a telephoto view of the cliff. Shot pulls back slowly

. . . AND YOU'RE GETTING A GOOD LOOK AT THAT, RIGHT NOW.
MEN IN A HELICOPTER IN THE FOG ALONG THE CLIFF.
THEY HAVE JUST TRANSFERRED THE BAG WITH SUPPLIES
TO THE MEN IN THAT TENT. IT LOOKS AS IF IT HAS BEEN
SUCCESSFUL BECAUSE THE HELICOPTER IS FLYING OFF.

SO THE GUYS IN THAT TENT WILL HAVE A MORE
COMFORTABLE NIGHT, TONIGHT,
THAN THEY DID LAST NIGHT,
OR THE NIGHT BEFORE.
THEY HAVE BEEN WET.
THEY HAVE BEEN COLD.

IT WAS A VERY BRUTAL STORM.

SO, THAT IS THE LATEST FROM EL CAPITAN. FIVE DOWN. TWO
MORE UP THERE, BUT RESCUE CREWS EXPECT TO GET THEM
TOMORROW.

After Yosemite, the station began looking to me as a front line guy for major breaking news stories. Inevitably, those assignments demand considerable live time. Hopefully, you will get to do some of that kind of work, too. Here are some guidelines to help you in any kind of live situation.

Live Shot Guidelines

Speak Naturally

Don't worry if you get nervous before going live. It's natural. Go easy on yourself. Relax. In live shots, you're just talking, the same as anywhere else. The words and sentence structure in my Yosemite live shot were less than perfect, but forgivable because they made sense and conveyed the moment.

Reporters get into live shot trouble when they try to speak as precisely as they write. Never try to memorize a live shot. Know your material. Talk it as you would to a friend, a producer, or the assignment desk. If that sounds difficult, look at it this way: Do you stumble in ordinary conversation? Do you stumble while walking down a street? Speak normally. Keep it simple.

Use Key Words for Notes, Not Sentences

You might have an easier time learning to talk a live shot if you limit your notes to a few key words. Follow them, the same as you would steps along a path.

I remember doing a live shot after a fatal collision between two fire-fighting planes. We stood outside the air base. On my notepad, I wrote "flowers" for my first key word, referencing the gate in front of the base:

FLOWERS AND NOTES PINNED TO THE GATE
TELL A STORY OF SADNESS AND LOSS.

For the second word I wrote "privacy," because the other pilots asked us to keep a respectful distance:

THIS IS A CLOSE GROUP OF PEOPLE.
THEY WORK TOGETHER AND PLAY TOGETHER.
TONIGHT, THEY'RE ASKING FOR PRIVACY
AS THEY GRIEVE TOGETHER .

I ad-libbed those words. For most live shots, I write only the roll cue in full, using big letters, which makes them easier to see:

FIGHTING FIRES WITH AIRPLANES HAS ALWAYS BEEN RISKY.
CREWS KNOW IT.
THEY ACCEPT IT.
TONIGHT THEY'RE DEALING WITH IT.

If you ever get lost or tongue-tied while doing a live shot, refer to your notes and use that one complete line to bail into a package or sound bite.

Beware of Typical Live Clichés and Crutches

AS YOU CAN SEE BEHIND ME…
EVEN AS WE SPEAK…
LET'S TAKE A LIVE LOOK…
WE WANT TO TELL YOU…
OF COURSE …
WE CAN REPORT…

Live reporters love spouting such phrases. They're a waste of breath.

One of the worst is the word *Now*. Watch certain reporters, and count the number of sentences beginning with, "Now . . ." The word is an affectation of immediacy, usually where none exists.

Reference Your Location

Even if you're standing in the dark for one of those notorious black-hole live shots with nothing visible in the background, give viewers a sense of what happened there. Set a scene. Paint a picture with words:

THE MEETING ENDED OFFICIALLY AT NINE O'CLOCK,

BUT, LONG AFTER THE DOORS CLOSED AND THE LIGHTS
WENT OUT, PEOPLE KEPT TALKING IN THIS PARKING LOT.

Go Mobile

When doing live shots in more visual locations, consider asking the photographer to hand-hold the camera. Use it to take the viewer somewhere. Reporters have done excellent live shots in which they stood outside a door, opened it a crack, and let the camera peek inside. That's good stuff. It's voyeuristic and looks live. The lens becomes a window and the reporter, a guide.

Change the Background For Your Introduction and Tag

When possible and appropriate, change the background between your introduction to a package and its tag. This is similar to the method we use when interviewing people. While the story runs, turn 180 degrees or move somewhere else. Give viewers a different look.

Photographer Doug Laughlin and I used the technique when a B-24 bomber flew into town for an air show. We shot and cut our story, then wrapped a live shot around it. For the introduction, we stood outside the plane. While the story played, we hurried to a second location inside the cockpit, where Doug had rigged a small camera. When the package segment ended with historical footage of a similar plane in a death spiral, we came back live and continued the narrative by showing viewers what would have been a crew's escape route from the cockpit to the hatch, two decks below. It wasn't so much a live shot tag as a journey, and maybe an experience.

Hide Your Earpiece

When doing live shots, every reporter uses an earpiece through which he hears the anchors, the producer, the director, and cues. We call it an *Interruptible Feedback Device*, or *IFB*.

The best of these are custom-molded to your ear and become almost invisible. Even so, wear the IFB on the side facing away from the camera. This will be one of those finesse touches that makes a good impression on résumé reels.

Match Your Voice

Early in their careers, reporters tend to read narrative tracks in a different tone of voice, or at a different energy level, than when they speak live. News directors regard this as a sign of inexperience. Seasoned reporters learn to sound the same, whether speaking or reading.

Here are three ways to sound more consistent:

1. Use the same microphone in your live shot as you did for your track. No two microphones sound exactly alike.
2. As you read your track, talk it. Look at the script, and imagine you're saying it to a friend. Actually, this applies to any track, anytime.
3. Use a short section of natural sound at the top of the story before that track begins. It does not need to be a sound bite. With as little as a two-second break, you can mask any vocal or technical inconsistencies.

Add a Production Element

Even if you're doing only a quick live hit with a voice-over into a sound bite, add a production element.

When a sewer line exploded in downtown San Francisco, the blast tossed two heavy manhole covers twenty feet into the air, shattering windows. Our producer asked for a live shot with a voice-over, followed by one or two sound bites. That's where I added the wrinkle. Rather than the conventional method of placing both sound bites at the end of a live voice-over, I used one of them, a witness who had seen the explosions, at the beginning.

Live on camera, I gave the director a roll cue and let that first sound bite run. On the back of it, we butted trailing video for a live voice-over. This enabled me to begin reading from the end of the sound bite, without waiting for a cue and risking an awkward delay. As that voice-over ended, the director listened for a second roll cue to yet another sound bite followed by even more trailing video. While it played, I took a few steps to my left to change the background, and then tagged the segment live on camera.

Sound complicated? It wasn't—just fast and efficient. From two separate cuts we gave the live shot four video components: a sound bite, a voice-over, another sound bite, and one more voice-over. When you count the live ledes and tags with slightly different backgrounds, we produced a 1:15 segment with six different looks.

Structure the Package: Every Story Should Stand On Its Own

Strive to make your live shot insert stand alone as a complete package. Give it a beginning, a middle, and an ending. Without such structure, we regress to the standards of forty or fifty years ago, when reporters produced packages with stand-up opens and closes. Sometimes, adding structure to a story requires only two extra lines, one for the beginning and another to conclude.

This notion of cut packages standing alone should apply to all of your work, not only live shots. Every story needs to make sense and be complete, independent of an anchor or reporter introduction. Your script should identify important people by name and role so that if the character generator fails or your director misses a cue, your viewers will know who they are. *When viewers don't have questions, they won't have distractions.*

These are small touches. They add up when you're building a professional reputation. A complete story that stands on its own is more likely to appear in subsequent broadcasts. If a network or feed picks it up, the extra effort may also put cash in your pocket.

Keep a Copy of the Package Script in Your Hand

We're always learning in this business, even after two or three decades. CBS News correspondent John Blackstone can attest to that. He was covering a major trial in San Francisco, and went live to introduce a package after a late-in-the-day verdict. As Blackstone set up on the bureau roof, he heard the producer in New York tell him, "Stand by, John. We have a problem with your feed."

Six or seven minutes passed. John waited, and finally heard the introduction from Dan Rather. Simultaneously, that same producer broke in on his IFB: "John, we never did get a clean version of the package. Just talk to Dan. You have a minute and a half."

Poor Blackstone. "That's not what I expected," he said. "I'd prepared two sentences as a lead-in." Now he would have to more or less recite the script, except that he hadn't brought the copy with him.

Despite his quickened heartbeat and elevated blood pressure, Blackstone did a flawless talk-back, "It certainly would have been easier if I'd had that script in my hand for reference," he said.

John has kept a script with him for every live shot since.

Speak with Your Anchor in Advance

Live shots should transition smoothly from the studio, to the field, and back again. Whenever possible, plan these segues in advance. Help your anchors by suggesting what they might say in their introductions to you. Recommend questions they might ask when you finish. By being smart, you'll look smart.

When you're live, it is not a good time for surprises.

Protect Yourself—Don't Tell the Anchors Everything

While it's good for a reporter and anchor to know what the other is doing, Don Knapp, who spent twelve years as a correspondent for CNN, warns about giving anchors too much advance information. "The network would fly me to a fire or whatever, get me on the ground next to the truck, and expect me to go live immediately. That was always their first priority."

As a good soldier, Don would call his producers in Atlanta and tell what he knew, even if it wasn't much. "I might say there was a fire, that people had been hurt, that we didn't know the extent of the damage yet, and that we were waiting for authorities to update the situation."

Inevitably, when leading into Knapp's live shot, the anchor would repeat all of those facts, leaving Don with nothing to add. "Protect yourself," says Knapp. "Save a detail or two—something you can work with."

Never Directly Correct Your Anchor

In my first week at KRON-TV in San Francisco, an electrical transmission box blew up downtown, spreading carcinogenic PCBs across two city blocks. Authorities closed the area for several days.

When tossing to my live shot one night, the anchor referred repeatedly to "PCPs," which had nothing to do with smoking electrical boxes, and everything to do with smoking marijuana. I made the mistake of correcting her while on the air, and smugly, at that. A more seasoned reporter would have handled her mistake indirectly, by mentioning the letters PCB as often as possible.

Later, back at the station, that anchor lay in wait with claws extended. I took maybe two steps through the door before she loudly and publicly ripped into me. "Don't you ever *dare* correct me on the air again, young man." She actually waved a flawlessly manicured red fingernail in front of my nose.

Beware the wrath of an embarrassed anchor. It leads to an even more embarrassed reporter.

A bit later, our broadcast's producer, Peter Spear, took me aside to break the tension with some hilarious and sage advice. "Welcome to big-market television, kid. Remember this lesson. Anchors ain't normal people. They like to believe they're normal people. They try to act like normal people, but they have this red-light fever affliction. After they stare at tally lights long enough, their brains scramble and they begin to believe they're special. So, here's the key to survival. Whatever you do and wherever you go in the rest of your career, never let on to an anchorperson that you know this secret. Indulge them. Make them feel wonderful, gifted, brilliant, and, most important, normal. But remember— normal, they ain't."

To be fair, I have worked with many anchors who do not fit Peter's generalization. If you are an anchor and reading this, it will be natural for you to assume that you are one of them.

Personal Horror Story

Like every other skill in this business, learning to go live takes diligence, hard work, and practice. Any honest reporter can tell his own personal live shot horror story, and maybe two or three. Hence the adage that it's always good to make your biggest mistakes early, in markets you can leave.

My worst live shot was also my first. It happened at WLKY-TV in Louisville, Kentucky, where news director Brian Norcross, who later became a revered weather forecaster in Miami, gave me my first job. Although Brian had hired me as a photographer, he promised occasional reporting opportunities.

It took two weeks for me to get my first big "break." A freight train derailed in western Louisville. Actually, "derail" might be too strong a word. One wheel of one empty car of a four-car train slipped off the track. Norcross didn't have anyone else available, so he sent me. When I arrived at the scene with the photographer, an old hand named Willie, we found a few railroad police and a gang of teenagers hanging around.

The newscast would sign off in a few minutes. Our producer wanted a live report. Willie established a signal in close to record time. Actually, he lit it up too fast. Willie put a microphone in my hand, crammed an IFB into my head and, before I knew anything pertinent, the control room told us to stand by. *The first rule of live shots is be prepared when you go on the air.* I was about to learn it.

I was already stressed. The giggling teenagers made it worse, so I tried reasoning with them. "We're going to be live in a minute, so please wait behind the camera and don't wave or anything, okay?" Like little angels, they smiled. But these kids weren't angels. Worse, I had inadvertently given them instructions for causing mischief. As soon as anchor Ken Rowland pitched to our live shot, they leaped in front of the camera, waving and howling and jumping. In an effort to get the kids off camera, Willie panned left. The kids followed.

He zoomed in tight. They clustered around me. Willie jerked right, then up, then down, trying to fake them out. Nothing worked.

In an out of control, hopeless situation that could have been my first opportunity to shine, I panicked. With the kids screaming, waving, and the camera moving, who could think? Mr. Rowland, a Louisville news institution, chose that moment to ask a pertinent question. "Wayne, you didn't tell us, but where, exactly, is that derailment?"

I should have said, "You're watching it, Ken." After rushing to the scene, and having lived in town barely two weeks, I honestly did not know.

Those are the gory details of how my first live shot inadvertently became my first humorous show-closer.

If only it had been funny at the time.

CHAPTER 13

We Interrupt This Serious Book . . .

Newsrooms can be funny places. Humor happens spontaneously when smart, quick-witted, often cynical people work together in close quarters, under pressure. In newsrooms, few topics or events remain off limits or sacred, assuming we keep the levity within reasonably good taste.

It's part of the newsroom mentality. While we live personal lives in the real world, reporters have an "observer gene" that kicks in once we cross an invisible, professional line. The job gives us front row seats to glee, tragedy, strangeness, mayhem, magnificence, and the mundane. Like emergency first responders, we journalists can step back emotionally, enabling us to keep clear, objective heads when doing our jobs.

Here, then, is one of the most retrospectively funny and twisted episodes I ever saw in a newsroom. It happened in 1975, not long after KABC-TV in Los Angeles took delivery of its first microwave truck. In the long term, this incident served a purpose by helping to hasten the use of supplemental cover video, or "b-roll," during live shots.

The industry still viewed live shots as a novelty in 1975. Reporters would stand at a scene, describing something or interviewing someone while, at the bottom of the screen, the station inserted large letters: "Live." Theoretically, this made a report more exciting. Soon, however, viewers and news managers realized that live talking heads in the field weren't any more fascinating than live talking heads behind a desk.

As a remedy, KABC-TV news director Bill Fyffe wrote a memo suggesting that photographers should pan a scene to give viewers a look around during extended reports or interviews.

Fyffe was a formidable boss—a newsman's newsman. He had a deep, fearsome, booming voice like a drill sergeant. When he issued orders, staff members practically jumped to carry them out. Bill Fyffe rarely closed his office door. Instead, he hung a traffic signal just outside. When green, a person could enter without risk. If yellow, best to make the visit quick. Red meant bad news.

As fair warning, Fyffe also hung a plaque on his office wall. It bore these words, a twist on the Twenty-third Psalm, "Yea, though I walk through the Valley of the Shadow of Death I shall fear no evil because I am the meanest son of a bitch in the valley."

Actually, there was someone meaner—a serial killer known only by reputation as the Trash Bag Murderer. In that summer of 1975, he had begun shooting and dismembering transient men, stuffing their severed body parts into plastic garbage bags, and leaving them along streets and highways between Los Angeles and the Mexican Border.

Late one sweltering afternoon, the Trash Bag Murderer struck again. Our assignment desk sent reporter Steve Lentz to the scene, along with a photographer who, in deference to his good name, shall remain unidentified. We'll call him Wally.

The crew arrived and fired a live signal. The newscast took them immediately. Lentz stood about twenty yards in front of the gruesome bag, questioning a Los Angeles police detective. Their interview went something like this:

> LENTZ: "How long has the body been here?"
> DETECTIVE: "The, uh, subject was discovered this afternoon at approximately 1637 hours . . ."

> LENTZ: "Do you have any idea who the victim might be?"
> DETECTIVE: "The, uh, deceased is not carrying any obvious identification."

> LENTZ: "Any motive behind these killings?"
> DETECTIVE: "Well, uh, no. But a motive might lead us to the perpetrator . . ."

Live or not, this interview could have a murderous effect on the ratings. "There, uh, have been several incidents of this nature in recent weeks," the boring detective elaborated.

About then, Wally remembered Bill Fyffe's memo and began one of those slow pans. In a corner or his picture, viewers could see a plastic garbage bag on the sidewalk beneath a highway overpass. The detective kept rambling. "The, uh, heinous nature of the crime suggests . . ."

After finishing the pan, Wally followed his photographic instincts. He hit the zoom button. At home, viewers saw their televisions fill with his image of the lumpy bag. It bulged from the middle and slumped over the edge of the curb. That bag was in shade, and Wally assumed too dark for clear viewing. Not so.

Back in the newsroom, Bill Fyffe stormed from his office. "Wally! Dammit! Wally! Get off the bag!" he bellowed, as if Wally could hear.

Wally couldn't, however. In those early days of live shots, crews had minimal direct communication with anchors, producers, or directors, and much less with management. At best, Wally had a two-way radio for speaking with the assignment desk. He and reporters took their cues from a pager tuned to the station's frequency.

Whatever their technical limitations, it was too late. Through the bag's opaque plastic, viewers clearly saw the outlines of a hand and other body parts.

Not so appropriately, a graphic at the bottom of the screen read, "Live."

"Dammit! Get off of it!" Back in the newsroom, Fyffe's face turned almost as red as the bag.

As if Wally heard Fyffe by psychic energy alone, he kind-of complied by panning, again, inadvertently revealing a trail of congealing blood that led from the sidewalk, to the gutter, and eventually into a storm drain.

Fyffe was spewing by then. The self-proclaimed 'meanest son of a bitch in the valley' had gone on a rampage, and my desk sat directly outside of his office. For the sake of self-preservation, I retreated to the microwave transmission room where, with the live shot mercifully ended, technicians rolled tape of Lentz asking a few more questions for the late news.

Even then, the detective never changed his dreary tone. Lentz, who has always been a joker, had endured enough. Steve knew nothing of his live shot's visual details or all the problems they caused, so he decided to tweak the detective and give the crew in transmission a little entertainment, as if they needed it. "Tell me, Detective," asked Lentz in his same somber tone, "Do you think this was, uh, suicide?"

"No," the detective replied seriously, "we have, uh, ruled out that possibility pending further investigation."

CHAPTER 14

Keep It Simple:
The Suitcase Theory of Story Packaging

Try to remember the last time you packed for a trip. Did you cram too many clothes into your suitcase? Did they come out wrinkled? And, when you opened the bag to grab an item, could you find it?

Now compare that suitcase to a television news package. We overstuff those, as well. *If a reporter puts too many twists, turns, or facts into a story, he risks obscuring its message.*

Here's a disconcerting truth—if an average viewer takes away the five facts of who, what, when, where, and why from a television news segment, he has beaten the average. Viewers like their news to be uncomplicated and digestible. This doesn't mean dumbed-down or lazy. It does mean clear and straightforward. Make it easy for your viewers to find what they want or need from a story.

How Viewers Watch the News

In your mind, you may see yourself as a television news version of Cecil B. DeMille, but don't expect John and Mary Viewer to buy into it. They will never give your work the same professional attention to detail that you do. A television news story is not a major motion picture. Most homes have no curtain, no giant screen, nor an earth shattering sound system. Television news audiences rarely dim the lights to watch your segment. Some of your viewers may not even be sitting down.

In many homes, the news blares from a set on the kitchen counter and competes with life's distractions. Your typical viewer listens more than watches, and comments more than he listens. As your piece runs, he's making dinner, talking on the phone, doing the kid's homework, finishing a crossword puzzle, or surfing the internet. Occasionally, if a story spikes his interest, he might glance up. By then, your masterpiece will be halfway over.

Are five facts beginning to sound like a pretty good goal? Most days, I will settle for three.

Report for Your Audience, Not Your Bosses

The Water Main Break

Not long ago, a reporter sent me samples of his work from a small market. He was twenty-three, still finding his way in his first job, and struggling. "I feel overwhelmed," he wrote. Translated, that means he had a problem focusing.

The reporter's clips included a late-news segment about a water main that cracked during a blizzard. Barring complications, a public works crew would replace the damage before the next morning's rush hour. They did have one concern—that the leaking water might freeze into a sheet of ice and block a major intersection.

In a small city on a slow night, that water main break made big news. The broadcast producer asked our young reporter for a live shot with a package insert. After watching the segment, it was clear that he tried hard with his assignment. If possible, he tried *too* hard.

The reporter began with a montage of running water accompanied by a symphony of jackhammers. In painstaking detail, he explained how workmen poked holes in the cement and used a special listening device to locate leaks. He filled the piece with so many facts, figures, and obscurities that after a while, it began to look less like a news story, and more like an instructional video about street repair. If a viewer had watched closely, he might have been able to pass a civil service test.

All of the reporter's problems trace back to one fundamental error. He never put himself in the place of the people at home. He forgot that most of them didn't care about the specifics of urban street repair. They simply wanted to know when Public Works would fix the break, and if they would need to find alternate routes for the morning commute. The reporter could have given them that basic information in the first fifteen seconds of his live shot.

Then, if he had thought past the assignment sheet, he might have told a narrative story to which anyone might relate—that on a frigid night this crew faced a mean, nasty job. Between their numb fingers, the freezing mud, and the struggle to keep flowing water from turning into sheets of ice, he had dramatic ingredients for a piece with universal appeal.

"Why didn't I think of that?" the kid asked later. Simple. We chalked it up to nerves and inexperience. He should have taken a figurative step back and trusted his natural curiosity. At that stage of his career, however, this young reporter didn't have the confidence. *He worried so much about missing an element that he overcompensated. Rather than errors of omission, he committed errors of congestion, and crammed too many facts into a ninety-second package.*

Put simply, he allowed his fear to confine him.

This is a common mistake. Learn to recognize it, and you will be well on your way to fixing it. When you find yourself in a similar circumstance, whether reporting on politics, economics, science, the law, a union dispute, or some local problem like a broken water line, identify a single theme, storyline, or character, and stay true to it. Get to the point. Write for your viewers, not your bosses. Just because the alphabet begins with "A" and finishes with "Z," do not feel obligated to detail all twenty-four letters in between.

The next time an assignment overwhelms your focus, that simple rule will help.

CHAPTER 15

Report What You Find: What IS Will Always Be More Interesting Than What You Make Up

How many times have you gone to cover a flood or imminent disaster, expected to find fearful citizens, and discovered them to be nonchalant, instead? Did you still try to do a story about fear, or did you adjust your approach? Reporters face this dilemma every day in all kinds of assignments. Due to time constraints or pressures from management, they ignore their own good instincts, and tailor stories to fit preconceived notions.

Have you heard of Guerneville, California? It's a free-spirited resort on the Russian River. Life might be perfect for residents if not for the rainy season. When winter storms blow in, low-lying Guerneville inevitably becomes the first place in California to receive a flood warning, although a media warning would be more appropriate. At any sign of danger, television crews and satellite trucks pour in, all looking for high water of Biblical proportions.

It rarely materializes. Guerneville's founding mothers and fathers built their town with floods in mind. When the river rises, most of the supposed damage remains cosmetic, even if it does make good pictures. But, because journalists don't usually report their own overreactions, Guerneville's flood warnings still lead the news. Worse, some reporters go out of their way to find or conjure flood threats, even when they don't exist. I once overheard an interview similar to this:

REPORTER: "How worried are you about the high water?"
RESIDENT: "We're not worried at all. This town is built for high water. It only looks bad. At this level, I'm not worried about the river."

REPORTER: "What do you mean when you say it only looks bad?"
RESIDENT: "Oh, the water comes up over the banks and goes under the houses, but we've built them up, now, after the last flood."

REPORTER: "So what would you define as a bad flood?"
RESIDENT: "Back in 1995, that was bad. That was what they called a hundred-year flood. I had mud in my living room after that one. The place took half the summer drying out."

REPORTER: "Do you worry about that happening again?"
RESIDENT: "Oh sure, I always worry. Who wouldn't? Live it once, you'd worry, too."

REPORTER: "And if it floods this year?"
RESIDENT: "I don't even want to think about it. Bad news. Nobody wants that kind of mud again."

Predictably, the reporter used only the "bad news" part of his interview on the air. Later, he was dense enough to wonder why Guerneville residents treat the press so cynically.

It never occurred to him that, if he'd looked around and listened, he would have found a better angle in Guerneville's blasé attitude toward high water. Such a story would have made the residents look hearty and brave. It would also have been the truth. And that's our job—telling the truth.

Vandalized News Coverage

In 1995, our assignment editor spotted a newspaper item describing how vandals broke into an eighth-grade computer lab in Middletown, a small community two hours north of San Francisco. The break-in angered students so much that Martha Webster, editor of the *Middletown Times-Star,* invited them to write open letters to the vandal, promising to publish those sentiments on the front page.

When she saw their grammar and spelling, however, Ms. Webster recognized a bigger story. *"You probly don't have the lightes ide how much truble you caused,"* wrote one pupil.

"Dear Stpied delttect dume lame low lef. I don't think nobody can every forgive you," penned another.

The letters left Martha Webster dumbstruck. Many kids couldn't even spell the word "vandal." "It was galling," she said on camera—so galling that when she published those letters she did not make a single correction. Parents, teachers, students, and ordinary citizens expressed outrage and embarrassment.

It appeared to be a good story, so the desk ordered me to rendezvous with photographer Randy Davis in Middletown. We found a different set of facts once we arrived. The break-in and subsequent letters had taken place two years earlier. Not two days, two weeks, or two months. *Two years!* I called the station and suggested we might want to reconsider our coverage. "Do a piece, anyway," ordered our executive producer. "We still like the spelling angle."

"This is a stretch," I told him.

"You stretch real well," he said.

The people of Middletown didn't see it that way. "This is sensationalism," a parent lectured.

"Why don't you find a real story somewhere else?" suggested another.

"It's old news," the school's principal told us. Randy and I agreed with her. Orders are orders, however. We still had to go through the motions of following up a two-year-old story we'd never covered.

Randy and I examined the possibilities. Could we do the piece without mentioning the two-year gap? No. That wouldn't be ethical.

We began by visiting the newspaper and interviewing Ms. Webster. Then we waited for school to let out and found some of those eighth graders, who had since become tenth graders. We asked them to spell "vandal." Surprise, surprise— even after the hullabaloo of two years earlier, many of those kids still got the word wrong. It was a start, so what else could we do to justify the story?

Exposing the Absent Villain

We found our angle by asking, "Why?"

Middletown did not make the news by accident, although if our assignment manager had read just a little more of the newspaper article, he would have caught the story's relevant context. A few days earlier, California State Assemblyman

Steve Baldwin had given a speech to make a case for stricter spelling standards in public schools. In so doing, he held up Middletown's woes as his example.

Fair enough. Politicians are experts at manipulating facts to make arguments. Baldwin, however, represented a district in Southern California, three hundred miles away. We called his office. "Has Mr. Baldwin ever visited Middletown?"

"No," said a staff member.

"Has he spoken with any residents?"

"He is familiar with the case."

Ultimately, this story wouldn't peg on a vandal, illiteracy, or a newspaper scandal, but on politics. Baldwin's speech gave us a better, more topical hook. Until we told them, Middletown residents never knew that a distant politician had shaken their old, dirty laundry in front of the rest of the state. When we presented the facts in those terms, they were more than happy to talk:

Middletown Spelling
Summer 1997

Pictures of various signs in town

HERE IS A SIGN OF PROGRESS IN MIDDLETOWN. THEY SPELLED "EXCELLENCE" RIGHT. AND "ACADEMICS."
ALONG WITH "STOP" . . .
"LIQUOR" . . .
"DELI" . . .
AND "SALOON."
IF THAT SOUNDS A LITTLE HARSH . . .

(SOT)
Wayne to a high-school boy: "SPELL 'VANDAL' FOR ME."

Boy: "I couldn't spell 'vandal' for you."

Wayne: "OH COME ON. SPELL 'VANDAL.'"

Boy: "No."

WE ASKED THAT QUESTION BECAUSE, TWO AND A HALF
YEARS AGO, A V-A-N-D-A-L BROKE INTO THE MIDDLE SCHOOL
AND WRECKED COMPUTERS. AT THE TIME,
ANGRY STUDENTS WROTE THE LOCAL NEWSPAPER,
WHICH PUBLISHED THOSE LETTERS. BUT LOOK CLOSELY
AT THE SPELLING. MANAGING EDITOR MARTHA WEBSTER
DECIDED TO PRINT THEM AS WRITTEN.

(SOT)
Martha Webster: "It said there might be a problem in the lower
grades when eighth graders are having this much difficulty with
simple words."

DURING THE NEXT THREE WEEKS, SPELLING BECAME THE
BIGGEST NEWS IN TOWN, EVEN AMONG THE KIDS WHO WROTE
THOSE LETTERS.

(SOT)
Female student: "I read them and at first thought they were a
joke. They were really bad."

(STAND-UP)
Wayne on Camera:
DIG A LITTLE DEEPER, THOUGH, AND YOU'LL DISCOVER THIS
STORY ISN'T SO MUCH ABOUT MIDDLETOWN AS IT IS ABOUT
HOW CALIFORNIA TEACHES ENGLISH TO ITS STUDENTS.
SPECIFICALLY, SHOULD THE STATE EMPHASIZE CREATIVITY
INSTEAD OF GRAMMAR? OR GRAMMAR INSTEAD OF CREATIVITY?
IN SHORT, ONE WORD, SPELLED . . .

P-O-L-I-T-I-C-S.

Narration continues over file video of assemblyman

. . . AS DEFINED BY ASSEMBLYMAN STEVE BALDWIN OF
RIVERSIDE, WHO REOPENED THE OLD WOUNDS BY USING

MIDDLETOWN'S LETTERS AS AMMUNITION IN HIS FIGHT TO
BRING BACK SPELLING TESTING TO STATE SCHOOLS.
HIS CAMPAIGN HAS NOT BEEN PLAYING WELL HERE.

(SOT)
Mother in a car: "I think he needs to go and dig up some new
news somewhere else."

(SOT)
Wayne asks another high-school boy:
"HOW DO YOU SPELL 'VANDAL'?"

He answers: "V-A-N-D-E-L?"

(SOT)
A second mother: "It's sensationalism, that's what's happening."

(SOT)
Wayne continues with the kids, trying to get a spelling of
"vandal": "DOES IT HAVE AN 'AL' OR AN 'EL'?"

Boy answers: " 'E.' No. 'A'?"

HOWEVER, IF YOU SPEAK WITH THE PRINCIPAL AT THE HIGH
SCHOOL THOSE KIDS NOW ATTEND, A BETTER QUESTION
WOULD BE HOW TO SPELL "CHEAP SHOT."

(SOT)
Principal: "The state assemblyman has never been here, never
talked to me, never bothered to call . . ."

IF MR. BALDWIN HAD CALLED, HE MIGHT HAVE LEARNED
HOW EVEN THE NEWSWOMAN WHO BLEW THE WHISTLE SAYS
ENGLISH LANGUAGE SKILLS, HERE, HAVE IMPROVED. JUST LAST
WEEK SHE RAN A STORY ABOUT A MIDDLETOWN GIRL WHO
SCORED IN THE TOP TWENTY IN THE STATE SPELLING BEE . . .

(SOT)
Wayne to Martha Webster: "IS THERE A PROBLEM HERE, NOW?"

Martha Webster: "I don't believe there is."

FAIR ENOUGH, BUT IF THAT'S THE CASE, LET'S PUT IT TO ONE, FINAL TEST. . .

(SOT)
Wayne asks a female student: "HOW DO YOU SPELL 'VANDAL'?"

She answers: "V-A-N-D-A-L?"

A second does the same: "V-A-N-D-A-L.

Postscript

If television news were a perfect business, we wouldn't have had to struggle so hard to make that story. Ultimately, I think we did right by Middletown. When the day began, its residents didn't like us. When it ended, they thanked us for giving them an opportunity to defend their reputation.

We made the best of a bad assignment by telling the truth, and reporting what we found. *What is will always be more interesting than what you make up.* Believe it. Work with it. When in doubt, that principle will lead you to credible stories, and keep you out of trouble.

CHAPTER 16
General Ethics:
Science Reporting, Arsenic, and Life In Space

On December 2, 2010, Dr. Felisa Wolfe-Simon, a geomicrobiologist working with NASA and the United States Geological Survey, held a press briefing after publishing a paper that challenged a basic tenant of science. She and a team of researchers had isolated the GHAJ-1 strain of Halomonadacae in California's Mono Lake, and extracted purified DNA from +As/-P cells. As Wolfe-Simon, wrote, in part, "Our NanoSIMS analyses, combined with the evidence for intracellular arsenic by ICP-MS and our radiolabeled $_{73}AsO_{43-}$ experiments demonstrated that intracellular AsO_{43-} was incorporated into key biomolecules, specifically DNA."

Lost, yet?

If I told you that stories do not get much better than this, you might roll your eyes and say to yourself, "It's not as if she discovered alien life on Earth."

Actually, she thinks that maybe she did.

Welcome to the challenging realm of science reporting, also known as science translating. In this field, reporters must respect research conducted by extremely smart people, and make it understandable for general audiences. Few reporters grasp all of the terminology, nuance, or math in a science story. That's okay. Just try to understand and explain the material well enough to make it relevant.

I like science reporting because the people in those stories appreciate the attention. They aren't crime victims, criminals, or media-trained politicians.

In an era when feature reporting has almost died, science stories present fun alternatives.

Dr. Wolfe-Simon's announcement caught most of the world by surprise, but not me. I had worked with her, known it was coming, and struggled because of that knowledge. Those difficulties had little to do with simplifying complex facts, and everything with maintaining professional standards while dealing with a source. Report long enough, and you, too, may encounter a similar dilemma, if not in science, then with some other kind of material.

A Tip and an Embargo

I initially found Dr. Wolfe-Simon while researching extreme forms of life on Earth. Her name appeared in one line of a *New York Times* article. She worked near San Francisco, so I called her as part of a beat check, and asked if she had a story.

Did she ever.

Dr. Felisa Wolfe-Simon was friendly, young, enthusiastic, a Harvard graduate, and open to news coverage. When she told me that she plays the oboe, and sometimes carries it with her on trips to pull extreme "bugs" from California's strange and primordial Mono Lake, I was sold. Dr. Wolfe-Simon invited me along, and hinted at how she might use that oboe to provide her own sound track.

Wolfe-Simon had been looking at what she called a "shadow biosphere," meaning life that followed a set of rules alien to our own. This life would self-replicate, have DNA, and be capable of Darwinian evolution, just like us. "It might be a distant relative or a remnant," she said. "The idea is that there could have been other options during life's early evolution on Earth. So, there are interesting implications, right? If a second genesis happened here, then perhaps it happened elsewhere."

I was still trying to get my head around the concept of such life when Dr. Wolfe-Simon confided that she thought she had found it. "I'm writing the paper, now," she said. "It might win me the Nobel Prize." Not that Wolfe-Simon wanted me to report her findings, yet. "My article in *Science* comes out in a few months."

That prestigious magazine can make or break the careers of scientific researchers. Essentially, Wolfe-Simon had placed an embargo on her discovery and pending paper.

Embargoes happen frequently in science and other kinds of reporting. They give reporters advance information with which to prepare a story, but restrict publication or broadcast until a specified date and time.

It is a hard-and-fast rule that reporters don't break embargoes—not if they hope to maintain credibility with sources.

"We could do an advance story, though, talk about your past research, and what you have been hoping to find," I suggested. "Then, after the article comes out, we could do a big one about your discovery."

Dr. Wolfe-Simon liked that idea. A couple of weeks later, I took my camera to her office and shot video of her writing the paper. "All life on Earth comes from the big six elements," she explained. "They're in the periodic table. Everything we know that is alive contains carbon, hydrogen, nitrogen, oxygen, phosphorous, and sulfur. All life is based on this."

Wolfe-Simon said she had found her exception in the mud of Mono Lake. "It has substituted the element phosphorous with arsenic." We went to her lab, where she showed me bacteria living in petri dishes. "All those dots you see are colonies of microbes that live on high levels of arsenic. Humans could not survive in such conditions."

Dr. Wolfe-Simon displayed candor and openness in that first visit. Surprisingly, she never routed me through NASA public affairs. We agreed to meet at Mono Lake six weeks later, when she conducted further research.

Mono Lake

If you have never visited Mono Lake, put it on your bucket list. The place is bizarre. Limestone tufa towers thrust high above Horseshoe Bay in craggy shapes. Because Mono Lake has no outlet, minerals have built up in the ultra alkaline, saline waters for almost a million years.

Arsenic is another of those accumulated substances. There are parts of the lake where it appears in concentrated amounts. One of them is Negit Island, our destination, a few miles offshore.

Once there, Wolfe-Simon began collecting her bacteria. While she worked, I shot sights and sounds of that barren, volcanic island, with its gurgling hot springs, and waters filled with moving white clouds of tiny brine shrimp.

Earlier, Wolfe-Simon had suggested I should interview Larry Miller, a research oceanographer with the United States Geological Survey. When I did so that day, he confirmed her arsenic-for-phosphorus theory. "They substitute arsenic for phosphorous," he said of the bacteria. "If it's proved, and it is shown to be a different form of energy exchange, then it really is another form of life. So, we are looking at something as alien as if it arrived on a meteorite."

That was one of the clearest descriptions, yet, of Wolfe-Simon's discovery. I would not be able to use it in the advance story, however, because of the embargo.

Another of his comments, "The questions she is asking are fundamental. Can life have survived in a different way than we are used to?" spoke to her general research, and would be fine.

Wolfe-Simon's colleague in the project, Dr. Ronald Oremland, also spoke on camera. "Is she on to something?" I asked.

"Very much so," he confirmed. While Oremland remained more circumspect, he put the research in perspective, "It says we should be looking for more than we're looking for."

If only Wolfe-Simon had been as cooperative. In the six weeks since our last visit, she appeared to have developed second thoughts about having said too much, too soon, to a reporter she hardly knew. She wanted little to do with me when we finally sat down for an interview.

Even then, she backtracked. "First we have to show whether it exists, or not," she said when I asked about the philosophical implications of her discovery. "First we have to find it. You can't attach a philosophy to something you haven't proved, yet."

Those sound bites and several others were safe and non-committal. They would fit the advance story. Nothing Wolfe-Simon said, however, admitted to the breakthrough.

I passed the rest of the morning by shooting more of Wolfe-Simon pulling samples from the shoreline muck, and then hiked off to find a suitable location for a stand-up. By noon, high winds forced us into the open boat and back to shore. They blew so hard and pushed the salty waves so high that it's a miracle my wet camera gear survived.

Our close call did serve as a bit of a bonding experience, though. Wolfe-Simon and I parted with smiles, on good terms.

Turning Obscure Science Into Pictures and Words

From a production standpoint, you might wonder how I planned to turn such obscure scientific content into a television news report. These would be long form stories, requiring as much different video as possible to keep the segments distinct and visually interesting.

For starters, I had shots of Wolfe-Simon in four main locations; writing the paper in her office, working with the microbes in her lab, riding in the boat, and collecting material on the island.

Her two colleagues had given good interviews.

And, I had enough video of Mono Lake to give it multiple looks. There were daytime shots of seagulls, brine shrimp, hot springs, and the landscape. I also captured a blazing, multi-color sunset with a full moon rising above the horizon and reflecting on calm, black water. That particular scene looked like an artistic rendition of some unknown world.

So how does a science reporter with his own camera visualize the biological roles of carbon, hydrogen, oxygen, nitrogen, phosphorous, and sulfur? I shot bugs and plants, and later spent an hour on the busy corner of California and Montgomery in San Francisco, shooting people. Additionally, I made time-lapse videos of the sun, the clouds, and the stars for an opening sequence about how nature's patterns have repeated through the eons.

Dr. Wolfe-Simon never did bring her oboe.

Fact Checking and Negotiations

Complications arose after I wrote the advance story and called Dr. Wolfe-Simon with one or two simple questions for a fact check. She said she would not answer them without seeing a copy of the script, which put me in a difficult position. To supply it would violate ABC News policy. And, she wanted seven days to read it before getting back to me. In television news, seven days are an eternity.

I would still have time before my deadline—barely. "I will send you a list of facts and quotes," I told her. "No script. Facts and quotes are the most I can do."

This did not sit well with Wolfe-Simon. She's a brilliant, precise woman, accustomed to getting her way. "Everyone else allows me to approve scripts. The BBC did."

"We are not the BBC," I said, without challenging her assertion.

"It doesn't matter," she said. "You cannot run the story, anyway, because I never signed a release agreement granting you the rights."

I was dumbstruck. In all my years of reporting, that was a first. "You agreed to do an advance story," I told her. "As part of it, you granted multiple interviews on camera. You put it out there. This is our story about your research. Trust me."

"I will call NASA and have them confiscate your tapes," she threatened. It occurred to me that Wolfe-Simon was bluffing. NASA would be unlikely to attempt such a move. It would lead to lawyers and a first amendment confrontation. I told her so. Our conversation did not end on pleasant terms.

I felt terrible. What had I done to turn a source against me? I had not broken any confidences, violated her embargo, or misrepresented her work.

Next, Wolfe-Simon's husband called about the video we would be using. They wanted to approve that, too. He lectured me about how the wrong video in the wrong place could give the wrong impression. He questioned my ethics and the station's intentions in hurrying our story. "Wouldn't you rather wait to get it right?"

"That is why I asked for a fact check." I said. "There are just a couple of questions. Your wife could have answered them by now. Can't she just do that?"

As a reporter, you will deal with problems like this from time to time. Subjects of stories may try to control content, retract comments, and delete scenes, unaware that once a proverbial genie has left the bottle, there is no putting it back inside. This happens with politicians, athletes, police, entertainers, or any ordinary person who feels that he or she has a stake in a story. They aren't bad people. They simply do not know the guidelines under which reporters operate.

Dr. Wolfe-Simon's request would have been normal for a public relations story, but not for news. Public relations people give editorial control to the subjects they write about. News people don't, and shouldn't. This is what separates us from them.

I deeply wanted to get this story on the air, not only because of the content, but also because it was visually stunning. To ease Dr. Wolfe-Simon's concerns, I followed up on my offer and did send the script's factual language, plus all of the sound bites, verbatim. It was the best I could do while maintaining company guidelines. "You may comment on the facts," I told her, "but not the context."

Wolfe-Simon had promised a response in seven days. Nothing came for two weeks.

All the while, my bosses needed a date for the advance story. I couldn't give them one. Without that fact check, I did not feel comfortable about airing the piece.

Getting the facts absolutely correct is crucial for any kind of story, be it science, a three-alarm fire, or a murder investigation. We put information on the air that can make differences in people's lives. Viewers and the subjects of our stories trust us. It is only proper that we make every effort to get those facts right. Facts are sacred.

Meantime, Wolfe-Simon changed her tone, and began sending polite emails, requesting that we not run any story until she announced her discovery. She said she worried that our coverage would cause *Science* to cancel her article, ruining her career. She also expressed apprehension that some of her co-researchers had spoken too openly at Mono Lake.

Obviously, she did not trust me with the embargo, even though I hadn't come close to breaking it.

I wrote back to Wolfe-Simon and tried to reason with her. I noted how previous magazine articles revealed more about her work than my advance story. On her personal website, she had even told readers to get ready for a big announcement. "What, exactly, is the embargoed material in our script?" I asked Dr. Wolfe-Simon. If she would clarify her issues, we could avoid conflict.

She never did, although after I called NASA Public Affairs, she finally responded to my fact check notes. Her corrections would have essentially gutted the story. When I made counter-suggestions, she cut off all communication. According to NASA, Wolfe-Simon said I had violated our agreement.

"I don't get it," said my news director, Kevin Keeshan. "Your story makes her look brilliant."

Keeshan is a reasonable and responsible journalist. "Minimize the harm to all stakeholders in a story," he has said many times. Those words are a mantra to him. Clearly, Dr. Wolf-Simon had changed her mind. She has serious concerns. Keeshan and I felt we had kept our part of the deal, but decided that the potential harm to her career outweighed our benefit from running the advance story. Out of prudence, we cancelled it.

Clarifications and Lessons

Fast forward to the December 2nd announcement. As we watched Dr. Felisa Wolfe-Simon on the NASA feed in her shining moment, the reason for all of her stalling and inconsistent behavior became abundantly clear. Aside from holding back some technical details and the name of the bacteria, she and her team had pretty much given me the entire story.

If only Dr. Wolfe-Simon had confided that information, directly and specifically. If only she had trusted us to keep our word. If only she had appreciated that we, in the news media, respect embargoes because our reputations depend on them.

When the press conference ended at a little past noon, California time, I wrote a web story and walked into Keeshan's office. "We can do this, now," I said. "We need to. We have this story better than anyone."

"It's huge," Keeshan agreed.

I banged out a script that utilized all of the good sound we couldn't use before the embargo, and buried myself in an edit room until airtime. It was tight.

What follows fits my definition of a damn good, long-form story explaining a complex and possibly seminal discovery. The piece does not explain the science as much as what that science might imply.

In retrospect, "The Seventh Element," as we titled it, might even have been worth the pain.

The Seventh Element
December 2, 2010

Video shows time lapse shots of clouds, the sun, and stars. We see shots of people in downtown San Francisco, and later, shots of bugs and plants

FOR AS LONG AS SCIENCE HAS STUDIED LIFE, ONE COMBINATION OF ELEMENTS HAS REMAINED POTENTLY CONSISTENT.

THEY CALL IT CHNOPS, FOR SHORT . . .
CARBON, HYDROGEN, NITROGEN, OXYGEN, PHOSPHOROUS, SULFUR.

YOU WILL FIND THEM IN EVERY PERSON, EVERY BUG, EVERY PLANT . . .

(SOT)
Dr. Felisa Wolfe-Simon at Mono Lake

Wolfe-Simon: "All life has those six elements. Period. The end. That's all we know . . ."

Video shows Wolfe-Simon working on the paper in her office

OR, ALL WE THOUGHT WE KNEW UNTIL DR. FELISA WOLFE-
SIMON'S RESEARCH AND PAPER WENT PUBLIC, TODAY.
NOW, ADD ARSENIC TO THE MIX. SHE HAS DISCOVERED
A MICROBE THAT SHE SAYS REPLACES PHOSPHOROUS
WITH HIGHLY TOXIC ARSENIC, AND THEN USES IT
TO MAKE DNA, FATS, AND PROTEINS.
THIS MICROBE WOULD BE ONE-OF-A-KIND.

(SOT)
In laboratory, holding up petri dish

Wolfe-Simon: "All those dots you see are colonies of microbes
that can live on arsenic."

NASA video from that day shows "the bug" under a microscope

HER COLLEAGUES DESCRIBE THIS AS A SUBTLE,
BUT MAJOR DISCOVERY.

(SOT)
On the shores of Mono Lake

Wayne to Dr. Ron Oremland: "IS SHE ON TO SOMETHING?"

Dr. Ron Ormeland: "Very much so."

(SOT)
On island

Larry Miller: "If it's proved and shown to be a different form of
energy exchange, then it really is another form of life. So, we are
looking at something as alien as if it just arrived on a meteorite."

(SOT)
Sound up and under
Video shows Wolfe-Simon on boat

IN FACT, DR. WOLFE-SIMON FOUND THE MICROBE WITHOUT
EVER LEAVING CALIFORNIA.

(SOT VO lede sound to full screen)
Wolfe-Simon: "If you want to look for something interesting on
Earth, then Mono Lake is the place to do it."

(SOT)
Up and under
Video shows bubbles and fumes from hot springs on island

IF NATURE KEEPS SECRETS, WHY NOT HERE?
IN BUBBLING, MILLION YEAR OLD WATERS FILLED WITH
ACCUMULATED SALT, ALKALINE, AND ARSENIC.
EXTREME CREATURES SURVIVE HERE. AND NOW
WE KNOW WHAT MAY BE THE MOST EXTREME OF THEM ALL.

(SOT)
Sits on shore

Wolfe-Simon: "An alternate biochemistry. An alternate
biochemistry."

(SOT)
On island

Wayne to Larry Miller: "THIS TAKES THE NOTION OF LIFE
AS WE KNOW IT?"

Miller: "And turns it on its head!"

(WAYNE STAND-UP *at Mono Lake*)
THIS RESEARCH COULD LEAD TO SOME INTENSE PHILOSPHICAL
DEBATE. WHAT IF, BEFORE LIFE AS WE KNOW IT ESTABLISHED
ON EARTH, NATURE ATTEMPTED SOMETHING COMPLETELY
DIFFERENT? A FORM THAT TRIED, AND FAILED? IT COULD
CHANGE EVERYTHING.

(SOT)
On island

Wolfe-Simon: "Let's say it's older. Were there multiple options for
the origins of life? Did it happen more than once? We have no idea."

File video shows galaxies as shot by the Hubble Space Telescope

IN THE LARGER SCOPE, THIS EXPANDED DEFINITION OF LIFE
CHANGES OUR SEARCH FOR IT, ELSEWHERE. THE POSSIBILITIES
. . . BOUNDLESS, NOW.

(SOT)
In office

Wolfe-Simon: "It would probably suggest there are other options
elsewhere in the universe."

(SOT)
At Mono Lake

Dr. Ron Oremland: "It says we should look for more than we are
looking for."

Video shows more shots of people downtown San Francisco.
Next, we cut to the beauty shots from that eerie sunset at Mono Lake

SINCE WE HUMANS FIRST BECAME AWARE OF OURSELVES, WE
HAVE LOOKED ABOVE AND WONDERED IF WE WERE ALONE . . .

IF LIFE COULD EXIST ELSEWHERE.

HOW IRONIC IF, AFTER ALL THAT TIME, WE MAY HAVE FOUND
 A VERY STRONG CLUE, RIGHT HERE.

(SOT)
Smiling by the shoreline

Wolfe-Simon: "It could be very . . . interesting."

FROM MONO LAKE IN CALIFORNIA'S SIERRA NEVADA,
WAYNE FREEDMAN, ABC7 NEWS.

Postscript

You might wonder what Dr. Felisa Wolfe-Simon thought about the story after it aired.

I do not know.

When this book went to print, scientists were still vigorously challenging the methods, merits, and possible implications of Dr. Wolfe-Simon's controversial findings. As a journalist working with it in the present, the story was certainly memorable, compelling, and challenging.

Historians will write the final chapter.

Part Four

PHILOSOPHY

CHAPTER 17

Craftsmanship and Restraint: Don't Mess with the Pope

The next time you come across a hand-made wooden chair, take a few moments to examine it closely. Look at the lines. Whoever made that piece was a craftsman, a person so much in touch with his medium that he left no evidence of his sweat and toil. You won't notice the joints, the glue, or the nails. To the eye, they will fit together as one.

For a finish carpenter, the work is about the furniture. For a television news reporter, the same standard applies. *His work should be about the stories.*

The Benihana Trap

It's only natural that people in a performance medium want to show off their skills, but sometimes they overdo it. Those of us who write, report, shoot, or edit can easily fall into what I call the "Benihana trap."

Never heard of it? What about the restaurant chain by that same name? At Benihana of Tokyo, diners sit around a large grill while the chef conducts a cooking exhibition. He tosses knives, food, and chop, chop, chops his way through the courses. If you've had the experience, which do you most remember? Was it the meal or the chef?

I use this example because reporters and crews sometimes make similar mistakes when producing television news stories. They obscure their material by over-shooting, over-writing, over-voicing, over-cutting, or over involving themselves. In trying to impress coworkers or win awards, they forget their intended audience. It's the equivalent of making a chair to look at, rather than sit in.

When you study some of the most effective television news stories, you will find that the craftsmanship looks effortless, assuming you notice it at all.

Growing Pains and Confessions

This chapter is really about growing up and maturing as a reporter. Experience is the best teacher. After some of the stunts I pulled early in my career, it is astounding that I still work in this business. The worst was the time I single-handedly offended most of the Catholics in San Francisco.

Never Try to Do a Funny Story About Religion, Politics, or Sex

Of all the truisms about reporting, remember this one—*viewers and readers have thin skins about religion and politics.* The more someone believes in a cause, the less likely that he or she will have a sense of humor about it. I learned this lesson the hard way.

In 1987, Pope John Paul II came to San Francisco as part of a national tour. For most of a week, KRON-TV followed the pontiff's every move. In the newsroom, we jokingly called it a "Pope-a-thon." His visit culminated in a mass for sixty thousand people at Candlestick Park. Both the crowd and reporters arrived hours before dawn. I interviewed the faithful as they waited. Never have I seen more devoted or content people. It was beautiful.

The day was so remarkable that we saved the tapes for posterity. That was my first mistake. I made the second, a near-fatal one in terms of my career, three months later. It began innocently enough. Actress Elizabeth Taylor had put her name on a new perfume, and, as part of a national promotional tour, she appeared at a local Macy's department store. The desk sent us to cover it.

We couldn't believe the turnout. The line to see and meet Elizabeth Taylor extended through the entire cosmetics department, out the store's front door, onto the sidewalk, and around the corner. Some fans had been there since before dawn—just as long as those Catholics had waited to see the pope. Moreover, it occurred to me that many of Miss Taylor's devotees wore the same blissful expressions on their faces.

Perhaps by now you see where this is going. As a self-appointed observer and critic of the human condition, and as a reporter in search of the elusive "different angle," I felt compelled to compare the visit of Elizabeth Taylor to Macy's with that of the pope to Candlestick Park.

Ouch.

The idea was tasteless, insensitive, offensive, and stupid, but I thought it was brilliant. I intended to do a commentary about literal and figurative cosmetic values, but forgot that viewers rarely appreciate sarcasm, particularly Catholics when the subject is their pope. *Sometimes, it's much smarter for a guy to suck it up and do the obvious story.*

Back at the station, I ordered two graphics from the art department. The first showed a map of the pope's journey across America. The second detailed Miss Taylor's multi-city perfume tour. Our Catholic viewers did not appreciate my effort.

Next, I used some of that file video of emotional Catholics glorifying the pope and genuflecting at Candlestick Park. It seemed clever to contrast those shots with the scene at Macy's, where gleeful fans gave similarly effusive praise to Miss Taylor before practically throwing themselves at her feet. We cut back and forth—Macy's, Candlestick, Macy's, Candlestick, Macy's. Again, our viewers never quite caught the intended nuance.

Of course I saved the "best" for last. While looking through the file video, I also found a sequence of church officials sprinkling holy water on members of the Candlestick crowd. In the edit room, it cut perfectly with new pictures of cosmetic saleswomen circulating through Macy's, spraying perfume on customers—spritz, spritz, spritz.

Somehow the script cleared review, but the news director at that time was my old nemesis, Herb Dudnick. When the pope story aired, Herb shouted so loudly that witnesses say the glass wall of his office bent visibly outward. They swear that Dudnick's face turned as red as a tomato, with veins bulging from his forehead.

In the newsroom, phones rang relentlessly for more than ninety minutes. The callers accused us of blasphemous heresy. If we'd lived in the Middle Ages, they would have burned me at the stake. Those callers swore they would never watch KRON-TV again.

Poor Herb. He came to rebuild a news department, and had begun to succeed. With his superior coverage of the pope's visit, Herb had won viewers. Then we aired my story, which shooed away most of the Catholics among them in one minute and fifty-three seconds.

After the piece aired, Herb rushed to the edit bay. In what must have been a futile effort to turn back the clock, he grabbed the master edit reel and bulk erased it. For that reason, no copies of this misguided story exist in the known universe. And yet, for unexplained reasons, the fearsome Herb Dudnick did not fire or even suspend me. No—in some ways, the punishment was worse. He relegated me to the medical beat, where a reporter with bad judgment couldn't possibly do more damage. Or so it seemed.

The AIDS epidemic was making major news at that time, and my very first story dealt with the development of a female condom. Explaining it required me to say "vagina" while sitting live on the set. After the pope fiasco, I was such a nervous wreck that, when it came time to utter the word, I began to stutter. "V-V-V-V-V-. . ." I couldn't get it out. "V-V-V—Vagina!"

In retrospect, Herb Dudnick was a good and patient man. Despite his temper, he practiced restraint as a manager, and also as a human being. A few years later, Herb even recommended me for my job at KGO.

I guess he never mentioned the pope.

CHAPTER 18

A Few Thoughts About Writing, Voicing, and Using Sound

C heck that. I have "a few" thoughts about writing the same way General Motors makes "a few" cars. In television news reporting, writing isn't everything, but it comes close. Good writing marries words with pictures, sounds, interviews, and concepts. With skillful writing, a reporter can take marginal material and breathe life into it. By writing badly, he'll take wonderful material and kill it.

If You Don't Like the Way You Sound . . .

If you already work in television news, you probably have a good or at least decent speaking voice, but that doesn't guarantee you like the way you sound. You would not be the first to fret about breathing, delivery, or inflection, never realizing that your problems have may have less to do with elocution than the words you choose. If you want to come across as an approachable, credible person on television, write the way you speak.

The News Dialect

Many news people transform when they get behind a microphone. Their voices pitch higher. They utter words and phrases they would never use in normal conversation. The news, as they describe it, becomes a series of:

- ironic new twists
- shocking developments
- stunning turnarounds
- and horrible tragedies

That kind of writing is awful.

- Do **books fly off shelves** because they have wings?
- Who is **Mother Nature**? Is she related to **Father Time**?
- What is a **makeshift memorial**?
- When an agency **beefs up security**, does it put cattle by the door?
- When **shots rang out**, did they play a tune?
- When **emergency crews raced to the scene**, did one of them receive a checkered flag?

Reflexive, exaggerated, clichéd writing puts invisible barriers between news people and an already skeptical, critical public. We don't speak that way in real life, so why does such hyperbole creep into our stories? When, for instance, was the last time you sat down to dinner and heard your spouse announce, "**Next up, the pot roast!**"

And what if that pot roast turned out burned? Obviously, "**Something went terribly wrong.**"

Active, Not Passive

What is the flaw in this sentence?

HE WAS SHOT.

We hear the verb SHOT, but never learn who pulled the trigger. Here's a possibility:

A COPY EDITOR WHO ABHORS
PASSIVE VOICE SHOT HIM.

To write in active voice, identify the subject first. State what he, she, or it did, does, or will do, and to what or whom. Passive voice sentences rarely tell a complete story. We write them because we're in a hurry, or lazy, or do not have all the facts. We should do better.

Non-Descriptive Linking Verbs

Avoid non-descriptive linking verbs:

> IS
> ARE
> WAS
> WERE

When they appear in your copy, challenge yourself to find descriptive action verbs. Let's say you're doing a medical story and find a passive phrase:

> AFTER BLOOD IS DRAWN . . .

By activating the verb, it becomes:

> AFTER DRAWING BLOOD . . .

Put a subject noun in front, and you might improve the copy even further:

> THE NURSE DREW BLOOD . . .

Which sounds most natural?

If, however, you must force such changes into sentences, move on. Rules are made to be broken, as evidenced by this very sentence. Even William Shakespeare used a non-descriptive verb once in a while.

Elocution Convolutions

Sometimes, we lapse into parenthetical phrases or use big words instead of writing simple sentences. Of an embattled congressman, a reporter might write:

> CONGRESSMAN JOHN DOE,
> MARRIED TO THE SAME WOMAN

> FOR THIRTY-FIVE YEARS, SAYS
> HE'S NEVER HAD AN AFFAIR WITH
> AN INTERN.

Would you speak like that to a friend? No wonder you might stumble while saying it. Try using short, declarative sentences:

> THE CONGRESSMAN HAS BEEN MARRIED TO THE SAME
> WOMAN FOR THIRTY-FIVE YEARS. HE SAYS HE WOULD
> NEVER CHEAT ON HER.

Nor do we use opening clauses in normal conversation:

> HAVING PARKED HIS CAR IN FRONT OF THE BANK,
> THE ROBBER WALKED IN WITH HIS GUN.

Could anyone read that and still sound natural? Or, does this sound better?

> THE ROBBER PARKED HIS CAR IN FRONT OF THE BANK,
> AND WALKED IN WITH HIS GUN.

While we're on the subject of indirect and convoluted television news sentences, here is my favorite of all time, from a broadcast in Sacramento, California:

> THE OBVIOUS CONCLUSION AND
> BOTTOM LINE WAS THAT SHE WAS
> A PARTICIPANT IN HER OWN DEATH .

Or, to put it another way:

> SHE KILLED HERSELF.

Mixed Metaphors

Avoid getting overly fancy or metaphoric with your writing. Sure, good metaphors can help you sound smart. Bad ones have will have the opposite effect.

Here is a glaring example from after the September 11 terrorist attacks. You might remember how the Federal Aviation Administration temporarily grounded airplane charter companies because of security concerns. In Denver, one reporter visited a local airport for an economic impact story. THEY'RE TAKING ON WATER AND IN DANGER OF SINKING, he wrote of one charter firm. Nice try. Had that company owned a seaplane, his line would have been pretty good.

Use a Thesaurus to Avoid Repeating Words and Phrases

In recommending that we write the way we speak, I do not mean we should do so, literally. To appreciate the distinction, examine a verbatim, sometime, from a so-called eloquent speaker going off-the-cuff. His verbiage may not impress you as much after you read it on paper. You're likely to find run-on, conjunctive sentences, and many repeated words or phrases.

Redundant words creep into much of what we write, including news scripts and Internet copy. The more words you use, the more likely that their duplicates will reappear and expose weaknesses in your vocabulary.

This stuff is important. It makes the difference between good writing and bad.

That is why I always keep a big thesaurus on my desk, or at least consult the digital one inside my computer. You should, too. A good thesaurus will make you more articulate. It can also help you out of a jam.

Use a thesaurus the next time you fall prey to writer's block. Open it up, pick a word that applies to your story, and go surfing. As one word leads to another and you write them down, they may inspire you to write a better script.

The thesaurus is a crutch, certainly, but it sure does work.

Enough Nitpicking

Hopefully, now you will look more closely at the words you choose. There are some excellent books on the subject. Read *Writing Broadcast News: Shorter, Sharper, Stronger* by Mervin Block. If you fancy yourself a good writer, Mervin will humble you, much as he did me while helping to edit the first edition of this book.

At least he kept me laughing. Well, most of the time.

Using Sound

Writing well for television requires more than words. In our visceral medium, viewers must also feel, sense, and hear. To achieve that, good writers learn to use sound effectively.

Write from Point-to-Point

By now, you have read a few of my scripts, and might have noticed that I rarely write more than two or three sentences before inserting a piece of sound. A photographer taught me that style. This should not surprise you. In smaller and medium markets, particularly, some photographers are more qualified to file stories than the reporters with whom they work. They bring a sense of ownership to the job. In such environments, no self-respecting photographer will let a newbie reporter ruin a piece. Ideally, they pair as a team.

Such was my relationship with Kerry McGee, a classmate at the University of Missouri. After graduation, he went to work at WAVE-TV in Louisville. When I joined that wonderful, energetic staff a few months later, we partnered together almost every day.

McGee used to pester me about writing long-winded scripts. "You're a vocal narcissist," he would taunt. It was true. I suffered from an irrational, unrequited love affair with my voice. For that and other reasons, McGee stuck me with the name, "Hollywood."

Kerry McGee could be merciless. The man carried a camera for a living, and also wielded a quick, sharp pencil. If he disapproved of a script, he pushed for revisions, deadlines be damned.

"Hey, Hollywood. What's this?" he would scold. "That's wall-to-wall words. Are we doing radio, here?"

Thanks to Kerry McGee, I developed a sense of pacing and blending sound that survives to this day. Short narrative tracks lead into natural sound pops or sound bites. Subsequent tracks continue those thoughts, as if in a dialogue.

Here is a section of script that blends narration with multiple kinds of sound from a story about the Fresno High School Warriors football team. The night we covered them, they had lost thirty-one consecutive football games:

0-31
September 1992

(SOT)
Tight shot: wrapping athletic tape around an ankle

IN A WORLD OF BONE, SINEW, STRENGTH, AND WILLPOWER,
THERE IS NOTHING MORE BAFFLING

THAN THAT STRING OF EVENTS KNOWN AS A "STREAK."

(SOT)
Two guys slap shoulder pads

STREAKS DEFY LOGIC.

(SOT)
Player: "Superstition is superstition . . ."

THEY TAKE ON LIVES.

(SOT)
Wayne: "HOW MANY TIMES HAVE YOU LOST, NOW?"

Second player: "I don't know. You'll have to ask someone else . . ."

SOME WOULD SAY STREAKS HAVE WILLS OF THEIR OWN.

(SOT)
Players in huddle: "We want a win! Pride!"

FOR A FOOTBALL TEAM, A STREAK CAN BE THE
BEST OF FRIENDS, OR THE WORST OF ENEMIES.

(SOT)
Team crashes through barrier and takes field

NO ONE KNOWS BETTER THAN THE WARRIORS OF
FRESNO HIGH SCHOOL.

(SOT)
First player: "It's more than just a game. By now, we have to
redeem ourselves as human beings."

What Reads Well Does Not Always Make Good Television

Did you notice the seamless transitions in that script? It's the same effect you sometimes feel when riding a train over a good stretch of track. The individual rails blend together, as if they were one. Television news stories link sections, too. Instead of rails, we build them from narration and sound.

What looks good on paper, however, may not lead to good television. Writing and editing a seamless script is a complex craft.

Among the more common mistakes: reporters or editors force sound bites or natural sound pops into stories—sometimes, even, between the words of sentences. The reporter may know what a subject said because he had the luxury of seeing the video three or four times, but his viewers get only one shot. Consequently, if a sound bite hits unexpectedly or is too short, or if viewers do not hear it clearly, then it becomes an unwanted distraction—a bump in the narrative that raises more questions than it answers. Hold yourself back. When in doubt, do without.

Find the Clean Edit Point

Edit your sound bites at the cleanest, most natural points, even if it means adding a second or two. When possible, avoid cutting a sound bite in mid-clause or mid-sentence. Preferably, let interview subjects begin and finish their own thoughts. Our viewers are suspicious enough, already.

Finding the clean edit point is part of writing, too.

Match the Background Sounds

Background sounds can wreak havoc with seamless editing. Listen for them in the field, when logging raw footage, and be aware of them during your writing.

Let's say you have a sound bite from a busy street with a jackhammer audible in the distance. Common sense dictates that this interview will not cut cleanly against another recorded in a quiet room. The jackhammer will be distracting and counterproductive. It will be worse if you hope to use audio from the jackhammer interview over video from another location. Then, you run the risk of making it downright confusing.

Whenever possible, conduct interviews in neutral audio environments. Remember to record a few seconds of room tone or ambient sound before leaving. It can open spaces between tight words or sentences during editing.

You might wonder why I consider such technical concerns to be a part of writing. Well, the more you, as a writer, pay attention to the technical process, the better you can work with a story's potential or limitations. As the writer, you become the architect of a story—the person who designs it on paper.

Blend the Sound: Be Truthful About It

Technology makes it easier than ever to blend audio from one sequence and shot to another. We've come a long way.

In the old days, we used to hover a pencil-tipped magnet over the sound stripe to erase "pops" from spliced, 16mm film.

Later, we advanced to twisting audio knobs and alternating tracks for frame-accurate machines making split-edits on two-channel videotape.

Now, we have non-linear editing systems that meld sounds with the press of a mouse. Those systems offer more audio channels than ever before. If you have time for post-production, use as many of those channels as you need, but remain truthful about it. Only pull sound from the location where you shot the story. We're still in the news business. If you cheat on a regular basis, someone will catch you.

Do not repeat the mistake of a venerated network correspondent who shamelessly compiled a sound effects library in plain view on an office shelf. He got away with using it for many years, until he added chirping birds to sweeten the audio for a story out of the northwest. Just one problem—the birds he used live only in the south, and our nation is filled with amateur ornithologists.

Somebody had egg on his face.

Inflections and Tones

When working with sound, use your writing to smooth transitions. Hear that sound in your mind as you commit to a line, and again before tracking. Change inflections as needed. Use your voice as an instrument. Listen to it objectively. If the track doesn't work, fix the copy, read it again, or both. Do not be ashamed of retakes, assuming you have time. They almost always improve a story.

Ideally, your voice will vary, slightly, from one assignment to the next. Take your cues from real life. When you listen to people in conversations, notice how their voices change with situations. Actually, it is a sign of inexperience when reporters write and read every story the same.

Pacing and Rhythms

Try to give your stories a musicality and a beat. Sad stories may have slower paces. Happier ones may move faster. As the noted voice coach, Dr. Ann Utterback, writes in her *Broadcast Voice Handbook*, "Sometimes, emotions can change in one sentence."

While every story should have an internal metronome, avoid inappropriate tempos. Don't cut a flashy, fast-paced open for material that cannot sustain such an energy level. Reporters commonly make this mistake when trying to liven up dry stories. They hope to add momentum. Instead, when the promised rhythm slows, the rest of the piece bogs down by comparison.

The Rule of Threes

My wife engraved a beautiful inscription into my wedding band. It reads, "My heart, my love, for life." Do you hear the rhythm in that sentence?

Da-da. Da-da. Da-da. The human ear likes threes.

The Rule of Threes also works when writing television news. Here is the opening to a piece about a fourteen-year-old boy who shot his classmates at Santana High School near San Diego, California:

> THE LUCKY ONES WALKED OUT OF SANTANA HIGH SCHOOL
> THIS MORNING. THEY WERE GRATEFUL
> NOT TO BE LEAVING ON GURNEYS,
> IN WHEELCHAIRS,
> OR BY HELICOPTER,
> AFTER ONE OF THEIR OWN TOOK A TWENTY-TWO-CALIBER
> HANDGUN AND OPENED FIRE IN A RESTROOM.

Do you hear the threes? GURNEYS—WHEELCHAIRS—HELICOPTER.

Here is another example, from a story about a cat named Stanley. In 2001, he made national news by climbing a power pole in his neighborhood and then staying there for days:

> IN THE LIFESPAN OF ANY STREET,
> THERE ARE BUSY DAYS . . .
> THERE ARE QUIET DAYS . . .
> AND, ON BOWLING GREEN STREET IN SAN LEANDRO,

THERE ARE STANLEY DAYS.

Certainly, you must hear the rhythm in that section. Try reading it aloud. You might like the way you sound.

Change the Cadence

Now a word of warning—threes become repetitious and ineffective when we use them too often. Sprinkle in some matter-of-fact ones or twos for contrast.

Below you will find a section of script that uses threes in combination with a pair of twos. Again, read it aloud and listen to the cadence:

> IF THE HIGHWAY TO HADES HAS AN EARTHLY OPPOSITE,
> THIS MAY BE THE PLACE.
> THE COLDER THE TEMPERATURES,
> THE HOTTER THE TEMPERS.

The rhythm words are: HADES, OPPOSITE, and PLACE, which accent the threes.

The words, COLDER and TEMPERATURES, paired with HOTTER and TEMPERS, accent the twos.

Alliteration

Susan's inscription had something else going for it. Those words, "My heart, my love, for life," have alliteration.

As with the rule of threes, too much alliteration can be gimmicky, but a few repeating sounds will occasionally fancy-up your writing. And, there's nothing wrong with that.

Here is an alliterative section from a story about drive-in movie theaters. It contains only a few words with repeating sounds. They're scattered. They're subtle. They find their own rhythm:

Excerpt from 'The Solano'
Summer 2010

(STAND-UP)
DRIVE-IN MOVIES PEAKED IN THE 1950S AND 60S. BACK THEN,

THERE WERE TWO-HUNDRED AND SEVENTY-TWO SCREENS IN CALIFORNIA, ALONE. NOW, ONLY EIGHTEEN REMAIN. IS THIS A REVIVAL? OR A REQUIEM?

(SOT)
Old black and white footage showing drive-ins from the 1950s, and then dissolves to a snack bar advertisement showing cokes and candies floating across the screen

DRIVE-IN MOVIES RODE IN ON A WAVE OF POST-WAR, UPWARDLY MOBILE CAR CULTURE—A TIME OF TECHNICOLOR DREAMS AND PANAVISION PROSPECTS IN A LAND OF PLENTY. BUT THAT WAS THEN.

(SOT)
Interview with a drive-in historian in an old projection room

Wayne to historian: WHAT HAPPENED TO THEM?
 Historian: Well, they pretty much turned into a cemetery, a trailer park, or a Walmart at this point.

(SOT)
Wind blows through an abandon movie theater screen

GO TO A DRIVE-IN, THESE DAYS, AND YOU'RE LIKELY TO FIND A CORRUGTED SCREEN, BANGING IN THE BREEZE . . .
A DEAD-END DERELECT WAITING FOR BULLDOZERS AND SUBDIVISIONS.
MOST DRIVE-INS EXIST ONLY IN OLD PHOTOS, NOW.
REMEMBER THE ISLAND AUTOMOVIE IN ALAMEDA?
LONG GONE. SAME FOR THE PARKWAY IN PETALUMA, WHICH USED TO FLOOD, ANYWAY.

(SOT)
Dan Tocchini, former owner: "It's a driving range, now."

(SOT)
Golfer hits shot

. . . AN INEVITABLE VICTIM OF ENTERTAINMENT EVOLUTON.

Connect, Connect, Connect

If there is one, most important concept for you to take away from this section, it would be "connection."

In the spring 2009, news photographer Dean Smith and I covered a commemorative telephone booth stuffing at Saint Mary's College in Moraga, California. The script from that story exemplifies most of what we have looked at in this chapter. The sound bites and narration connect. The story has pacing, rhythm, a small amount of alliteration, and a reporter who enjoyed playing with his words:

Booth Breakers
March 2009

Shots of campus and kids forming a line

YOU MIGHT ASSUME THAT AT SAINT MARY'S COLLEGE IN MORAGA, THE ONLY KIND OF CRAMMING THESE KIDS DO APPLIES TO EXAMS.

(SOT)
Kids begin filing into booth and crawling on top of each other

. . . NOT AFTER THE SPECTACLE WE WITNESSED TODAY.

(SOT)
Female student says: "It was just like being really, really squished."

YOU KNOW THAT LINE ABOUT HOW THOSE WHO FORGET HISTORY ARE DOOMED TO REPEAT IT? AT SAINT MARY'S, THE ONES WITH GOOD MEMORIES GOT STUCK WITH A REENACTMENT.

(SOT)
Ray Motta, an elder alumni: "Back in my day we had a real booth. A real booth with real people."

Video shows Ray today, and then cuts to his image in a life size photo of the first booth stuffing

RAY MOTTA TODAY, AND FIFTY YEARS AGO,
WHEN A DIFFERENT CROWD OF KIDS
FROM HERE STUFFED A TELEPHONE BOOTH
AND SET A WORLD RECORD.
THEY DESCRIBE THE PHOTO AS 'ICONIC.'

(WAYNE ON CAMERA standing by photo)
THE ORIGINAL RECORD WAS TWENTY-TWO.
A QUARTER OF A CENTURY LATER,
ANOTHER GROUP OF STUDENTS UPPED IT TO TWENTY-FOUR.
TODAY, THESE KIDS ASPIRE TO TWENTY-FIVE.

(SOT)
Natural sound of kids jamming into the booth

FOR MOST OF THESE KIDS, TODAY MARKED A FIRST.

(SOT)
Question to student holding a cellular telephone:
"HAVE YOU EVER EVEN BEEN IN A BOOTH, BEFORE?"

"No."

Close-up shots of faces crammed against the glass

SO THEY LEFT THEIR CELL PHONES OUTSIDE, PILING IN,
TIME AND AGAIN. AN ASSAULT OF HEADS, APPENDAGES,
AND FLESH LEAVING OILY STAINS UPON THE GLASS.

IT WASN'T SO MUCH A MATTER OF THESE NICE, CATHOLIC KIDS
TAKING THE LORD'S NAME IN VAIN . . .

(SOT)
Kid shrieks:
"Oh my God, Oh my God . . . "

. . . AS IN PAIN.

(SOT)
Another student: "Ow! Ow! Ow!"

More shots of arms, legs, hands and heads clearly not in the booth

THE GOOD NEWS . . . NO INJURIES.
THE BAD . . . THESE STUDENTS ONLY TIED THE ORIGINAL RECORD
OF TWENTY-TWO, AND THAT, WITH A PROTEST.

(SOT)
Ray Motta says:
"We didn't have bodies hanging out. Our record stands."

*Another shot of kids in the booth, and one leg, in particular,
flopping outside*

TELL THAT TO THEM.

(SOT)
Kids in unison: "Nooo!!!!!"

It Takes Time and Practice

To help find natural rhythms and inflections in your writing and delivery, read
poetry, experiment, and rent movies in which narrators move the plots forward.

For a casual style, listen to Ray Liotta in *Goodfellas*. That voice has credibility.

Morgan Freeman does a wonderful job in *The Shawshank Redemption*. He
reads with no rush, no hurry. His pacing is perfect.

Nor should you miss Robert Redford's narrative sections in *A River Runs Through It*. His read during the final scene is a classic of understated cadence.

It might help if you copy the scripts, play the movies back, and read along with them. Or do the same with some well-written television news stories. Watch the classic work of Charles Kuralt, sometime. When you match your voice to those of the masters, quality can be infectious.

Who knows—when you get good enough at establishing your own style, maybe some young reporter will emulate you, someday.

CHAPTER 19

Writing to Pictures: Seek the Simple Truths

Television news requires reporters to write differently than for any other medium. They write to be heard. They write parallel to pictures. The best pieces create lifelong impressions, sometimes with one line and one shot.

Greg Lyon, a reporter at KRON-TV, once did a story about hard economic times for California's salmon fishermen. His photographer/editor, Lou D'Aria, wanted to use a low, long-lens shot of a seagull pecking at a morsel of food between the planks of a pier. That darn bird simply wouldn't give up. Peck, peck, peck.

Greg tortured himself finding a line to fit the image. He wrote a few words and ripped them up. He tried another line and tore that up, too. After a while, he came up with this:

THE LIVING IS WHERE THEY FIND IT.

Those were seven choice words—short, simple, and descriptive. They spoke to the picture, and also beyond it.

At about the same time, John Hart of NBC News wrote another telling line. In a piece about illegal immigrants slipping across America's southern borders, Hart described the frustrations of customs officials. He compared their job to that of someone trying to catch . . .

. . . PEBBLES IN AN AVALANCHE.

Quite an image, isn't it?

Watch Steve Hartman's work at CBS News. In a story at the Grand National Rodeo, he wrote of an overmatched cowboy needing . . .

> . . . THE RIDE OF HIS LIFE, THE FOURTH NIGHT IN A ROW.

With one simple line, Steve described hope and impossibility.

Hartman transcends journalism. "Sometimes I feel like such an imposter," he likes to say. Hardly. Steve is an old soul, wise beyond his years. He brings it to his work.

Simple Truths

All three of those lines communicate *simple truths*. Rather than stating the obvious, *simple truths* are empirical in nature. They empower viewers to make discoveries and reach conclusions for themselves. It's the equivalent of leading a person to a threshold, and letting him take the final step to a realization. Usually, he appreciates it more that way.

Simple truths can be elusive, however. Their resonant details or connections may be so obvious that we look right past them. Where, for example, is the simple truth in an urban murder?

> IN OAKLAND, THEY'RE NOTING THE YEAR'S NINETIETH
> HOMICIDE VICTIM MORE FOR HIS NUMBER THAN HIS NAME.

Later, we learned that number ninety was McKinley Williams, a thirty-three-year-old construction worker with two children. He'd been playing basketball before being shot, and still wore his gym clothes. Those would have been good details, but, in the absence of them, *we described intangibles*. I didn't need a press release or a fact check to write that line. It's the kind of *simple truth* that comes from connecting your humanity with your material.

Writing at the Highest Level

In this book, I have shared my essentials for telling memorable, narrative stories. It is an incredibly complicated process. We've looked at the basics— structure, characters, interviewing, contrast, spontaneity, the mechanics of writing, editing, performance, and many other fine points in between. *Simple truths* are the last major piece to the puzzle. When we frame stories in *simple truths*, we rise to the highest levels of our calling.

Early on, I suggested that you look for stories of life in your everyday work. *Simple truths* cut to the heart of that. *They make stories approachable. They create the essence of universal appeal.*

The Grateful Deadhead

Simple truths might appear anywhere in stories. They can be as uncomplicated as small observations.

In 1997, we spent a day with the late Dick Latvala, whose name means a great deal to fans of the Grateful Dead. Thirty years earlier, he had chucked his job as a mailman and dropped out of society to become, as he described it, "a full-on, Deadhead hippie freak." Dick dedicated himself to following the Dead around America, taping their concerts. Eventually, when the band needed an archivist, his dedication paid off. The Grateful Dead hired Dick:

FOR DICK, THE DEAD BECAME A LIVING.

That simple truth worked as a play on words. It came to me in an instant of *relaxed* clarity. You cannot summon such a state when writing. A line like that arrives only when you're ready to receive it.

The Zone

Is there a sport at which you're exceptionally good? Do you play a musical instrument? If yes, you may have visited that place called "the zone." It's where you forget about mechanics and lose yourself in the moment. Once, while playing golf with PGA Tour player-turned-television analyst Brandel Chamblee, I asked how he stayed in the zone to hit a particularly delicate shot from a thin lie on tight grass, over a bunker, and made it spin to a stop next to the hole.

"Here's the example that sports psychologist Bob Rotella gave me," said Chamblee. "Imagine you're single and you get a call from, oh, I don't know, pick some sexy actress you've never met."

I gave him a name.

"Okay, now imagine now that she calls you on the telephone, says you're her lifelong fantasy, she wants to fulfill it that night, and you only have to do one thing to make it happen."

"One thing?" I asked.

"Yes. And the one thing is that you cannot think about her," said Chamblee. "Because, if you think about her and what might happen, it will inevitably change you or your behavior, and then she won't want you. So, you just have to keep being yourself until she shows up."

That's how *simple truths* come to writers in the zone. *They get immersed in the process, not the outcome.*

Experience the Story

Ernest Hemingway used to say that before expressing an idea, a writer must free himself by experiencing it. Live the moment fully.

Neil Armstrong certainly did so when he set foot on the moon. "That's one small step for a man—one giant leap for mankind," he said. Armstrong wasn't a great writer, and yet no one ever spoke wiser, simpler, more truthful words.

Think It, Write It

It doesn't take a moon walk to find simple truth clarities. A few years, ago photographer Michael Clark and I shot a story about small boys playing a Pee Wee Little League game. During a lull, Mike rolled video of a kid waiting at the plate with a bat on his shoulder. The youngster surprised us by blowing a wad of gum into a bubble as big as his head. Then, it popped all over his face.

"At this level, even the inaction is action packed," I quipped to Mike. When he laughed, I scribbled the line into my notebook.

Later, it worked for the piece.

Listen to Your Inner Voice

The World's Newest Oldest Human

We had a similar moment when covering Chris Mortensen, who took one-hundred-fifteen years to become a household name. By then, he had outlived his wives, his children, and most of his grandchildren. Finally, after the death of a woman in France, he ascended to the title of World's Oldest Person.

By the time we met Mr. Mortensen, he had gone blind and almost deaf. He lived in one room of a retirement home. After one-hundred-fifteen years, his remaining worldly possessions filled less than a chest of drawers. Being the newly recognized World's Oldest Person did not appear to impress Chris Mortensen.

He didn't say much for the interview.

On our way back to the car, I commented, "If a person hangs around long enough, I guess he earns the title by default." We chuckled about that. Later, the thought led to an opening line which fit our video of a disinterested old man in a wheelchair:

> THERE ARE SOME TITLES FOR WHICH WE WORK . . .
> OTHERS FOR WHICH WE ASPIRE . . .
> AND SOMETIMES, TITLES FIND US.
>
> FOR CHRIS MORTENSEN OF SAN RAFAEL, THE LAST OF THOSE
> THREE HAS HAPPENED, ALTHOUGH, AT ONE-HUNDRED-FIFTEEN
> YEARS OLD, TITLES DON'T IMPRESS HIM MUCH.

The Freeze-Dried Dog

A few years ago an innocuous AP story crossed the wire. It mentioned a new method for disposing of dead pets—freeze-drying them, just like instant coffee.

Kevin Keeshan found the item back when he was our executive producer in charge of special projects. That article prompted both of us to wonder, "What kind of person freeze-dries a deceased dog?"

We found our answer in Pam Kiefer from Tracy, California. Within moments of arriving, I realized this would not be the simple consumer story we expected. Everybody gets attached to pets, but Pam's relationship with a twelve-year-old dead toy poodle named Beast had entered another realm. "Was this a normal dog?" I asked.

"No," answered Pam.

"What did Beast she think she was?" I asked.

"A person," said Pam of the stiff, stuffed, furry, freeze-dried dog that had died, unexpectedly, from heart problems. Pam spent $500 for the preservation, and appeared to have become stuck in the denial part of her grieving process. "The neatest thing that I didn't know is that she still smells just like her."

Maybe it all sounds weird, but not by Pam's standards. This was a woman who tended artificial flowers behind a plastic, white picket fence just outside her door. Inside, the dog had become a decorating motif. Beast's prize winning portraits hung from the walls. Her voice barked from the computer when emails arrived.

"We haven't gone to extremes, here?" I asked.

"No," answered Pam, so innocently.

It was awkward. The assignment would never have happened if we had known what we would be walking into, but by then it was already too late. When a station sends a crew, it will get a story, somehow. Our shoot ended with Pam standing in her kitchen, holding and stroking that freeze-dried poodle. With the camera rolling, I suggested that she might want to get another dog.

"No, no, there will never be another Beast," said Pam, who then paused for a beat. "And I have a dog," she added emphatically.

At that moment, I understood completely how she felt. Pam was still grieving, unable to let go. Beast still gave her comfort.

The piece I eventually wrote might never air today, but it was remarkable for 1997. Viewers have said that "The Freeze-Dried Dog" takes them from surprise, to laughter, to incredulousness, to pity, and then to empathy—all in a little more than two minutes. We make the final turn with two simple truth lines and two sound bites as the story ends. They acknowledge the weirdness while trying to make sense of it all:

The Freeze-Dried Dog (Ending Sequence)
August 1997

IT IS BOTH AMUSING AND SAD. YES, PEOPLE DO GRIEVE THIS WAY FOR LOST PETS. PAM NEVER HAD CHILDREN.

SHE SAYS REMEMBERING THE LOVE OF BEAST REMAINS PRIMARY, AND THAT BEAST WAS A DOG, SECONDARY . . .

Wayne dips fingers into Beast's filled water bowl

(SOT)
Pam Kiefer: "And there is still water in there, yes. I still fill her water bowl."

OF COURSE SHE DOES. IF YOU DON'T UNDERSTAND, YOU NEVER WILL. AND, PAM KIEFER WOULDN'T CARE ANYWAY BECAUSE, EVEN IN DEATH, A PET PROVIDES COMFORT.

(SOT)

Wayne to Pam as she stands in kitchen, holding and petting Beast: "YOU'RE NOT GOING TO GET ANOTHER DOG?

Pam: "No. No. There will never be another Beast."

Long pause as she looks down and continues petting dog

"And, I have a dog!"

The station's telephones lit up after we aired this piece. Was our audience angry? Appalled? Disgusted? No. Most of them called with the same question: "Where can I go to get my dog freeze-dried?"

Summon Your Muse

If you're having a hard time with inspiration, help the muse along. I once asked Devorah Major, the poet laureate of San Francisco, how she teaches children to write metaphors. "You use your senses and comparative thinking," she said. "Look at a pink sunset. Of what would the color remind you? Cotton candy. What would it sound like? Quiet. If the pink color had an emotion, what would it be? Calm. It leads to a calm, cotton candy sunset."

Despite my admonition in the previous chapter about metaphors, sometimes a script begs for them, as long as we use them constructively. After a tsunami rolled through Santa Cruz harbor in 2011, I described the challenge for clean-up crews as:

A JIGSAW PUZZLE OF BOAT PIECES.

Writing "About" Instead of "What"

A strong metaphor goes deeper than merely describing *what* a shot shows. It tells *about* the image. This is an important distinction. Writing *what* addresses the obvious. Writing *about* conveys a stronger impression. It's more narrative.

Here's an example from our coverage of an earthquake in Montclair, California, in 2008. When I saw hundreds of broken bottles on the floor of a vintner's store, the wine lover in me wondered how such a mess might taste. I turned the thought into a metaphor at the end of a track that described quake damage from several locations:

... A RIP IN THE EARTH THAT CRACKED WINDOWS,
BROKE CHINA,
RIPPLED CEILINGS,
READJUSTED MIRRORS,
AND RELOCATED TOILETS.
AT THIS VIDEO STORE, THE QUAKE TOSSED HUNDREDS OF
HOURS OF VIEWING ONTO THE FLOOR.
IN THIS BOOKSTORE, IT DID THE SAME TO SEVERAL YEARS
WORTH OF READING.
AND, AT VILLAGE WINES AND SPIRITS, THE QUAKE WASTED
A LIFETIME'S WORTH OF GOOD DRINKING ...
IT TURNED VINTAGE CABS, ZINS, AND CHARDONNAYS
INTO ONE BIG HOUSE BLEND AWAITING THE MOP.

Finding A Simple Truth Theme: "Things to Remember"

Strong, clean writing with *simple truths* can be a laborious process. Often, our most challenging stories become some of our best. They demand more of us, particularly when we're trying to write up to extraordinary material. At such times, self-doubt may actually make you a better writer.

I got mired in a project like that on a Thursday night in 1991. Five days earlier, the Oakland Hills had caught fire, burning thousands of homes. Most of us working in the San Francisco Bay Area had covered other big disasters, including the Loma Prieta Earthquake of 1989, but inch for inch, block by block, victim by victim, few of us ever saw a more devastating force than the Oakland Hills firestorm.

It began on a Sunday afternoon, with a charcoal cloud covering the eastern hills. In a few hours, wind-driven flames consumed entire neighborhoods. Many of the people who lost their homes had only minutes to escape. They left behind pets, important papers, photographs, and memories.

The rest of that week, we covered the aftermath. Late on Thursday, Milt Weiss, KGO-TV's news director at the time, asked for what he called "a think piece."

"We'll run it tomorrow," he said. I appreciated Milt's confidence, but after five days of coverage it seemed we had shown and said all we could about the fire. More daunting, Milt wanted the segment to fill three or four minutes.

I began my research by reviewing the week's stories. Our staff had done some fine work. Several pieces stood out. Among them, we profiled Oakland fireman Gary Paccini. His own house had burned to the ground while he helped to save seven others. In another segment we met local families who opened their doors to fire victims. Lauren and Maureen Bybee, for example, adopted a family with five children.

I must have looked through every newscast, searching for stories, pictures, interviews, and spontaneous moments. Then I went back to the field tapes, hoping for new material we might have overlooked, or not had time to use.

Collectively, they had the makings of a storytelling gold mine, but such richness came with a price. There was too much material. I tried every possible way to jump-start a script, including compiling a list of words from a thesaurus, but made little progress. After a week of doing and watching fire stories, my attempts seemed overstated or trite.

Two hours after sitting down to write, my computer screen had just as many words as when I started—none.

I thought about the fire victims who would see this segment. Who was I to speak for them? How could anyone else appreciate what those people had endured? Impossible. If a person wasn't a victim, it made him an outsider.

The concept struck a chord. It felt almost original. "That's the first clear thought you've had all night," I told myself, and wrote it down:

> NO ONE CAN APPRECIATE WHAT THESE PEOPLE ARE GOING
> THROUGH, UNLESS THEY HAVE DONE SO THEMSELVES.

I looked at the numbers of planes and fire trucks, the crews, and the dollars spent. In spite of our best men and machines, the fire had run us over:

> EVEN WITH ALL OUR TECHNOLOGY,
> THERE WAS NOTHING WE COULD DO . . .

I reflected on the loss of life and property. Earlier in the week we had used long-distance video of firemen poking through rubble and finding what appeared to be human remains. I connected that with another shot, of a burned doll inside a little girl's hope chest:

> THERE ARE SOME THINGS THESE PEOPLE HAVE LOST
> THEY HAVEN'T EVEN THOUGHT OF YET.
> SOME WILL SAY THEY'RE ONLY OBJECTS,

BUT THEY'RE THE STUFF THAT TRIGGERS MEMORIES.
THE FIRE REDUCED THEM ALL TO BURNSCAPE.

That line dealt with feeling overwhelmed. Anyone who has suffered a loss knows how, for days, weeks, and years, forgotten details resurface and reopen old wounds.

From those three thoughts, the theme began to find itself. It became a story of observational details and memories.

Things to Remember
August 1991

FROM THE BEGINNING, WE KNEW THIS WAS DIFFERENT . . .
AS IF WHAT HAD BEEN A QUIET FIRE SEASON DECIDED
TO MAKE UP FOR LOST TIME, ALL AT ONCE.

FROM ACROSS THE BAY IN SAN FRANCISCO,
THIS BILLOWING CHARCOAL SKY LOOKED OMINOUS.
IN THE EAST BAY HILLS, IT WAS OVERWHELMING . . .

(SOT)
Woman cries: "My home, my home."

Full sound and pictures of flames

FOR THOSE WHO LIVED THROUGH IT, THESE SIGHTS AND
SOUNDS ARE SEARED INTO MEMORY.

THE FUTILITY OF A GARDEN HOSE . . .

(SOT)
Man tries to save his roof with a hose

Neighbor shouts: "Get away!"

THE FURY OF THE WIND . . .

(SOT)
Wind and flames crackle; fire blows across highway

AND, FINALLY, THE REALIZATION THAT, EVEN WITH ALL OUR
TECHNOLOGY, THERE WAS NOTHING WE COULD DO.

(SOT)
Plane drops fire retardant

THROUGH A LONG AFTERNOON AND ON INTO EVENING,
THOUSANDS OF HOMES BURNED.

(SOT)
Natural sound as the camera drives past several burning homes;
the sequence continues with more houses;
we dissolve into shots of the fire at sunset, and then night

IF WE FOUND COMFORT IN THE DARKNESS,
IT CAME FROM WHAT WE COULDN'T SEE . . .

(SOT)
We see a fleeing family loading a car

The woman gasps: "Oh, dear God."

IF WE FELT ANGER,
IT CAME FROM WHAT WE COULDN'T CONTROL . . .

(SOT)
A distraught man puts his head in his hands

AND, IN THE SHELTERS ALL THAT NIGHT, IF WE KNEW FEAR,
IT CAME FROM WHAT WE DID NOT KNOW . . .

(SOT)
Woman: "You don't know if you'll ever see your home again.

Maybe it isn't a palace to someone else, but it is to me. It's all I have. This is ripping out my heart."

(SOT)
Pictures from sunrise, the morning after, show people and ruins; we hear the trickling sound of water pouring down a storm drain.

NO ONE CAN APPRECIATE WHAT THESE PEOPLE ARE GOING THROUGH UNLESS THEY HAVE DONE SO THEMSELVES. THEY HAVE LOST FRIENDS AND FAMILY, SOMETIMES WITHOUT A TRACE.

(SOT)
We see a long-lens shot of firemen looking for human remains in a charred house

THEY HAVE LOST SECURITY . . .

(SOT)
Another long-lens shot: a mother and son walk away, carrying suitcases

THERE ARE SOME THINGS THESE PEOPLE HAVE LOST THAT THEY HAVEN'T EVEN THOUGHT OF YET. SOME WILL SAY THEY'RE ONLY OBJECTS, BUT IT'S THE KIND OF STUFF THAT TRIGGERS MEMORIES. THE FIRE REDUCED THEM ALL TO BURNSCAPE.

(SOT)
We talk to a little girl

Wayne asks if she's seen her house: "No, I couldn't look. I didn't want to go."

(SOT)
We dissolve to pictures of rescue crews removing a burned cat from beneath wreckage; the cat meows

THERE ARE NO SILVER LININGS IN A STORY LIKE THIS, BUT,
FOR THOSE WHO LOOK, THERE CAN BE HOPE AND INSPIRATION.
FOR EVERY PERSON MISSING A PET, THERE IS THIS SIAMESE WHO
HAS A NEW NAME—PELE, AFTER THE HAWAIIAN GODDESS OF
FIRE. SHE'S GOING TO BE ALL RIGHT . . .

(SOT)
*We dissolve to video of fireman Gary Paccini as he surveys his
burned-down house*

FOR THOSE WHO BELIEVE IN HONOR AND DUTY,
THERE IS OAKLAND FIREMAN GARY PACCINI,
WHO HELPED RESCUE SEVEN HOMES,
BUT RETURNED TO FIND HIS OWN HAD TURNED TO DUST . . .

(SOT)
Gary: "I was already committed where we were . . ."

AND THEN THERE'S THE GOODNESS OF HUMAN SPIRIT. THE
VOLUNTEERS WHO, WHEN NEEDED, GAVE OF THEMSELVES . . .

(SOT)
We hear a crying baby and see a crowded living room

. . . PEOPLE LIKE LOREN AND MAUREEN BYBEE, WHO OPENED
THEIR HOME TO PERFECT STRANGERS, THE SILVA FAMILY . . .
HENRY AND JACQUELINE AND THEIR FIVE KIDS.

(SOT)
Wayne asks Maureen what she got out of this: "You feel good
about yourself. What you put out you get back, and sevenfold."

(SOT)
*Helicopter sound—an aerial shot looks down upon a landscape of
burned homes*

TWO YEARS AGO, WE SURVIVED AN EARTHQUAKE.
THEN CAME THIS.
NATURE HAS SHAKEN US.
SHE HAS BURNED US.
BUT SHE HAS NOT BROKEN US.

Simple Truths as Endings

Finally, here is a simple truth we used as an ending. Every year, thousands of hopeful and often misguided amateurs ask professional sports teams if they may sing the national anthem before a game. In 1991, the Oakland Athletics held an open tryout. Dozens of them auditioned.

For reporters and photographers who covered this event, the experience proved to be excruciating. Why? Because in order to succeed at singing the national anthem, a person must nail that high note in "O'er the land of the free . . ." Some squeaked it. Others screeched it. Most who tried never reached it.

Adding to our pain, the Athletics piped the singers through a loud public address system. With every new performer, we anticipated the horrible sound.

We cringed.

We cowered.

We covered our ears.

We ground and teeth and grimaced.

"Freeeeeeeeeeeeeeeee!"

At least I took a good closing line away from the painful experience:

> . . . THE NATIONAL ANTHEM
> BELONGS TO ALL OF US.
> BUT, IN THIS LAND OF THE . . .

> (SOT)
> A montage of auditioners missing the high note in "free," and people holding their ears: "Free/Freeeee/Freee . . ."

> . . . ONLY THE BRAVEST SHOULD TRY TO SING IT.

CHAPTER 20

Look Beyond the Superficial: Write Your Stories on Multiple Levels

Anyone who leads police on a 110-mile car chase must imagine he has a good reason. He's either running from something, or to it.

Curious yet? News Director Kevin Keeshan certainly was. When he learned we had purchased freelance video of such a pursuit and the subsequent arrest, he pushed the story my way.

"Something's going on with this," Keeshan said.

I wasn't too keen on the idea. "It was a car chase."

"No. It was 110-mile car chase. Sometimes, we have to do this stuff." He wondered if there might be more to the story.

I still didn't care much for it. Nobody had gotten hurt. Police had the suspect in jail. And, most irritating for me or any journalist, we suffered from a dearth of information. The arresting officers had worked late, gone home, and not yet filed reports. Aside from a few minutes of shaky, grainy stringer video and one paragraph of wire copy, we knew nothing. But even when an assignment doesn't thrill you, work it, anyway. That particular day, my motivation had a lot to do with trying to prove the boss wrong.

The suspect had led police through five counties and more than a dozen small cities. I telephoned detectives in every one of them. Nobody told me much. Cops tend to confirm only as much as you know, and then, maybe, tell a little more.

Still, when a reporter spends three hours asking questions, one piece of information leads to another. If he's lucky, the puzzle pieces click together and a picture emerges. That's what happened with this story.

One detective disclosed that the suspect had been driving a stolen green Ford Explorer. A second officer, from another city, boasted that his department's auto theft task force played a key role in making the arrest.

"But the chase began thirty miles south of you, in San Jose," I mentioned.

"It was a stakeout."

"A stolen vehicle stakeout?"

"Can't say."

"Is that a good guess?"

"That's a good guess. And I've told you too much already."

I called a third detective in another city. "So, we know it was a stakeout and a stolen truck, but who owned it?"

"Peninsula Ford," he said casually.

Bingo. He'd opened the door. I could call the dealer, ask questions, and, most important, extract firsthand information from someone other than a police officer. I rang Peninsula Ford and spoke with the sales manager, Elliott Negron. "That's our truck, no doubt," he said. "I knew it when I saw it on the news."

"Were you surprised?"

"We already knew something was going down."

"And why is that?"

Negron explained how the Explorer had disappeared two nights earlier. "The thieves cracked the key out of the lock box and drove it off the lot."

"That has to be maddening."

"We're getting used to it," he said. "Local dealerships have lost twenty cars that way in the last month."

"Dealerships? As in, more than one?"

"You don't know about this?"

With that, the puzzle began to take shape. No wonder the police hadn't said much. "You're saying that when they stopped that suspect in your truck last night . . ."

"Yeah," finished Negron. "They busted a stolen car ring."

Suddenly, the story wasn't just about a police chase anymore. "Can you clear something up?" I asked. "Why did the chase of your stolen truck begin thirty miles south, in San Jose?"

"That's the other part of this. I have a mechanic with sharp eyes."

"Tell me more."

"Well, he knew about the thefts. Everybody did." Negron described how thieves had stolen so many cars from so many dealers that their "inventory" exceeded both manpower and storage space. Sometimes they would heist a car, leave it in the neighborhood, and pick it up later.

Enter Negron's mechanic, who took a lunchtime walk and spotted what looked like a new Chevrolet sitting on a side street. The mechanic informed Negron, who called the police, who confirmed the car as stolen. Inside its glove box they found a receipt from a San Jose hotel. Detectives drove down, looked around, and found a fleet of stolen cars in the parking lot. They set up their stakeout, and when the bad guys returned later that night, our 110-mile car chase began.

It was basic connect-the-dots reporting, but the exercise reminded me of how stories can be interesting on several levels. What began as a one-line item about an extraordinarily long chase became a tale of stolen cars, persistent cops, and, best of all, a little guy, the sharp-eyed mechanic, who set events in motion. If we wanted to push the piece further, we could have added the element of a twenty-seven-year-old suspect who'd bounced in and out of jail since age eighteen because of a drug habit.

That's a story with universal appeal and a little something for everyone. I must grudgingly and respectfully acknowledge that my news director had darn good instincts.

Look at the Bigger Picture

Galaxy 4

Do you remember a communications satellite called Galaxy 4? In 1998, it malfunctioned, causing many Americans to lose their wireless communications. Until then, most of us had taken our devices and emails for granted. Galaxy 4 changed that. Its loss of signal left us technologically exposed. For a culture still coming of age in an era of connectivity, this marked an uncomfortable first.

As did most media outlets, KGO-TV covered the basics of Galaxy 4's failure. We explained how the satellite worked, described the problem, and explored solutions.

I began the story by visiting San Francisco's financial district. "How's your email?" I pointedly asked one man.

"Smoke signals would work better right now," he said.

Beyond the who, what, when, where, and why of our inconveniences, Galaxy 4 led me to examine our newfound reliance upon technology. Was this story about a broken satellite, or also about us? It seemed to me that, until recently, the human race had managed just fine without wireless communication, and I had a small piece of local knowledge to make the point.

Fifteen years earlier, I had purchased a mattress from San Francisco's McRoskey Airflex Company. When it eventually wore out, I remembered telephoning the company to ask about a replacement. In seconds, the receptionist quoted what model I had bought, the date of purchase, the warranty, and the price. "That's a fast computer," I remarked to her.

"We don't have computers." Nor, she added, did the company use email, voicemail, printers, terminals, or pagers. Nothing. In ninety-nine years of business, the McRoskey Airflex Company never felt a need to modernize. Employees still filed paper receipts, used carbon copies, and alphabetized customer information on three-by-five cards.

When Galaxy 4 failed, I called McRoskey Airflex again and spoke with the same receptionist. "What does Galaxy 4 mean to you?"

"Nothing," she said.

That day, we rounded out the basic news story by visiting the mattress company and showing its fault-free, low-tech methods. While Galaxy 4 knocked the rest of us back to the 1960s, McRoskey Airflex remained unaffected. Our comparison and contrast treatment told the specifics of a broken satellite, and also addressed how much we rely on technology.

What People Take Away:
Sometimes, A Good Story Can be About Something Else

"The Lawn"

Sometime, somewhere, you must have played the telephone game. One person whispers in the ear of another, who then passes that message to the next person, who passes it again, and on down the line. By the time the message goes full circle and comes back to you, it has often taken on another meaning or context because every person put a slightly different spin on it.

Based on the telephone game, you shouldn't be surprised that no two viewers approach or interpret any news story the exact same way. They pick up shades, tones, and build on them. Where one person might see a piece as a straightforward description of events, another might find humor in it. Skillful reporters work this to their advantage. *They recognize that a good story can sometimes be about something else.*

This theory works particularly well for feature reporting. There is no better example than the segment I did in 1999 after assignment editor Bill Magee brought a press release to my desk. "I don't know if this is a story or not," he said. "It has a public relations element, but you might find an angle." He was right.

That release came from a fertilizer company, and announced the winners of a national lawn contest. Lo and behold, a second-place winner lived in our viewing area—one of ten second-place winners, I should note, and most of them just happened to reside in major television markets. It was a blatant commercial ploy, but before throwing that press release in the trash, I remembered a neighbor who had been a compulsive lawn addict. Have you ever lived next to one? If our local second-place "winner" was at all like my neighbor, then there might be a story. I played the hunch and made a call.

Our second-place winner's name was Ralph Gillibert. His lawn, in nearby Oakland, did not disappoint us. It measured twenty-by-twenty feet and blazed green beyond golden light dreams. One could safely say that Ralph's lawn made artificial turf look ragged by comparison. In just describing it, I still have not done it justice.

That lawn was so grand, so magnificent, that it had become a neighborhood tourist attraction. When nearby residents hosted company, they routinely brought those people by for special viewings. Photographer John Griffin and I watched as one group of visitors stood piously in front of Ralph's meticulously painted fence. They peered, pointed, gawked, said, "Ooh," then, "Ahh," and snapped pictures.

You would think they were visiting the Sistine Chapel of grass. Ralph certainly treated it that way. When he trimmed the edges, he got down on his hands and knees, and used scissors. When he mowed, he did so based not on the day of the week or the time of day, but on the position of the sun.

Even Ralph's dog gave the lawn deferential treatment. The pooch never set a paw on it. Ralph had trained him to circle around.

Only Ralph's wife of thirty-four years, Alice, had yet to become completely subservient to that grass. Actually, it may have been the other way around. Early in their relationship, Alice Gillibert recognized she had married an obsessive perfectionist. "Dinner must be ready precisely at six," Alice told us. "We must finish by six-thirty."

She recalled an incident in which Ralph yanked a dessert fork from her hand during a meal. "It was time to wash the dishes," she said he said.

Maybe it was then that Alice decided she could either fight Ralph's tendencies, or deal with them. That's where the lawn entered in. "It's a good place for him," Alice told us.

John Griffin and I quickly recognized that Alice Gillibert would play a big part in this story. We shot it as a give-and-take, moving between Alice in her kitchen and Ralph in his yard. Outside, he patiently explained the merits of mowing patterns at optimal blade settings of three-eighths of an inch. Inside, Alice showed wedding pictures and described the trials of life with Ralph. In terms of personality, the two of them were polar opposites—a perfect match, and they played off it. Thanks to the Gillibert's honesty and humor, we took an award-winning lawn and used it as the centerpiece of a character study:

The Lawn
November 1999

IF OUR LAWNS WERE CHILDREN, MOST OF US WOULD BE
DELINQUENT PARENTS.

THEY'RE THE WAYWARD STUFF OF BEST INTENTIONS
GONE TO SEED, OR AS RALPH GILLIBERT WOULD SAY . . .

(SOT)
Ralph Gillibert: "Goat pasture."

*We see Ralph on his hands and knees, edging his lawn with
a small scissors*

IF THOSE WHO LIVE IN GLASS HOUSES SHOULD NOT THROW
STONES, THIS IS A MAN WITH EVERY RIGHT TO BE CRITICAL.
HERE, IN A TWENTY-BY-TWENTY-FOOT SECTION IN FRONT
OF HIS OAKLAND HOME, RALPH SEEKS NOTHING LESS THAN
BLESSED PERFECTION.

(SOT)
Wayne: "ISN'T THIS SCISSOR BIT A LITTLE OVER-THE-TOP?"

Ralph: "Quiet. I'm concentrating . . ."

YOUR BARBER SHOULD BE AS METICULOUS.

YOUR MATE AS PATIENT.

(SOT)
Wayne asks Alice: "HE'S A PLANNER, AND YOU'RE A . . . ?"

Alice: "Procrastinator."

HE'S A NEAT FREAK. SHE'S . . .

(SOT)
Alice: "Loose."

HE'S REGIMENTED. SHE'S . . .

(SOT)
Alice: "Casual."

We see their wedding picture

RALPH AND ALICE ARE A CLASSIC EXAMPLE OF OPPOSITES
STILL ATTRACTING AFTER THIRTY-FOUR YEARS.

HOW COULD SHE HAVE KNOWN THAT,
WHEN SHE MARRIED THE MAN,
SHE WOULD SHARE HIM WITH A LAWN?

(SOT)
Alice interrupts: "Every day. Every day he's working on the
lawn . . ."

(SOT)
Wayne to Ralph: "WHAT LENGTH OF BLADE DO YOU USE?"

Ralph: "Three-eighths of an inch."

Wayne: "EXACTLY?"

Ralph: "Exactly."

(SOT)
In the kitchen

Wayne to Alice: "WHAT IF A NEIGHBOR COMES BY WALKING
HIS DOG, AND THE DOG GETS LOOSE?"

Alice: "Heeeh! That would be serious."

IF LAWN CARE EVER BECOMES AN EXTREME SPORT,
RALPH WILL QUALIFY.

TO KEEP AN EYE ON IT, HE RARELY TAKES LONG VACATIONS.

TO PROTECT IT DURING DROUGHTS, HE DUG A WELL.

AND, WHEN NEIGHBORS HAVE COMPANY, THEY BRING THEM
BY TO LOOK WHILE ALSO KEEPING A RESPECTFUL DISTANCE.

(SOT)
Alice points to the bricks that surround the lawn: "Our own dog
walks around the bricks . . ."

Wayne walks the bricks surrounding the lawn

. . . OR ANYONE. IF "POINT A" IS ON ONE SIDE . . . AND "POINT
B" ON THE OTHER, AN AVERAGE PERSON WOULDN'T EVEN
CONSIDER TAKING A DIRECT ROUTE . . .

(STAND-UP)
Wide shot: Wayne stands on the bricks, looking at the lawn

TO DO SO WOULD SEEM . . . SACRILEGIOUS.

(SOT)
Cut to a tight shot of Wayne's shoe. Its toe extends onto the grass. He snaps it back

(SOT)
Wayne to Ralph: "IF SOMEBODY WALKS ON THIS LAWN, IT BOTHERS, YOU, DOESN'T IT?"

Ralph: "Not really. Depends on who it is."

Wayne: "OK, LET'S SAY A SUMO WRESTLER WALKED ON YOUR LAWN."

Ralph: "No, I wouldn't like that."

BUT IF YOU LOOK AT IT, THERE'S A LITTLE OF RALPH'S YARDENING OBSESSION IN EVERY ONE OF US. WE ALL HAVE QUIRKS. MOST OF US WANT TO DO AT LEAST ONE THING REALLY WELL . . .

(SOT)
Wayne to Ralph: "IS THERE REALLY SUCH A THING AS A PERFECT LAWN?"

Ralph: "I don't believe so. I've never seen one."

BUT HE'S CLOSER THAN HE THINKS BECAUSE, SEVERAL MONTHS AGO, ALICE READ AN ADVERTISEMENT FOR A NATIONAL LAWN CONTEST . . .

(SOT)
Alice: "I took the pictures of it and filled out the forms."

AND RALPH WON. IT WAS NOTHING LESS THAN A BENEDICTION. HE GOT A T-SHIRT, 250 DOLLARS CASH, AND BRAGGING RIGHTS BECAUSE NOW IT'S OFFICIAL . . .

RALPH GILLIBERT'S LAWN FINISHED BEST IN THE WEST.

(SOT)
As Ralph sits on his lawn, Wayne asks: "WAS THERE A POINT IN YOUR LIFE WHEN YOU MIGHT HAVE KNOWN YOU'D GONE OVER THE TOP WITH THIS?"

Ralph: "No." (laughs) "It just snuck up on me."

Wayne: "WELL, IT'S A BEAUTIFUL LAWN."

Ralph replies with dignity: "Thank-you very much."

AND MAYBE THAT'S ALL HE EVER REALLY WANTED. NOTHING LIKE A COMPLIMENT TO KEEP A MAN HAPPILY MOWING INTO THE SUNSET.

Write Up To Your Viewers

Viewers still mention Ralph and Alice from time to time, which is satisfying. It's nice to hear compliments on stories, especially when so many viewers complain about the news. They resent being told how to feel or what to take away from a segment. They appreciate "The Lawn" because it allows them to decide for themselves.

I have shown "The Lawn" to groups of regular people and professionals many times, and always make a point to ask them what it was about. Answers range from obsession, to marriage, to patience, to the attraction of opposites. All are correct.

No one, yet, has suggested that the story is about an immaculate lawn.

CHAPTER 21

Finding Unique Stories:
Just Ask, Look, Listen, and Think

If you haven't heard of Fred Medill, someday you will. At fourteen years old, he had already become a force of nature.

Some kids play baseball with their fathers. Others go fishing. Not Fred Medill and his dad Carey. They hung around Hollywood red carpets with the paparazzi. "Maybe you could say we're fishing for a few celebs," Carey suggested.

The Medills' Tinseltown adventures began when Fred requested a star-studded home video to celebrate his bar mitzvah. Carey, a Beverly Hills attorney, obliged by scoring interviews for him with Neil Sedaka, George Foreman, and Cameron Diaz. After young Fred's experience with her, in particular, he was hooked. He declared himself to be an entertainment reporter, and his father, a photographer. From then on, after homework two or three nights a week, father and son joined the gaggles of Hollywood press watching stars, starlets, and wannabe stars and starlets preening, posing, and passing at movie premieres.

Give the youngster credit for being a fast learner. "They're just here to be seen and photographed," said Fred of the celebrities. "Some of them don't even know the name of the movie."

But they did know Fred, who was five feet, four inches tall and didn't even shave yet. He had a knack for leaning in, looking cute, stretching out his microphone, and getting the beautiful people to talk. Of Tom Cruise he once asked, "When you go on vacation, do you and Nicole take the kids with?"

Talk about chutzpah—as a ninth grader, Fred Medill notched an exclusive interview with President Bill Clinton next to Air Force One. "Do you think the new generation of American youth is more apathetic to the political fervor that existed in your time?"

"No," replied the president. Interview over. Fred used it.

Once a week, he would download his interviews into a home computer and host his own webcast called Fred TV. What Fred lacked in ratings, he gained in experience.

In December 1999, KABC-TV photographer David Busse and I followed Fred around for a day. I remember asking this remarkable young man about what his adventures had taught him about life and reporting. "Just ask," said Fred, "because you never know what's going to come of it. Even if they say no, it never hurts. Just ask."

That's darn good advice for any journalist, whether he's fourteen and collecting movie stars, or forty and looking to do a segment for the evening news.

They're On to Us

It's challenging for reporters to find original, memorable stories five days a week. Anyone who pretends otherwise isn't telling the truth. Most reporters are naturally curious, but we tend to get tunnel vision when focusing on the next daily deadline.

Avoid that trap. We need to take responsibility for at least some of our assignments. The stories we choose define us as reporters, and our industry as a whole. For the viewers to respect us, we must respect them. When you wonder why television news is losing audience shares, look at your coworkers, your competitors across the street, and perhaps at yourself.

If, as critics say, television news caters to the lowest common denominator, it is partly because we have driven many of the smartest people away. They're on to us. Every day, we cast the seeds of our own irrelevance. Some of us have become like Chicken Little shouting, "The sky is falling!" If all you knew of life came from certain television news broadcasts, you could easily believe we live in a frightening, dangerous world. You might not want to risk going outside, even in daylight.

To serve our viewers, we need to do more stories about issues, substantive politics, and that neighborhood around the corner. I also believe strongly that television news stories should be observational. Even though most of our viewers never make headlines, they live noble, interesting lives. Stories about their relatively minor concerns, quandaries, struggles, and victories can be rich in simple truths and universal appeal.

Granted, television news is a mainstream medium intended for a general audience, but let's try to expand the envelope. Take some risks. Everyone likes surprises, even viewers. If we don't shake up the format once in a while, then why should we expect them to come back regularly?

Find Your Own Stories

You will find good stories as a by-product of listening, reading, using your common sense, and following your own interests. Look around. What are people talking about? What are they writing about? What are they wondering about? What are you wondering about?

When you ask questions and pay attention, story ideas begin to connect. One day's work can provide research for the next. While shooting a piece about teenage pilots, for instance, a woman mentioned in casual conversation how she had purchased a ticket on a new, regional, one-plane airline. That story, in turn, led to another about an eighty-year-old former stewardess.

The same process works with follow-up stories. For instance, when unemployment peaked during the 2009 recession, I covered a massive "boot camp" for laid-off workers who met to exchange contacts, strategies, and mutual support. While there, I found an even better story in John Henion, an out-of-work Gen-X writer who had started a seriously funny blog, http://UnemployMentality.com.

What began as a way to pass the time became a new enterprise generating tens of thousands of hits a week.

Emails: Little Kabul

You can find many good stories in the letters and emails that viewers send to your station. Look through them as often as possible.

During the war in Afghanistan, residents of Fremont, a suburban city south of San Francisco, complained about how the media referred a small stretch of Afghan-owned storefronts and restaurants as "Little Kabul." One viewer wrote, "That section of town is in Fremont, and it will always be Fremont. Why did the media change the name?"

The media didn't. After a couple of telephone calls I learned that those Afghan merchants gave the name "Little Kabul" to themselves, and we, the media sheep, simply repeated it. Those emails led to a segment that exposed the controversy, and explored how names or labels needlessly divide people.

Newspapers and Other Outlets: The "No-Swear" Lady

Every day, television news reporters adapt stories from newspapers, the Internet, and other outlets. We may resent those ideas when managers force them upon us, but who says we must follow a print story as originally written? Instead, use the article as a starting place or tip sheet. Those items often contain the seeds for new angles and better stories.

I recall reading one piece about minor league baseball in California's Central Valley. It made passing reference to a "no-swear lady" who attended games and chided players for saying dirty words. Whoever she was, the "no-swear lady" appeared to be an intriguing character. I made a couple of calls to teams and found her in Visalia, California.

True to the article, Helen Luttrell sat behind the first base dugout at every Visalia Oaks home game. She always brought along a loud voice, a squirt bottle, a pail, and a brush. "The brush is for filthy language. When they swear, I tell 'em I'll wash their mouths out with soap like their grandmothers would do."

Can you imagine?

Helen's late husband had been a baseball fan, too. After he died, she continued attending every home game, and with renewed conviction, apparently.

I asked her a baited question. "What exactly do you define as a filthy word?"

Helen fixed me with a stern look. "You know darn well what a filthy word is. I don't have to tell you." It was absurd. Swearing comes to baseball players as casually as tobacco chewing, spitting, and crotch scratching. Helen Luttrell might as well have gone to a church and asked the preacher not to preach.

As interesting as the day had been, so far, it got even weirder when Rick Burleson, who managed a rival team, walked by. Helen did not like him. More specifically, she made Burleson out to be the devil incarnate. He did not care much for her, either.

Their feud had begun two years earlier. Burleson's squad gave up six runs in one inning, prompting him to make more than a few loud, indelicate remarks. Helen heard every detail. "If he used the f-word once, he used it twenty times," she said. "The way he yelled at his team made me want to cry. They're just boys."

She made a point of telling him so, loudly.

Burleson, a seasoned ex–big leaguer, had little patience for Helen's bucket, her soap, her brush, her opinions, or her mouth. He stepped from the dugout, stared up at her in the stands, and said in a way that everyone could hear, "Ma'am, mind your own damn business."

What gall! Helen wrote an angry letter to the league, which forwarded it to Burleson, and that sealed their grudge. From then on, whenever his team came to town, Helen Luttrell dogged Rick Burleson. They refused to make up.

More specifically, he ignored her. "I walk to the other side of the dugout so I won't have to listen to her," said Burleson.

"You could make peace with him," I suggested to Helen.

"No, he's the one who should come to me and apologize."

Burleson wouldn't talk of reconciliation. I asked him, "If a man can't play baseball and say a dirty word or two, what good is the game?"

"I dunno," he said.

We presented the story as a major league feud in a minor league setting. "He won't even look at me," said Helen, with hurt in her eyes.

"Maybe if she brought me cookies, or something," suggested Burleson.

Not likely. And yet, from one line in a newspaper article, we found a human interest story with a poignant simple truth. Helen Luttrell merely wanted a small amount of attention and a place in the game. When she crossed the invisible line that separates fans from players, she went too far.

In the words of Rick Burleson, she should have minded her own damn business.

Ask A Question Stories

Most reporters are inquisitive. Not all of them bring it to their work. They separate personal interests from professional ones. They may see something and wonder about it, never realizing how, by asking a question, they might turn that curiosity into a story.

My favorite "ask a question" story came about during my first year of marriage. Like many other newlywed males, I said and did a lot of clueless stuff, which left me needing to apologize to my wife quite often. Usually, I did so by purchasing flowers from a small sidewalk stand along Union Street in San Francisco.

There, a hip young lady sold twenty-dollar bouquets while, four feet away, on the other side of a picture window, a very classy thirty-something woman worked in a real estate office, selling million-dollar homes. Four feet—they spent their days so close to each other that I always assumed they'd met.

They hadn't.

One evening, during a casual conversation, my flower selling friend admitted she wasn't even sure of the real estate woman's name.

"Really?" That sounded odd. I went inside and spoke with the real estate woman. She didn't know the flower lady's name, either.

"That's fascinating," I told her. "Don't change anything just because I asked, but would you mind if I bring a camera and do a story about the two of you, sometime?"

"Give a call if you want."

More than a few news managers have said, "There are no slow news days, just slow news reporters." Well, the very next day really was slow, so I pitched that flower stand to our managers in the morning meeting. My bosses approved the idea, and quickly. There are no slow news managers, apparently.

The story I produced with photographer Pam Partee had nothing to do with traditional news, and everything with a simple truth, universal appeal theme— that in a big city, the closer we are to some of our neighbors, the more distance we may need:

Strangers
July 1991

(SOT)
Cynthia, the real estate woman, on phone: "I'm calling for Stephen Clark . . ."

CYNTHIA CUMMINS IS INTENSE AND PROFESSIONAL.

SHE LIVES IN A WORLD OF BIDS, ESCROWS, AND CLOSURES.

A BUSINESS LIFE OF APPOINTMENT BOOK INCREMENTS.

(SOT)
Cynthia says: "Well, today my calendar is just completely booked."

(SOT)
Outside we see Carol handing flowers to a customer:

"These are two dollars a stem. They came in this morning and are really fresh . . ."

CAROL GRAMADOS IS LIGHT AND BREEZY.
HER'S IS A WORLD OF BUDS AND STEMS AND BLOOMS.
A BUSINESS LIFE BASED ON WHIMSY.

(SOT)
Carol says to customer: "And thank you . . ."

THEY'RE TWO WOMEN, IN TWO DIFFERENT WORLDS
SEPARATED BY JUST FOUR FEET AND A PANE OF GLASS.

(SOT)
We pan from Carol outside to Cynthia, still talking on the phone: "You haven't heard from her yet?"

(SOT)
Carol: "Sometimes we smile, once in a while."

Wayne: "ANYTHING ELSE?"

Carol: "No."

(SOT)
Inside the office

Cynthia: "When I'm in here it's important that I concentrate on what I'm doing. So I really have to tune her out."

(STAND-UP)
On the street

IF YOU LOOK AROUND, YOU MAY FIND A CAROL OR CYNTHIA
IN ALL OUR LIVES. MAYBE WE PASS THEM ON A HIGHWAY
OR SHARE AN ELEVATOR WITH THEM.

MAYBE THEY EVEN LIVE RIGHT NEXT DOOR.
IT'S ALMOST AS IF THE CLOSER WE ARE TO SOMEONE,
THE MORE DISTANCE WE NEED.

(SOT)
Cynthia: "I think that's typical of life today.
Most people don't even have a pane of glass between them.
They're just sitting next to each other in an office or on the bus.
I mean, how much do any of us know about each other?"

CAROL AND CYNTHIA HAVE NEVER BEEN FORMALLY
INTRODUCED, EVEN THOUGH THEY'VE WORKED
WITHIN FOUR FEET OF EACH OTHER ABOUT TWO YEARS NOW—
ONE SELLING TEN-DOLLAR BOUQUETS,
AND THE OTHER, MILLION-DOLLAR HOMES.
THAT MUCH, WE KNOW.

(SOT)
Carol: "She's married. She works there. She's been there a long
time."

(SOT)
Cynthia: "Well I think she's a teenager. And she's very sociable.
She has a lot of friends who come by . . ."

(SOT)
Carol: "She's into her work and I'm into mine. She's really quiet
and . . ."

(SOT)
Cynthia: " . . . Sometimes she plays her music a little loud and I
have to knock on the window and motion to turn it down."

NOW THE BIG QUESTION . . .

(SOT)
Wayne asks Carol: "DO YOU KNOW THE NAME OF
THE WOMAN IN THERE?"

Carol: "Cynthia."

(SOT)
Wayne asks Cynthia: "DO YOU KNOW THE NAME OF
THE WOMAN OUTSIDE?"

Cynthia: "No."

CYNTHIA AND CAROL. SUCH FAMILIAR STRANGERS.
JUST AN OBSERVATION ABOUT LIFE IN THE BIG CITY.

(SOT)
Wayne to Cynthia: "YOU DON'T KNOW WHERE SHE LIVES
OR ANYTHING ABOUT HER FAMILY?"

Cynthia: "No."

Wayne: "DO YOU WONDER?"

Cynthia: "I do now. But I think I better bone up."

The Red House

My family lives on a ridge in San Anselmo, California. It's a nice house perched along environmental open space. We would like to paint it different color, but our planning commission dictates the guidelines. Only natural and bland will do.

We abide by the rules, however, so a few years ago my family and neighbors couldn't help but notice when, on an opposite ridge filled with equally bland homes, someone painted his house bright barn red. "It's a crimson eyesore," the neighbors said.

My daughter, Lauren, was three years old at the time. "Why did he do that, Daddy?"

"Because he's a goofball." We had a big laugh and, from then on, referred to the red house as "the Goofball House."

Lauren had posed a good question, though—the most important one—"Why?" From that moment on, we just had to know. My daughter and I drove to the bottom of the red house's long driveway, left a note in the mailbox, and waited.

The next day, a man named Claude Reboul called. "Yes, I own the red house," he announced in a thick French accent.

"We were wondering why you painted it red."

"I cannot give you a straight answer. There is no such thing as a straight answer in life," said Claude.

A few days later, he proved it. Photographer Charlie Jones and I visited Reboul and found him to be a robust seventy-six years old, going on twenty-six. And, he was anything but a goofball. Claude loved life to the point that he even insisted on popping a bottle of champagne to celebrate our meeting. "I live just outside the city lines," he explained. "I can paint my house any color. I can paint my house white. I can paint my house fluorescent green. I can paint my house orange-orange!"

As Claude explained, he'd painted it red in memory of his wife, Edith, with whom he'd spent forty-four years before her recent death. And that only began his story.

Claude Reboul grew up in France before World War II. When the Nazis invaded, he joined the underground movement. Before long, Claude dreamed of fighting Germans while wearing the uniform of the Free French, so he crossed the Pyrenees on foot. "It took twelve nights and thirteen days. I escaped from France and walked to Spain."

"You make it sound like a stroll through the park."

"Well, when you are sixteen years old, it is fun!"

Once in Spain, Claude surrendered to authorities, who put him in a prison he describes as more of a resort and a bureaucratic formality. The allies needed soldiers. Spain needed food. In return for one hundred pounds of flour, the Spanish traded Claude to the Free French, who sent him to Corpus Christi, Texas, for pilot training. Claude's first flight changed his life. "The instructor took me upside down, and I looked up, and there was a train above me!"

"You were hooked?"

"Completely."

The war ended before Claude could fire a shot. He made his way to New York City, intending to take a ship home, but fate intervened once again. Just before the scheduled departure, Claude met Edith. The ship sailed. Claude stayed. He married her and lived happily ever after in the United States.

Finally, as we walked around outside, I asked the direct question. "Specifically, Claude, what is it about red?"

"Her favorite color," he answered. "Red is the color of joy and happiness. Look at the gold of the hills. Look at the blue sky. Look how beautiful it is. Red!"

It seemed we'd found our answer, but the day held one more surprise because my wife, daughter, and I had noticed one other strange feature about the red house. Every Sunday afternoon, a small airplane flew from a nearby airport, and buzzed the house in low circles. We'd always wondered about that. After Claude told his story, I think I knew why.

"Is that you, Claude?"

"Well, of course!"

"That's the other reason?"

"So I can see my house!"

We asked a question, and found a story. Claude Reboul taught us a lesson about how one turn in life leads to another, and how men become the sum of their experiences.

A teenager.

A war.

A lifetime adventure.

A red house on a hill.

CHAPTER 22

One Story, Start to Finish

High-wire acrobats and television news reporters have plenty in common. Acrobats take risks every time they go to work. Reporters take risks every time they push a deadline.

Acrobats cannot function effectively without confidence.

Neither can reporters.

If an acrobat slips or loses his balance, he knows instinctively where to catch the wire and save himself. When a reporter slips while working a story, he "catches the wire," too, but in an editorial way.

For both the acrobat and the reporter, failure is not an option.

New York City to Ground Zero

That describes my challenge in New York City in the fall of 2001. A month after the September 11 attacks, KGO-TV photographer Michael Clark and I had just crossed the nation by train. As news of terrorist threats and anthrax scares dominated a grieving nation, we'd picked small communities at random and found nine small stories reflecting the much bigger one. Did the attacks change people? Could normal life still exist? Had the experience pushed Americans further apart, or pulled them closer together? Later, *Stories from the Heartland* became an award winning half-hour special.

In keeping with the trip's sense of unplanned discovery, Mike and I had only vague ideas about what we would do for our New York City story. We figured we would visit Ground Zero, among other places, to see what we would find, and that was about it. How naïve. We conveniently forgot that New York City is more complicated than, say, Mount Pleasant, Iowa. We didn't know the local geography. As a reporter from out of town, I had no name or face recognition, nor the home-field connections for gaining access.

Mike and I did have an expense account, however, so we ditched the rental car and hired a limousine. If that sounds extravagant, follow my logic. The limo would cost less than keeping a taxi all day. The driver would know his way around town, we wouldn't have to find parking, and because he would be working for us, we could use his trunk to store equipment. Should we require more gear or need to move quickly, we could do so easily.

Here, then, is what happened as we searched for a story at Ground Zero. The experience reinforces many lessons in this book, from characterization, to interviewing, to following spontaneous leads, to creating your own luck, to reporting what you find, to writing, structure, simple truths, and universal appeal. When you read the script, you'll see what we discarded, what we kept, and how the story came together.

Police State

The car met us at ten in the morning and delivered us into heavy financial-district congestion one hour later. With every passing block, the neighborhood surrounding Ground Zero looked more like a police state. Howard Price, the assignment manager at our sister station, WABC-TV, had said to expect as much: "There's plenty of security, but it leaks like a sieve."

Police and military guarded every intersection. They scrutinized buses, trucks, and people. We carried San Francisco and California press credentials, but nothing from New York City. Mike and I gambled that we could walk and talk our way in.

"We're from ABC in San Francisco," Mike or I would tell police.

"Where's your identification?" they would ask.

"Sir, we've traveled across the country by train, stopped in small towns along the way, and now we have one day left in New York. We can spend it in bureaucracy or we can try to find a story. Do we look like terrorists?"

This worked, several times.

Ten blocks from Ground Zero, our car could approach no closer, so we exchanged mobile telephone numbers with the driver, left him to orbit the area, and set out on foot.

Possible Stories Everywhere

When beginning this kind of shoot, your story is like a blank canvas. Whatever you see and hear has potential. You're looking for a focus, a thread, a theme, a main character. Like that wirewalker, you rely on your confidence. "See what you can find" stories move you around like waves or gusts of wind. Catch them. Ride them. See where they take you. Trust your curiosity.

Within two blocks, we came upon a basketball court surrounded by a chainlink fence. Inspectors had attached a note to it declaring the area free from asbestos contamination. That seemed a bit odd, so Michael took pictures. Inside, young men played a pick-up game. We were ten blocks from a mass grave, and they could turn their backs on the tragedy to shoot hoops. Why?

"We've got to move on with our lives," explained Anthony Torres while taking a break. "We can't stay depressed."

A second kid, Demetrius Padmore, joined in. "If we sit here and mourn, they get the best of us, you know?"

Both comments made good sound bites. I hoped they might say even more, and tried to push the first kid, Anthony, to another level. "Let's say you got Osama bin Laden in a room, just you and him, one-on-one . . ."

He cleared his throat. He stammered. His gentle face turned hard and mean. He paused, and said with resolve, "I'd end him."

A Look Inside

We moved on, keeping close to Ground Zero's fenced-off, guarded perimeter. The place looked more like a demolition zone than the scene of a terrorist attack. Construction cranes performed a repetitious ballet against a backdrop of ripped, torn, and gutted buildings. American flags billowed from poles and hung from facades. Workmen wore the stars and stripes on hats and clothes.

"Is there a better vantage point for looking inside?" I asked a policeman.

"Keep going that way," he pointed. We moved along, passing through temporary barricades that seemed to stretch for miles.

By now, you have certainly seen pictures of Ground Zero's destruction. They don't do justice to the width, the depth, or the tickling sensation from a fine dust that coated the backs of our throats. September 11 turned the World Trade

Center into a ghost city of eerily empty skyscrapers with chained and padlocked revolving doors.

Photographically, Michael couldn't miss.

We spotted a few civilians wandering around. The WABC-TV assignment manager had said, "It's become a tourist attraction," but this wasn't like any other tourist attraction you've ever visited. It did not have the slightest hint of commercialism. No one hawked souvenirs. No one acted loud, rude, or disrespectful. These "tourists" walked quietly, and spoke solemnly.

We approached several people, but nobody cared to talk until Rose and Bob Lamano, from Bedford, Virginia, kindly gave us a few minutes. "I grew up in New York," she said. "I never expected such a large area. To me, it's a little like stepping on holy land. I just felt like I wanted to be here."

Bob finished. "Initially, I didn't want to come here at all. It was like an invasion of privacy for those who died, but it's something we wanted to see to make us stronger. I just feel for all the people who lost loved ones, is all I can say."

After the Lamanos wandered away, Mike and I hiked along the Hudson River until we rounded a corner roughly one hundred yards from what used to be the World Trade Center's atrium. Above and beyond, we stared at blue sky where the Twin Towers had stood before September 11. It looked like a friendly, familiar face, only with the teeth knocked out.

"Hard to believe they used to be there," I remarked.

"Yep," Mike said.

The Story Finds Us

Often, when doing this kind of piece, a storyline will find you if you remain open to it. Thus far, we'd come across useful material, but nothing exceptional. Then we noticed a disheveled, frenetic woman taking pictures of the gap between the buildings. "There?" I asked in confirmation, hoping for a conversation.

"Behind that last arch," she pointed. "To the south of that crane was a tower. No hole. No hole. No death."

The woman's name was Deborah Ortega. She used to live in the neighborhood and still considered Ground Zero as home. "Were you here on September 11?" I asked.

As if bearing witness, Deborah pulled a well-thumbed photo album from under her arm and turned page after page of pictures showing the burning skyscrapers. "This is what we saw from the window," she said, pointing to a photo of the second tower. "I show these to people and tell them that this is my home, and this is my view, and then they kind of get it."

Deborah Ortega needed people to understand what she and her neighbors had survived, and continued to endure. She spoke of the destroyed World Trade Center the way others might describe a divorce or a dead family member. "I try to come back as much as I can just to get used to the idea of this place as it is now."

"Sounds like you have a lot of baggage . . ."

"Big baggage," she nodded through blinking, teary eyes. Deborah had a lost look on her face. It froze me. As happens so often, she took that as a cue to open up. "I saw about twenty people fall from those towers, and I felt like such a coward as I rode my bike away and knew I couldn't help them. But then I felt so bad for them up there. You could see them at the windows and see them wanting to get out. And we knew this was not a Bruce Willis movie where everything ends so happily, you know?"

As Deborah spoke, I recognized that this could provide a pivotal moment in our story—one which we might build to, or else from. Deborah Ortega was definitely a person worth following. "What are your plans for today?" I asked.

"Helping a friend move."

"From where?"

"Up there." Deborah pointed to an apartment tower across the street. "She lives on the thirty-second floor. You can see everything from there."

With Deborah Ortega, our piece began to take shape. In addition to being a good character, she was an insider who would take us deeper into Ground Zero than any press pass.

"Will your friend talk to us?" I asked.

"I'll call." Deborah dug a telephone from her purse and handed it over. After a few minutes of gentle persuasion her friend, Anita Glesta, invited us up.

"This way." Deborah hurried us along, never pausing or even looking as we came upon a mountain of teddy bears, flowers, and photographs. Emotionally, it stopped Mike and me cold. That memorial must have been shoulder high and seventy-five feet long. Those teddy bears, piled on top of each other, might as well have been bodies. In a visual way, Mike and I then understood how many people died in the Twin Towers on September 11. It was the first time I had seen teddy bears used as a memorial. They made a sobering tribute.

Deborah, understandably, did not want to dwell there, or even look. "We have to go now," she said. "Anita's almost finished with the movers."

One Story, Start to Finish **279**

Mike wanted to stay and shoot a sequence, but doing so might have meant losing Deborah. Besides, we could return later. She led us past a barricade, through a courtyard filled with chirping birds, then a building, and finally into an elevator. As the door closed, an officious apartment worker tried to force his way in with us. "Who the hell are you? You're not allowed in this building!" he protested.

I felt protective of Deborah Ortega, and also of our story. "We're the news. Who are you?" Deborah explained that he was the assistant building manager. She said he had ignored her for a month, until that moment.

"You'll have to leave," the assistant manager said. "You need written permission before entering the building."

I didn't buy it. "You don't know the law, do you? A resident invited us. That's all we need. You're way out of line. Now smile for the camera." He stammered in mild protest as the elevator door closed.

A Second Main Character

Deborah's friend, Anita Glesta, was an artist, a mother of twin boys, and looked the parts. As we entered her apartment, movers carried out the last of her furnishings and sculptures. We'd planned only to use her window for an overview shot of Ground Zero. That changed after one look at Anita's frown-frozen face. We knew she would have plenty to say.

Michael went to the window for his shot looking down. Next, Anita showed us around her empty apartment, explaining where the furniture used to be. On the kitchen doorjamb, we traced the growth spurts of her twelve-year-old boys.

"This was the living room, this was the kitchen, and this is where the boys slept."

"Quite a view," I observed while standing at the big window. "And I'll bet you paid a lot for it."

"We paid New York City prices. It is still impossible for me to look at the view now. And to think of moving back is inconceivable."

I asked the inevitable, obvious question, "Were you here?"

"Yes, I saw everything," Anita said stoically. "I heard the noise and saw the tail of the plane disappear into the building. Then I saw fire and knew immediately that we were in big trouble." Anita described stuffing her passport and telephone into a purse and running to the elevator. "About halfway down, the whole building started vibrating and then the door opened." She told how she took stairs the rest of the way, emerging just after the second plane hit. "When I got to ground level I kept running. I was struck by how everyone was just standing there in shock. They stood in utter disbelief, just watching this."

Michael and I moved Anita to a second angle and asked more questions. I suggested that, if one could come up with a physical description of her mental state, it would be "battered and bruised—emotionally black-and-blue."

"Scarred," she corrected.

"Will you ever get over this?"

"I don't know yet. I don't know," said Anita, almost wistfully.

It was enough. We thanked both Anita and Deborah for trusting us with their stories. Before meeting them, Michael and I had not imagined Ground Zero as a neighborhood. After, we thought of the entire country that way.

"We're victims, too," Anita added as we left. "We're victims of a crime, but we're not getting any help. The Red Cross won't give us anything without receipts, and, at best, then we get bread crumbs." Michael rolled video while Anita spent five minutes venting about the Red Cross, the government, and their general lack of understanding. "There has been no emotional—no umbrella support either financially or emotionally for people who lived at Ground Zero. It's outrageous and shocking."

I was still trying to figure out how to include Anita's closing tirade when Michael's camera began misbehaving. To fix it, he would have to walk down and meet the car, roughly a forty-minute round trip. He would never get past the assistant building manager again. That simplified our decision.

I left with Michael and waited for him at the teddy bear memorial, watching a cross-section of Americans wander past: civil servants, executives, blue collar people, men and women in uniform. They looked at the pictures, read the tributes, and got misty-eyed. Most of the men kept walking. But the women would move close, take a long look, build up a torrent of tears, move away, and then return, as if filling up with more grief to purge again.

When Michael came back he spent twenty minutes taking pictures of the teddy bears, the visitors, and their reactions. He simply set the camera on his tripod and let action work through the frame. Later, I asked a few people if their residual emotions surprised them. "I had that week of sorrow," confided one woman. "But coming here brought it back."

"Had you thought you were over the pain?" I asked another.

"When I came here, I thought I was over this, but not at all." She began to cry.

Finally, and mostly because KGO-TV had sent us across the country to New York City, we shot a stand-up. I didn't think we would use it:

> (STAND-UP)
> AND YET THERE IS MORE HERE THAN THE OBVIOUS GRIEF . . .
> IT GOES BEYOND THIS BEING A WAR ZONE AND ALSO A CRIME
> SCENE. IF YOU LOOK ABOVE, THOSE ARE APARTMENT BUILDINGS.
> GROUND ZERO IS ALSO A NEIGHBORHOOD.

Putting the Story Together

Three hours earlier, we had entered the area around Ground Zero without a story. Three hours later, a very strong story had found us—maybe too much of one. The challenge would be in writing it. I did have time on my side. The segment would air two weeks later as the conclusion of our series. Two weeks to analyze and over-think it. Two weeks to describe three hours in three minutes. Three minutes is a long time in television news, but not when trying to combine the following elements:

1. The kids playing basketball
2. The sense of Ground Zero being a police state
3. Pictures of the demolition zone
4. Pictures of the hole in the ground
5. The tourists
6. The teddy bear memorial
7. People reacting to the teddy bears
8. Two main characters, Deborah and Anita
9. The concepts of Ground Zero as a neighborhood, and how what happened there unified the nation

Three minutes.

Writer's Block

On Thanksgiving Day 2001, I sat down at my desk in San Francisco to write the story. How would it begin? My head told me to start with teddy bears because they were the strongest element.

In the first draft, I aimed for something dramatic:

NEW YORK HAS BECOME A CITY OF HOLES.
THERE IS ONE IN THE SKY, ANOTHER IN THE GROUND,
AND, AT WHAT USED TO BE THE WORLD TRADE CENTER,
THERE IS THE BIGGEST HOLE—
IN ITS HEART.

That had potential, but it didn't lead anywhere. It established a mood, but might also convolute the timeline. After a trip for coffee and a walk around the building, I tried a different open:

NEW YORK CITY'S NEWEST TOURIST ATTRACTION HAS AN
UNOBSTRUCTED VIEW OF THE STATUE OF LIBERTY,
AND NOT THE SLIGHTEST HINT OF COMMERCIALISM . . .

I worked with that for a while, added a couple of sound bites, looked at the copy again, and hated it. This was no time for writing to a formula. Our experience at Ground Zero defied one. The story required understatement.

Finally, a concept took shape. Every installment in our series had been a travelogue, eschewing more fancy techniques in favor of linear progressions. Why stop now? It goes back to the theory of writing what you find. I would describe our day at Ground Zero as it happened.

Isn't that strange? After two weeks of internal debate, I began the story at the beginning. Once I made that commitment, the words took over, pouring themselves out through my fingertips in less than thirty minutes.

From "Stories from the Heartland"
Ground Zero
November 2001

Basketball game

IF YOU LISTEN TO THE PUBLIC RELATIONS PEOPLE,
NEW YORK CITY IS GETTING BACK TO NORMAL.
TEN BLOCKS FROM GROUND ZERO,
A PERSON MIGHT ALMOST BELIEVE IT.
BUT, ASK A POINTED QUESTION.

(SOT)
Wayne to Anthony Torres: "LET'S SAY YOU GOT OSAMA BIN LADEN IN A ROOM, JUST YOU AND HIM, ONE ON ONE . . ."

Anthony: "I'd end him."

FOR TWO WEEKS, WE HAD TRAVELED EAST BY TRAIN.
THE CLOSER WE DREW TO NEW YORK CITY,
THE STRONGER THE PULL OF WHAT HAPPENED HERE.

GROUND ZERO IS NOW, EFFECTIVELY, A POLICE STATE . . .
AN OTHER-WORLDLY NO-MAN'S LAND THAT HAS ALSO
BECOME A TOURIST ATTRACTION—BUT THERE'S
NOTHING COMMERCIAL ABOUT IT.

(SOT)
Bob Lamano: "Initially, I didn't want to come here at all. It was like an invasion of privacy for those who died, but it's something we wanted to see to make us stronger. I just feel for all the people who lost loved ones, is all I can say."

We cut to pictures of people grieving by the teddy bear memorial

NOTHING YOU HAVE READ OR SEEN CAN PREPARE YOU.

NOTHING CAN WARN YOU ABOUT ROUNDING A CORNER
AND SEEING A MOUNTAIN OF TEDDY BEARS . . .

TO THIS DAY, GROUND ZERO REMAINS A GRAVEYARD WHERE THOUSANDS OF PEOPLE DIED. FOR NOW, THESE ARE ITS INNOCENT, FUZZY TOMBSTONES.

(SOT)
One of the women: "When I came here, I thought I was over this, but not at all . . ."

EVERY DAY, WORKMEN CARRY AWAY MORE OF THE PHYSICAL
DEBRIS, BUT THE EMOTIONAL KIND REMAINS.
IMAGINE LIVING HERE AND WATCHING THE ATTACK HAPPEN.

(SOT)
Deborah Ortega points to the wreckage: "Behind that last arch.
To the south of that crane was a tower. No hole. No hole. No
death."

IT SPEAKS VOLUMES ABOUT DEBORAH ORTEGA THAT, AS SHE
WALKS AROUND TOWN, SHE CARRIES A SCRAPBOOK WITH
PICTURES OF THE ATTACK AS SHE SAW IT FROM HER APARTMENT.

(SOT)
Deborah: "I saw about twenty people fall from those towers,
and I felt like such a coward as I rode my bike away and knew I
couldn't help them. But then I felt so bad for them up there. You
could see them at the windows and see them wanting to get out.
And we knew this was not a Bruce Willis movie where everything
ends so happily, you know?"

EVEN TODAY, PEOPLE WANT TO GET AWAY.

DEBORAH TOOK US TO A NEIGHBOR'S PLACE, ANITA GLESTA . . .
MOVING, FINALLY, FROM AN APARTMENT VIEW SHE CANNOT
BRING HERSELF TO LOOK AT.

(SOT)
Wayne: "YOU SAW IT HAPPEN?"

Anita: "I saw everything. I heard the noise and saw the tail of
the plane disappear into the building. Then I saw fire and knew
immediately that we were in big trouble."

WE ALL KNEW. WE ALL SAW.
AND THAT TROUBLE SPREAD ACROSS THIS LAND.

MAYBE, UNTIL NOW, YOU NEVER THOUGHT OF
GROUND ZERO AS A NEIGHBORHOOD.
IT IS.
MAYBE, UNTIL NOW, YOU NEVER THOUGHT OF
ALL AMERICA AS BEING PART OF THAT NEIGHBORHOOD.
EMOTIONALLY, WE ARE.
WHAT HAPPENED HERE EXTENDS TO EACH OF US.

(SOT)
Wayne to Anita: "IF ONE WERE TO DESCRIBE YOUR EMOTIONAL
CONDITION IN A PHYSICAL STATE, IT MIGHT BE BATTERED AND
BRUISED—EMOTIONALLY BLACK-AND-BLUE."

Anita: "Scarred."

IF YOU COME TO NEW YORK CITY, GROUND ZERO IS SOMETHING
TO VISIT, TO MOURN, AND THEN PUT SOMEWHERE SAFE.

IF YOU LIVE HERE, IT'S A HOLE IN THE SKY . . . ANOTHER IN THE
GROUND . . . AND A BIG ONE IN THE HEART.

(SOT)
Wayne to Anita: "WILL YOU EVER GET OVER THIS?"

Anita: "I don't know yet. I don't know."

IT JUST TAKES TIME.

Postscript

After the story aired, my daughter, who was then seven years old, asked about it at bedtime. "Daddy, who were all those teddy bears?"

"Moms and dads, sons and daughters, brothers, sisters, aunts, uncles, neighbors, friends, and friends of friends," I answered.

In retrospect, I wondered if that might have made a nice line. Or, maybe it wasn't necessary. All I really knew is that sometimes, it takes a while to turn a story off, and let it go.

CHAPTER 23

Change the Small Worlds First

M any people enter journalism and television news with the notion of changing the world. In reality, most of us of us will hardly nudge it. Instead, the world we cover is more likely to change us.

Take heart, however. There is a distinction between the world as a whole, and the countless small worlds of individual men and women. Those are where, as a journalist, you can make a difference. If your work informs, enlightens, influences a person, or touches someone's life for the better, then you can change personal worlds every day. With that goal in mind, treat every story, and every world, with care and respect.

Take them one at a time.

The One Book Bookstore

In 1991, I did a segment for CBS News about Walter and Deloris Swan, who had lived quiet, earnest, and honest lives in Bisbee, Arizona, a small tourist town just north of the Mexican border. Then, in old age and much to their surprise, Walter and Deloris became the main characters in a sweet and inspiring story.

Bisbee is a long way from anywhere else. To get there, photographer Dave Dellaria and I flew to Tucson, and headed south across the great emptiness. Few moments stir the soul more than an arid, dusty desert sunset when your only contact with civilization is a rental car, a black ribbon of striped asphalt, and a two quarts of bottled water.

Walter, in his eighties, worked his entire life in Bisbee, as a plasterer. He and Deloris had been married for more than fifty years, and raised nine children.

"Money was always tight," Walter told us. The family never had a color television, or videos, or much for entertainment. Just him. Walter would coax those children into bed every night with true stories of growing up in Bisbee with his brother, Henry. He told about the first time he saw an airplane, or about his first pair of shoes, or how a goat ate his schoolbooks.

Walter's pollywog story remains a classic. After heavy summer rains, he and his friends would go to a nearby "puddle hole," as they called it, and cool off in the water. One day, the kids found that puddle hole filled with blue-belly polliwogs. Like typical boys, Water and Henry took the critters home as pets and put them in a big water bucket on the kitchen counter.

No one paid any notice to the pollywogs, again, until well past midnight. That's when Walter's father got up for a drink of water. He stumbled to the kitchen, fumbled around in the dark, and found a glass. "Then," said Walter, "I was woke by somebody coughing and gagging in the other room. I had the funniest feeling in the pit of my stomach. I knew just what had happened."

Sure enough, Walter's father had dipped his glass into the polliwog bucket instead of the drinking water, and taken a big gulp.

Now imagine a childhood filled with such bedtime stories from Walter, who was an artist with the spoken word.

Years later, after the kids moved out, when Walter and Deloris had only themselves and not much to do, she made a suggestion. "Walter, you should take those bedtime stories and write a book."

"But I can't write," he replied, and it was true. During our visit Walter pulled out his childhood report cards. Sure enough, he made a string of Ds in composition.

Walter Swan might have been a bad English student, but, as a natural storyteller, he innately knew the rules of structure better than almost anyone. He rose to the challenge and spent nights at the kitchen table, writing his old tales in longhand. Deloris deciphered his chicken scratches, corrected them, and entered his work into a computer.

When they finished, the couple sent copies of their manuscript, called *Me 'n Henry*, to fourteen publishers. In return, they received fourteen rejections.

Many authors would have given up after that, especially if they'd spent most of their lives in an old mining town thousands of miles from those lofty New York publishing houses. "Still, we had faith in it," Deloris said. They were naïve, but the couple had courage, too. Walter and Deloris believed in *Me 'n Henry* so much that they used most of their life savings to publish a few hundred copies.

"The first time I held that book, I got all choked up," said Walter, who fought tears again when describing the moment.

He and Deloris made a novel plan. They took their book to the Arizona State Fair, set up a booth, and began doing business.

Me 'n Henry sold out.

Encouraged, the couple printed more.

This time, they rented space on Bisbee's main drag and opened a small storefront called the One Book Bookstore. On the shelves, piled high, they placed thousands of copies of *Me 'n Henry*. Walter's book was the store's only commodity. As at the state fair, it sold.

It was an ingenious marketing plan. Tourists would wander in. Walter, with his long gray hair, smiling face, and faded blue overalls, would spin a yarn or two, charm them, and then ask innocently, "Would you like to buy a book?" How could anyone refuse? Walter Swan, the author, personally autographed every copy.

"It was more money than we'd ever seen before in all our lives," Deloris said.

I asked what difference the money had made for them. "Oh, I can go to the grocery store now and buy anything I want," Deloris told us. "No more counting pennies. We can afford anything."

And what was her favorite indulgence?

"I just love that artificial crab," Deloris confided.

The Swans epitomized optimism, perseverance, and success. Anyone can learn from their story, including those of us who work in television news. When you believe in yourself, act on it, work at it, and never give up, good stuff happens.

The Most Important Lesson

Reporters often receive their greatest satisfactions from the simplest stories. "The One Book Bookstore" did that for me. The Swans' sweetness, honesty, and innocence touched me. Our segment certainly did not make much of a difference to them at that point. After all that Deloris and Walter had been through, being on the network news amounted to little more than gravy on top of a rich, loving, wonderful life.

But, there was one more twist to their story. It happened the night after our piece aired on *CBS This Morning*, when I stayed up late to watch David Letterman. Either he or someone on his staff had seen our segment, and they must have liked it, because who do you think Letterman flew all the way to New York City to be his guest?

It was Walter Swan telling bedtime stories again, and not just to his kids this time, but to the biggest audience of them all, America.

He looked like the happiest man on Earth.

It made me happy, too.

Watching Walter on the screen, that night, reminded me how the most profound rewards of this work come from sitting back and seeing what happens when we set a process in motion.

The Swans had already changed their world with their own actions. Our story changed it a little more, and for the better. By my definition, that's a good kind of day.

The best.

Acknowledgments

Writing a book is like someone asking if you can swim twenty miles. You figure a mile a day—anybody can work up to that. But this is in the open ocean to a proverbial promised island, with winds, storms, fog, and currents to push you off course. In the end, the distance is more like a thousand miles, and lonely. About halfway there, you realize you don't have a lifeboat. You just keep swimming, hoping you're heading in the right direction. When you finally reach the island, you circle it a couple of times, looking for a place to land. Then, when you do, no one meets you. It's still a long walk to the nearest settlement.

The first edition of this book sold well, but became prohibitively expensive once it went out of print. That was just plain wrong. For me, this project was never about gouging television news hopefuls or getting rich. Instead, it's about a guy having his say, sharing old-school values, and making a contribution to the craft he loves so much.

Thanks to my dear wife, Susan, for encouraging me to write this book and for naming it at the dinner table one night. Neither of us anticipated how much time and attention the manuscript would take from us as a couple. Susan, you got the short end of this deal. You already knew you married an obsessive man. This book forced you to new levels of sainthood—twice.

I thank my daughter, Lauren, for going to bed on time (mostly), which allowed me to get to the computer on time. After a few months of writing the first manuscript, she mounted a toy plastic horse atop the monitor. From then on, she referred to this project as "Daddy's brain-sucking horse." Lauren, thanks for sitting in the office and keeping me company on those early weekend mornings. And thanks for listening again, this time as a young woman.

Thanks to my parents, Mike and Alicia Freedman. Parents are unconditional fans. Kids need them, even when they're all grown up. Dad, I wish you were still here to hold this book in your hands.

For his practical help, deep thanks go to Mervin Block, who connected me with a publisher and made the first edition happen. That took faith and courage after Merv saw some early chapters. "Needs work," he said. Merv, you showed me what it takes to write a book. You challenged me. You influenced my work in broadcasting. At forty-nine years old, it was nice to find a mentor.

Thanks to my first editor, Devon Freeny, who never complained about my multitude of small changes. Thanks, even more, to my new editor and publisher, Renée Robinson—who empowered me to tackle this project again. Renée, I so much appreciate your consistent good humor through another multitude of changes.

I must acknowledge all the fine professionals with whom I have worked though the years. Editors like Jim Joy, Herb Bennett, Jim Sudweeks, John Odell, and Darrell Holdaway are masters at the subtleties of their craft. Photographers Dave Busse, Dean Smith, Randy Davis, and Pam Partee taught me, by example, how to shoot. As a guy who now shoots and edits, thanks to all of you for unselfish inspirations.

I owe Ken Swartz an enormous thank-you. At KRON in 1981, Ken mentored me in the ways and traditions of long-form storytelling. Among photographers, Ken is a Rembrandt with impeccable standards who also produced, edited, and won so many major awards that he simply tired of entering. Ken, we have not seen each other for many years, but I still hear your voice when working on complex projects. If my work is good, it reflects directly back to your influences.

Finally, thanks to my dear friend, KGO-TV photographer Michael Clark, who won't have to read this book because he's already heard it, over and over, through blizzards, floods, fires, baseball playoffs, cross-country train trips, and on, and on, and on—twice, now. A kinder, more patient photographer never roamed the Earth.

As for the people listed on the next page—thanks for listening, thanks for looking, and, in many cases, thanks for saying less instead of more. To some of you, thanks for showing me right from wrong in television news. To others, thanks for having faith and putting yourselves on the line for me. Most of you share something in common. You learned through experience to never again ask Wayne Freedman, "How's the book?"

Here's your answer. It's finished.

Again.

Scott Arthur
Jaie Avila
John Blackstone
Scott Buer
Ron Brown
Cathy Cavey
Krisann Chasarik
Lucille Clark
CoCo
Darryl Compton
Dave Dellaria
Herb Dudnick
Mike Ferring
Craig Franklin
Lynn Friedman
Joe Fryer, Jr.
Ron Guintini
George Griswold
Todd Hanks
Steve Hartman
David Hazinski
Anne Herbst

Heather Ishimaru
Carolyn Johnson
Kevin Keeshan
Don Knapp
Leonard Koppett
Brian Kuebler
Greeley Kyle
Don Langford
Doug Laughlin
Adrienne Laurent
Art Linkletter
Steve Lentz
Dierdre Lynch
Devorah Major
Kerry McGee
Bill McKnight
Mackie Morris
Dick Nelson
Karen O'Leary
Dr. Robert Papper
Lloyd Patterson
Phyllis Pecorak
Larry Pond

Dave Pera
Ike Pigott
Lou Prato
Stephanie Riggs
Karina Rusk
Mark Sanchez-Corea
John Sheehan
Andrew Shinnick
Valari Staab
Randy Steinman
Rick Swanson
Eric Thomas
Tim Tison
Al Tompkins
Elsa Trexler
John Turner
Max Utsler
Bobby Vermiglio
Tracey Watkowski
Milt Weiss
Catherine Welch
Leigh Wilson

Scripts

About the Author

Wayne Freedman has written and reported most of his life. In ninth grade, he published his first column for what became *The Los Angeles Daily News*, and continued writing it through high school.

He earned his Bachelor's degree in Political Science from UCLA while working as a network page assigned to the newsroom at KABC-TV in Los Angeles. In 1978 he received a Masters Degree in Journalism from the University of Missouri.

Wayne has been on San Francisco television for more than thirty years. He began at KRON-TV in 1981, after jobs at WLKY-TV and WAVE-TV in Louisville, and KDFW-TV in Dallas. He moved to CBS Network News in 1989, producing and reporting national feature stories while based in San Francisco. In 1991 he joined KGO-TV.

Since 1990, Wayne has conducted hundreds of writing and visual storytelling seminars for newsrooms and national organizations.

Wayne has been honored with fifty-one Emmy® Awards by the Northern California Chapter of the National Academy of Television Arts and Sciences. He received thirteen of those Emmys for *Writing*, and fourteen in the *On Camera News Talent* category. He has received other multiple Emmys for *Breaking News, Feature Reporting, Feature Series, Sports Reporting,* and *News Programming Special*. Wayne is also a member of that organization's Silver Circle. In 2011, he earned his 50th Emmy for shooting and editing his own stories as a *Multi-media Journalist*.

Wayne is a dedicated and frustrated golfer who has been known to shoot an occasional round at scratch. He is a member of the Golf Writers Association of America, having produced articles for several national publications.

Wayne Freedman lives in Marin County with his wife and daughter.

CPSIA information can be obtained at www.ICGtesting.com
Printed in the USA
LVOW04s1810050815

448964LV00020B/1206/P

9 780984 312535